"Everyone knows government isn't working. But what can we do about it? Drawing on her experience of working inside Downing Street and her tireless work outside the system, Caroline Slocock explains how we can quite easily turn 'bad' into 'good' government."

Anthony Seldon, author and historian

"A brilliant and easy-to-read guide to what makes good and bad government by someone who deeply understands it. All voters should read this – and give it to their MP."

Krishnan Guru-Murthy, broadcaster

"Part memoir, part political history, this beautifully observed book offers a rare glimpse behind the closed doors of British political life. Drawing on years spent in the Private Offices of Margaret Thatcher and John Major, as well as at the Equal Opportunities Commission, the author combines sharp insight with humanity, wit and compassion. Rich in personal anecdote and animated by a lifelong commitment to equality – especially for women – it is both an important record and an absorbing read."

Sayeeda Warsi, politician, lawyer and former co-chair of the Conservative Party

"Caroline Slocock has worked at the heart of government and knows where the bodies are buried – and how trust turns to dust when 'country before party' becomes 'party before country'. *Bad Government* is required reading for everyone interested in why UK politics feels broken. Starting with our politicians."

John Crace, *Guardian* columnist and author

"This is essential reading for anyone struggling to understand why government doesn't work as well as it should."

Gus O'Donnell, former Cabinet Secretary

"Is Britain becoming ungovernable? This book presents a vision for government to overcome distrust and the extremes of populism. Through dramatic behind-the-scenes glimpses of how government actually works (and doesn't), Slocock provides a hopeful alternative to the broken status quo. Brilliant."

Polly Curtis, CEO of Demos

"Packed with fresh, urgently relevant insights about how to govern more effectively, combined with a compelling personal account of what it's like facing the impossible challenges at the heart of power."

Steve Richards, author, columnist and presenter

"I've been struck over and over again by Caroline's combination of immense knowledge and experience and her firm moral compass. They're all here in spades. Let's hope politicians and civil servants are bracing themselves!"

Polly Neate, social sector leader and commentator

CAROLINE SLOCOCK

BAD GOVERN-MENT

(AND HOW TO MAKE IT BETTER)

\Bb\
Biteback Publishing

First published in Great Britain in 2026 by
Biteback Publishing Ltd, London

ISBN 978-1-83736-050-5

10 9 8 7 6 5 4 3 2 1

A CIP catalogue record for this book is available from the British Library.

Set in Minion Pro

Printed and bound in Great Britain by
CPI Group (UK) Ltd, Croydon CR0 4YY

FSC
www.fsc.org
MIX
Paper | Supporting responsible forestry
FSC® C013604

To all those who died in Grenfell Tower, and to my grandson,
Fred, who has just entered this world.

CONTENTS

PREFACE

When Keir Starmer became Prime Minister in 2024, trust in government in the UK was at a record low;[1] levels were among the lowest in the world in 2023, having been undermined by Brexit's extravagant promises and the subsequent chaos of Partygate – those illicit gatherings at No. 10 during the Covid pandemic – not to mention Liz Truss's disastrous premiership.[2] Like many new Prime Ministers before him, Starmer promised to put country before politics and restore that trust. But trust has continued to fall, and many are now saying that Britain is broken. These are often the very same people who are at each other's throats and inflaming tensions across the country.

Is Britain ungovernable? We're used to ministers fighting with themselves, but the relationship between ministers and civil servants had very publicly exploded before Labour took power, with one resigning Permanent Secretary threatening to take his Home Secretary to an employment tribunal, a former top official from the Foreign Office calling out a serving Prime Minister for lying and a Cabinet Secretary's WhatsApps revealing complete chaos inside No. 10 while Covid raged. No wonder these relationships broke down, after civil servants were accused of being a 'Blob' (in Dominic Cummings's words), full of activists with their own agenda, while ministers broke so many rules. It wasn't long before Starmer, who on entering government told the civil service that 'together, as one team, we can deliver our mission of national renewal and change', was publicly berating civil servants for being 'comfortable in a tepid bath of managed decline'. He then went on to sack his chosen Cabinet Secretary, amid briefings that he was blocking reform, and ended up being publicly berated by former senior civil servants for sacking the Head of the Foreign and Commonwealth and Development Office, Olly Robbins, without the chance to defend himself. Some saw this as an attempt to deflect blame to the civil service for his own disastrous decision to appoint Peter Mandelson as an Ambassador and save his own skin.

The hidden wiring of government has been sparking for all to see. Over decades, No. 10 has sucked ever more power into itself, micro-managing, while the business of government seems to lack purpose and direction and deep-seated problems remain unaddressed. When things go horribly wrong, as they did at Grenfell Tower and the Post Office, no one seems to be accountable and lessons are rarely learned. People with money and power seem far better at getting a hearing from government than people at the sharp end of its policies. The Mandelson and Greensill scandals leave many wondering, who is government really for – them or us? And when more and more Prime Ministers catastrophically fall, it begins to feel like no one is up to the job.

If governments don't get their act together, Donald Trump's 'strong man' approach to politics might take hold. We have seen how easy it is for Prime Ministers like Boris Johnson and Liz Truss to ignore democratic norms. Some politicians, including ministers under the last Conservative government, are portraying judges, lawyers, charities, campaigners and protesters as a block to democracy rather than key components of it. Rights are being attacked, communities are being divided and the truth is being inverted in the service of US-style culture wars.

Is it possible to turn the ship of state around?

Part memoir, part history, part manifesto for a different kind of governing, this book looks at what's wrong with government and how to make it better. It takes a long view of government from Margaret Thatcher's administration to the present day, through my eyes, as a former civil servant who in a minor way has also been part of that history. I was the first female Private Secretary in No. 10, the only other woman in the Cabinet Room when Thatcher resigned, and I welcomed a new Prime Minister into No. 10 a few hours after she left. I took forward key reforms to how government works under Thatcher and Tony Blair that remain in place to this day – and are now themselves urgently in need of reform. I championed advances in childcare, equal rights and working practices, including as CEO of the Equal Opportunities Commission, which helped establish new social norms that are now under increasing threat. Since I left government, I set up and led a think tank, which seeks to deepen government's connection with civil society. I've been working with people who are transforming public services; campaigning for ways to improve government and democracy; and critiquing government initiatives, like the Big Society, that may have had good intentions but failed. More recently, I have been working with government to help it join forces with civil society to strengthen our democracy and make it better.

I joined the civil service because I believed that government can be done well or it can be done badly, regardless of who is in power, and that I could make a difference. It is this same belief that lies behind this book.

I am passionate about the changes that are needed and believe that a new model of government is possible – but don't expect this book to be a treatise. It's more of a journey. My aim is to make you feel what it is really like to be in government and to experience its myriad challenges as if you were there yourself. Now you're in these shoes, I'd like you to explore with me how we can make government better.

Chapter 1

HOW GOVERNMENT BEGINS

Do you remember your first day in a new job? That excitement, and also that nervousness? Am I really up to this job? Will they still like me when they really get to know me? Will I like them? Will there be buyer's remorse? And what am I going to wear?

One thing's for sure: you won't have stayed up all night to hear whether you've been appointed only to find yourself just a few hours later standing outside the door of your new workplace, in front of a bank of television cameras and journalists who are waiting for you to tell everyone what you're going to do, before you've even got your feet under the desk.

But that's how government in the UK begins.

• • •

'Our country has voted, decisively. For change. For national renewal. And a return of politics to public service.'

Sir Keir Starmer, our new Prime Minister, is speaking from a podium outside the door of No. 10. The nation is hanging on his every word. Can he turn the tide after the collective traumas and psychodramas created by Brexit, Boris Johnson, Liz Truss and even Rishi Sunak, who promised when he was on the steps of No. 10 to deliver 'integrity, professionalism and accountability at every level' but failed to deliver a government which the people could trust? Will Starmer's government be any better?

And so we listen and hope to believe.

'When the gap between the sacrifices made by people and the service they receive from politicians grows this big, it leads to a weariness in the heart of a nation. A draining away of the hope, the spirit, the belief in a better future that we need to move forward, together.'

'Weariness'? Or is it anger and exasperation? But weariness is not a bad word for the many who've 'drained away' and stopped voting. Around 40 per cent of the eligible population didn't turn up the previous day, a massive decline since the last high of 1997, when over 70 per cent voted. But many of those probably won't be listening to what he's saying today, because they've literally switched off. We're still listening, though…

'Now, this wound, this lack of trust, can only be healed by actions not words. I know that. But we can make a start today with the simple acknowledgement that public service is a privilege…'

That subtle use of the word 'we' creeps in. It's not just Keir Starmer who's starting a new job, but a whole government, the first Labour government in fourteen years, but does he also mean us?

And then comes a pledge:

> Politics can be a force for good – we will show that. And that is how we will govern. Country first, party second. You have given us a clear mandate and we will use it to deliver change. To restore

service and respect to politics, end the era of noisy performance and tread more lightly on your lives…

But what about us?

'So with respect and humility, I invite you all to join this government of service in the mission of national renewal,' he says.

There it is: government is not just them, but us, and we're all in it together.

'Our work is urgent. And we begin it today.'

• • •

Set aside any feeling that we've heard it all before, or that politicians are all the same. This is a fresh start, a moment of optimism, and I for one am buying it, glad like many to see the back of some spectacularly bad government in recent years.

But there's a slight feeling of déjà vu. OK, it's a much more sober moment than Tony Blair's triumphant entry into Downing Street in 1997 to the tune of 'Things Can Only Get Better'. In 2024, there's no money and very little growth. But the words are similar. Blair promised 'a government that seeks to restore trust in politics in this country. That cleans it up, that decentralises it, that gives people hope once again that politics is and always should be about the service of the public.' Many good things followed in 1997, including investment in public services, peace in Northern Ireland and action to end child poverty, and the electorate voted him back two further times. But those non-existent weapons of mass destruction and the highly unpopular invasion of Iraq, not to mention the Westminster expenses scandal in 2009, did little to restore trust in politics.

In 2010, David Cameron also said something very similar to Starmer on becoming Prime Minister:

> One of the tasks that we clearly have is to rebuild trust in our political system. Yes, that's about cleaning up expenses, yes that is about reforming Parliament and yes it is about making sure people are in control – and that the politicians are always their servant and never their masters. But I believe it is also something else. It is about being honest about what government can achieve. Real change is not what government can do on its own – real change is when everyone pulls together, comes together, works together, where we all exercise our responsibilities to ourselves, to our families, to our communities and to others.

Rather than the country pulling together, his Brexit referendum ripped families – and Britain as a whole – apart, to the point that, even today, many people can't bear to speak about Brexit for fear of coming to blows. Cameron's 'Big Society' initiative fizzled out, and many felt it simply offloaded responsibilities to others as he cut the state back. But he did an enormous service for society by introducing gay marriage, to the surprise of the many in his party who were against it. Now that was good government: showing leadership by doing the right thing and serving the whole country, not just your narrow political ends.

'Restoring trust', 'returning government to the service of the people' and 'pulling together' are common words on many a new Prime Minister's lips. Even Boris Johnson, who probably did more than any Prime Minister to undermine trust in politicians, promised the people when he first took power in 2019 that he would 'restore trust in our democracy' – by finally delivering Brexit, of course.

There was no whisper about illegally proroguing Parliament or of setting rules for us that he had no intention of following himself.

As Rishi Sunak, the last Prime Minister before Keir Starmer, said in his Downing Street speech, 'Trust is earned. And I will earn yours.' Which, sadly, he didn't.

Do I believe that new Prime Ministers simply rehash the same material for their first speech, like Joe Biden's plagiarism in 1987 of words from a Neil Kinnock speech, which some believe cost him the nomination for the presidency first time around? No. I believe trust, public service and the country pulling together so often feature because they are the foundation of good government, and it's right that an incoming Prime Minister should solemnly promise to deliver them, particularly when these qualities have in the past been so conspicuously absent.

Pledges on the steps of No. 10 are one thing, being in government is another. Despite what Keir Starmer has promised, politics, not country, often ends up first – and bad government inevitably follows.

• • •

It's a massive shift from being Leader of the Opposition to becoming Prime Minister, with no pause for breath, let alone training, and, as Starmer concludes his speech, he's about to make the leap by walking through the door of No. 10.

A few hours earlier, I'd been talking on the *Today* programme on Radio 4 about that difficult transition. I was inside No. 10 when John Major had taken over from Margaret Thatcher and I remembered how excited – and slightly nervous – we were about a change of boss. We were watching Major's speech outside No. 10 from within.

I told *Today*'s listeners how, from that moment, Starmer would be 'Prime Minister', not 'Keir'. Instead of a small circle of trusted political aides, he would have the whole civil service machine – ultimately around half a million people – at his disposal to put his plans into action. As a former civil servant, he'd have a better idea than most of how the civil service works, and he'd be accompanied by his Chief of Staff Sue Gray, also a former civil servant. But, however well prepared he was, it was still going to be a shock.

He was about to hand over much more of himself to the office of Prime Minister and No. 10 than many of us would feel comfortable with. How he spends his time, what he reads and what he says will now in large part be controlled by those working for him, and absolute trust in his team is going to be critical. They are there to serve, but if Starmer is not careful it will feel more like he's being driven than being in the driving seat. And then, of course, there are 'events, dear boy, events', as Harold Macmillan put it, and the media constantly finding fault on a news cycle so fast it can make your head spin. A Prime Minister can be thrown off course, unless they keep a clear head and know exactly what they stand for and who they are.

And there would be a loss of personal freedom, too. Out and about, Starmer would never be alone, a security detail with him at every turn. Where he goes and who he talks to will be mapped out for him in advance, with briefs that tell him what to do, what to say and where to stand to be photographed.

But then Starmer had already surrendered something of himself on his path to No. 10. The suit and glasses that he's wearing today, donated by Labour peer Lord Alli of Norbury, are designed to make him look the part, or at least as smart as his opponent in the general election, multi-millionaire Rishi Sunak.

He's not alone. I'll never forget my surprise when I met David

Cameron, back when he was Leader of the Opposition, and saw he was wearing foundation on his face. Here was a man who was primed for television cameras and a mass audience, and who was prepared to look faintly ridiculous in front of everyone else.

But then there is the insecurity that many feel when they take on a public-facing role which seems so much bigger than they personally are. When Margaret Thatcher became Leader of the Opposition in 1995, she confessed in an interview with Radio 2 presenter Jimmy Young how hard it was at first to reconcile her private self with the mantle of the new role: 'I don't think that one has still come to the surface because there is so much to do that one hasn't really realised the Leader of the Opposition is me! I think it's only "me" still.' Her voice and tone are self-effacing, girlish even, and she's prepared to show vulnerability. But it wasn't long before she received voice coaching to lower her voice and slow down her words, so she could take on the gravitas of a man, which her male advisers thought was essential if she was to be taken seriously. The greatest actor of her day, Sir Laurence Olivier, had a session with her on how to act and 'project herself' into her words. She was also told how to dress so that she looked less like a 'Tory wife' and more like the potential leader of a country. She ditched the hats and fussy clothes, as advised, but kept the pearls that her husband had given her. With Thatcher, you were always going to get her authentic self, however inauthentic her voice had become. This was one reason why she still connected to the people who voted for her.

But not every candidate to become Prime Minister dresses themselves up for the role. Boris Johnson – the man 'born to be king' – felt there was no need and continued with his trademark dishevelled style. Voters seemed to like this 'devil may care' indifference to political and social norms, giving him a hefty majority in 2019, but many were turned off when they saw what that meant in practice. Jeremy Corbyn also took little care over his appearance, like Michael Foot before him, and was dressed down by Prime Minister Cameron, who said that his mother would tell Corbyn to 'put on a proper suit, do up your tie and sing the national anthem', during Prime Minister's Questions (PMQs).

Labour politicians generally know they have to look the part, believing voters do not see them as the natural party of government. That's why New Labour representatives in 1997 suddenly adopted sharp suits and good haircuts before the election, and Labour politicians in 2024 did the same. People like their politicians to look like politicians, not themselves, and then blame them for all being the same. Those who have a natural sense of entitlement, like Boris Johnson, don't need to bother. They project themselves, and that's enough.

Johnson didn't need to speak about his personal life in public to come across as authentic with the electorate, and he had plenty he could have said about his childhood to get sympathy – about how his mother had to spend eighteen months in a psychiatric hospital and later his parents split up – but he had a better tactic: to make people laugh. He didn't need to invite the media into his kitchen and open up his cupboards, like Thatcher did to demonstrate she was a good housewife. Nor did he need to sit on the *One Show* TV sofa with his spouse and talk about 'girl and boy jobs' in the home, as Theresa May felt obliged to do. (Philip May, we learned, takes out the dustbins. Boris, one suspects, does not.)

Making their private lives public is what politicians – especially those who are naturally buttoned up – are often encouraged by their spin doctors to do. Poor Theresa May, known for her stiffness, was forced to go on LBC radio and tell the whole world that she and

Philip had been unable to have children and how sad this made her feel. Did we need to know? Or that she owned about 100 recipe books and would cook Donald Trump a slow roast shoulder of lamb if he were to go to her house for dinner? Imagine what she must have felt inside, after that, even if her political advisers were patting her on the back for showing the public who she truly was. It was possibly up there with Donald Trump holding her hand as her top cringeworthy moment.

This is how many politicians now attempt to connect with the public, as face-to-face contact has become increasingly rare. Gone are the days when a Prime Minister could directly address the electorate in person, as when John Major stood on a soap box on a street corner during the 1992 election, talking to anyone in the crowd who came to listen, and successfully (despite predictions) winning the public over to gain the Tories another term. Understandably, voters want to get close to judge a future Prime Minister's character, but for me that character is shown by what they stand for, their vision and how well they respond to pressure, not personal details given in set-piece interviews and speeches, or footage of them embracing and kissing their spouses while the audience applauds, as often happens now. It's so common it's becoming something of a cliché. A live TV audience laughed when Starmer told them during the 2024 election that his father was a toolmaker. I don't think this was because they thought this was funny, but because they were sick of hearing him making the same point, again and again. I feel for him. When he became Leader of the Opposition, according to the book *Get In* by Gabriel Pogrund and Patrick Maguire, he employed a voice coach who tried to train him to sound authentic when he spoke about himself and his private life. It was a struggle for such a private man to get the words out without it sounding scripted (and maybe that was because they were).

Becoming a Leader of the Opposition and, if you're lucky, a Prime Minister, can mean sacrificing a part of yourself. Your 'me' is now a 'we', with everyone telling you how to be you.

It's not just Starmer himself but his family whose lives were about to be sucked even further into the machine. They would shortly be moving into one of the two Downing Street flats, along with their rescue cat JoJo, with enormous upheaval all round. Not everyone wants to live above the shop, but for PMs there really isn't another option. At least they get Chequers at weekends, with its considerable space, gardens, grounds and a swimming pool, and servicemen and women to cook meals. Leaving their former family home is the only way to ensure their security and privacy; had they stayed in an ordinary London street, they would be surrounded by photographers and have to put up with invasive security to protect them from any intruders, or (as happened after they had moved out) arson attacks.

What would his two teenage children make of all of that? A new home, far from their friends, inside their father's workplace, with many eyes on their comings and goings. Perhaps Starmer's children may already have heard the story about Euan Blair. Euan, aged sixteen, was taken into custody by the police for being incapacitated on a pavement the day he finished his GCSEs. He tried to keep it quiet, giving a false name and his old address, but it ended up all over the newspapers. It's hard being the child of a Prime Minister, but especially terrible during the teenage years.

To navigate this, Starmer has tried to protect his children by not releasing their names to the public, and also offering them the carrot of a pet dog. Some weeks later – and after what Sir Keir himself described as 'long negotiations' – the promised dog instead became a Siberian kitten, Prince, who gained huge attention from the media, appearing in a photograph with the new Prime Minister, looking startled and uncomfortable (but also very cute) on the PM's desk. What would the Downing Street cat, Larry, make of it? Lots of speculation naturally followed, and the official spokesperson informed the media that the two cats hadn't yet met. We loved Prince, but did it make us feel any closer to the Prime Minister? Maybe just a tiny bit. The spin doctors must have loved it.

• • •

But all this is yet to come…

The door of No. 10 opens and Starmer enters. He'll be greeted with the words 'Prime Minister' by the Cabinet Secretary, Simon Case, clapped by Downing Street staff in the lobby, watched by cameras (a new development, making this so much more stage-managed than in my day) and will be taken to the Cabinet Room and, after meeting his Private Secretaries, he will be briefed on security. There will be enormous goodwill, too much detail and too many faces, just like on any other first day at work. But those first days do not involve giving written instructions on when to use nuclear weapons, appointing Cabinet members and junior ministers, or receiving congratulatory calls from heads of state around the world. All on very little sleep, but massive doses of adrenaline.

At some point in that first busy day, he and his wife will be shown the two Downing Street flats and will reach a decision about which one they will move into. The smaller flat is above No. 10, the bigger one above No. 11, accessed via the corridor that connects the two buildings (so, for all practical purposes, it might as well be in No. 10). Decisions will need to be made about when to move and whether to redecorate first or just accept what's there. Make bad decisions, and public criticism may follow.

Boris Johnson spent at least £112,000 redecorating his flat, on top of the (checks notes) £30,000 annual allowance already given from the public purse for that purpose. According to one visitor, the couple had inherited a 'John Lewis furniture nightmare' from Theresa May. Boris Johnson later said that, after he'd removed the carpets because their dog Dylan was being housetrained, it looked like a 'crack den' and needed refurbishing.[1] The money initially came from Conservative donor Lord Brownlow, who the PM personally approached via a WhatsApp message saying 'the flat is still a bit of a tip'. He asked if Lord Brownlow could provide the 'approvals' to their interior designer, Lulu Lytle, so she could get on with it, also mentioning in the same message that he would get back to him about a pet project Lord Brownlow had been promoting.[2] A scandal eventually ensued and the Prime Minister repaid Lord Brownlow from his own purse when all of this came to light. Photographs were published to demonstrate the result of this expenditure. One Twitter user commented, 'It looks like a Moroccan brothel' – it certainly was distinctive.[3] The allegedly gold wallpaper, which cost £840 a roll, was painted over by Liz Truss when she became Prime Minister and the next inhabitant, Chancellor Jeremy Hunt, told the press the wallpaper was starting to peel off.[4]

It was very different in Margaret Thatcher's day. Public records show that Thatcher, who took the No. 10 flat (as all Prime Ministers before Tony Blair did), was not happy with the provisions already made by the public purse on her behalf. Too much had been spent, and she was worried about public criticism when the numbers came out. The £1,836 expenditure included cleaning and relaying carpets and cleaning a furniture cover but also new bed linen and pillows for the two bedrooms, as well as £19 on a new ironing board. She told her Private Secretary that she would pay for the ironing board herself and only needed bed linen for the one bedroom they used.

Hopefully Jeremy Hunt, the last inhabitant of the No. 11 flat, left it in good condition, as this is the flat the Starmers eventually chose as their own, unsurprisingly as it has four bedrooms and the teenagers would be able to have their own rooms.

• • •

What is it like saying goodbye to one Prime Minister and hello to a new one, a few hours later? Sad, exciting and busy, in my experience. It's what civil servants are there for, to seamlessly work for whoever is sent to us and help them settle in.

When Margaret Thatcher left No. 10, she had been there for eleven and a half years. I was a civil servant, specifically the Private Secretary (Home Affairs) to the Prime Minister, and one of five Private Secretaries who at that time formed her small inner circle of civil service support. In this case, it wasn't an election but a resignation that led to a change of Prime Minister. She had won three elections, but her popularity was falling due to a disastrous new form of council tax: the community charge, generally known as the poll tax, since anyone who could vote would have to pay it. To avoid what looked like certain defeat at the next election, her colleagues turned against her and an ill-judged speech in the House of Commons railing against Europe was the final nail in her coffin for a then pro-EU party. Her resignation was a major trauma for the Conservatives and tears were shed in the Cabinet Room when she informed her ministers of her decision, including by some of those ministers themselves, even though the night before they had advised her to step down. I know this because I saw it, the only other woman in the Cabinet Room that day.

As a fresh leadership election was launched, flowers from

well-wishers flooded in; eventually there were so many that she sent them down from the flat to line the corridors of No. 10, and we were told to take some home, which many of us did, wrapped in bin bags so the media outside would not see them. There was a leaving party involving everyone in No. 10, at which we gave Mrs Thatcher a present which I had chosen with help from one of her friends (a rare volume of Rudyard Kipling poetry, a favourite poet of hers) and a shortwave radio which the BBC gave us for free (so that – as the head of No. 10 Andrew Turnbull told her at the party – she could get angry with the BBC wherever she was in the world).

Work was suspended for a while, as government was in limbo. The removal company was already taking possessions away and had given each of us a miniature version of their van, which I had left on my desk. I felt bad when Margaret Thatcher looked down on it, wistfully. But she knew the score – ministers come and go, and we remain.

She was with us in the office when the news of the election of the new leader of her party was announced. John Major was her chosen candidate, and she said enthusiastically, 'Come on, let's go over to No. 11 and congratulate him.' We traipsed after her, our eyes on her rapidly advancing back as she went in a huge burst of energy down toward No. 10's front door, then turned right into the connecting corridor to No. 11, and up the stairs to the first-floor reception room where people were gathering. John Major dashed up the stairs beside us in his shirtsleeves, full of excitement, and stopped to kiss some of the women – including me – on the cheek. When we reached the room and started milling with the other well-wishers, I looked over to Mrs Thatcher, who was now on her own in a corner. Power drains away so quickly.

That night, she invited the Private Office up to the flat to share their last meal, moussaka, with us. It was a painful affair. Upbeat, she spent the whole time giving us her thoughts on who John Major should appoint to his Cabinet and some of us chipped in, while her husband Denis told her repeatedly to let it be.

The next morning, she walked down the Downing Street stairs with Denis and their son, Mark, to the Private Secretaries, including me, who were waiting for her at the bottom. Her first words to us were, 'We'll throw a party, when you are all less busy.' She looked down the well of the staircase to the basement at the great globe that the French President, François Mitterrand, had given her. It was too big to take away. Then they shook our hands, and we were in tears. She said, 'I'll go quickly, Andrew', aware of the crowds of staff lining the long corridor to the front door. It was too much for her. And, when she walked along the hallway, the flashlights outside began to go off, the light coming through the windows above the No. 10 door. As she left, many were in tears, and her own shone in her eyes as she gave a final, short speech to the press outside.

And then, just a few hours later, John Major came through the door. The flowers were long gone, the stage had been reset and he was happily clapped in, with no sense of the emotion that had earlier filled the air.

I was glad to see the new PM, despite my empathy at the sadness of Margaret Thatcher's departure. I was not a political supporter but, in any case, I thought it was right that she should go. She had been in power too long, and ultimately power corrupts.

With one exception (Bernard Ingham, her longstanding and ever-loyal press secretary, who chose to resign), the civil servants remained in power when she lost hers and left the building, along with her political staff.

We adapted to the new man immediately, because that was our job – to get to know him and what he wanted and to deliver it. Our submissions came out of the box signed 'J', not 'MT', reflecting not just a change in personnel but also in personal style. The rate of turnaround of decisions also changed, but the decisions eventually came, and that was what we needed to do our job.

He quickly settled in, perhaps helped by a private meeting with Jim Callaghan, a former PM who like him had gained power through the resignation of his boss and knew what it was like to come suddenly into office. They were chasms apart politically, but were also united in being that rare thing in modern times: a Prime Minister who had never gone to university. OK, the police protection officers did complain to me at first that he would sometimes slip away from their protection, but I guess he must have bowed to the inevitable loss of freedom, as the complaints soon stopped. He was more approachable and less dogmatic than his predecessor, and unlike her, he clearly liked women, so I preferred working for him. He didn't just watch cricket, as she did, but he also played it, and we saw him practising his cricket moves in the Private Office. But when we gave him the Wisden for the year of his birth for his birthday, quite uncharacteristically he didn't thank us. We weren't the home team anymore, as we were with his predecessor. In his case that was his Cabinet, who seemed happier too, and it all made sense to me.

• • •

Back to 5 July 2024: the defeated Prime Minister had probably said his farewells long ago, so inevitable had the result seemed. Did the civil servants feel like we did back in 1990 – sad to see someone you'd worked with closely go, but excited by the prospect of a new boss? Yes, probably.

The new Prime Minister will walk up the staircase and see the previous Prime Ministers who have done his job: Margaret Thatcher, John Major, Tony Blair, Gordon Brown, David Cameron, and then like a merry-go-round going faster and faster, Theresa May, Boris Johnson and Liz Truss – but not yet Rishi Sunak, whose official portrait will be taken and added in due course. Each new Prime Minister has to walk past these ghosts of Prime Ministers past: a potted history, as it were, of government in this country, good and bad.

Each frame is roughly the same size, so they can easily be shifted to a new place as the next ex-Prime Minister joins them. Liz Truss, who was Prime Minister for only forty-nine days, occupies a similar size plot as the longest-serving Prime Minister of the modern era, Margaret Thatcher, who served eleven years and 209 days. However spectacularly bad your government, however painful your defenestration, the No. 10 staircase is forgiving. They were all masters and mistresses of this building once, and that is never to be forgotten. Every ex-Prime Minister has a serene face, the highs and lows of office evened out through an official portrait.

But it's very different when you are actually inside No. 10, doing the job, with so much that is unexpected being thrown at you and everyone piling in to tell you where you're going wrong…

So, there it is. The set in No. 10 is cleared for another government once again, for a new drama, each time different but with some familiar elements, like the plots of romantic comedies or Shakespearian tragedies. Which is it to be here, as Keir Starmer settles in? We take our seats, and wait to see what emerges from the wings: the ministers who resign in protest or have to be pushed, the overmighty adviser who has to eventually fall on their sword, the rebellious MPs who turn against a policy before eventually turning against the PM, the unexpected events that throw all best laid plans off course, the promises that are broken and the hopes that end, as with all Prime Ministers, with a speech outside the doors of No. 10, opening a new chapter for a building that has seen it all, and always carries on, as Prime Ministers and their governments – good and bad – come and go.

Chapter 2

NO. 10 AND THE USE AND ABUSE OF POWER

'Country first, party second.'

KEIR STARMER AS HE ENTERED NO. 10

***Bad government**: performative politics; focusing on holding on to power rather than working with others to deliver lasting change.*

***Good government**: governing through vision and values; orchestrating, rather than seeking to do more and more yourself.*

How many times, particularly over the last decade, have we seen reporters outside No. 10 speculating about intrigue or dysfunction, talking about the premature departure of advisers, MPs rebelling and ministers resigning, or Prime Ministers being forced out, only for another to take their place and start the cycle all over again? Often, we see a weak Prime Minister seeking to gain political control by changing the staff at No. 10, only to find that it is not No. 10 that is the problem – but them. Meanwhile, many of the nation's biggest challenges, the things that fall squarely on the Prime Minister's desk, are neglected, and unexpected crises like the Covid-19 pandemic are handled chaotically. They have power, but their focus too often seems to be on how to keep it, rather than on how to use it for the good of the country – on campaigning rather than governing. All eyes are on No. 10, instead of what government should really be for.

It generally starts so well, with those promises delivered on the steps of No. 10, and a wave of public goodwill often follows the new Prime Minister as they walk through the door, wanting to believe that a new chapter has been reached. So how do we get to the point where that same person becomes the very figure that the public comes to hate? What goes wrong inside No. 10 itself that prevents government from being good?

Is it the people within or, as some think tanks advise, No. 10 itself that needs reform, with an expanded Department of State merged with the Cabinet Office, for example? Or is it that it has become too big and instead should concentrate on what only it can do – leadership – and provide a clear sense of vision, purpose and direction? It should be the conductor of an orchestra, rather than trying to play every instrument itself.

• • •

There are those who think the building is the problem.

Four months after Starmer first entered Downing Street as Prime Minister, the journalist Tom McTague wrote of

> many of those inside No. 10 who have already come to see the creaking, mice-infested building of No. 10 Downing Street as a symbol of Britain's failed state. There are a number of senior figures close to Starmer who have even concluded that the building

> is not suitable as the hub of a 21st-century government and needs to be closed down, and turned into a ceremonial museum.[1]

This came some six weeks after the spectacular resignation of Sue Gray, Starmer's first Chief of Staff in No. 10 on 6 October 2024, preceded by many weeks of bitter, hostile briefing against her clearly coming straight from inside No. 10. It had not been a happy place. But according to many inside, it's the building that's the issue, not those who inhabit it.

I take a different view. On 20 November 2024 I found myself in a BBC studio talking with Matt Chorley and Tom McTague on BBC Radio Five Live about whether No. 10 is no longer fit for government. Tom explained that 'senior figures close to the Prime Minister' think it is too old-fashioned, with its nooks and crannies and its many rooms. It was very far from the open plan that Labour had enjoyed when it was in opposition, particularly during its election campaign. In an open plan everyone would know what was going on and could be on the same page. If there had been an open plan, his sources were suggesting, this falling out between Sue Gray and the others might not have happened.

Gray, of course, was already all too familiar with the dark corners and secrets of No. 10, and probably had her own views about whether it is the people inside or No. 10's working environment which is the ultimate source of Britain's ills. Her bland but informative Partygate report into what happened during Boris Johnson's tenure during the pandemic found that there were 'failures of leadership and judgement in No. 10 and the Cabinet Office.'[2]

One of these now infamous lockdown parties, on 18 December 2020, was billed as an 'end of year meeting with wine & cheese' and took place in the foyer just outside the press office. A custodian and a Downing Street police officer dropped by when one attendee set off a panic alarm and found 'a large number of people in the area outside of the main press office and one individual giving a speech. Inside the press office a further fifteen to twenty people were present.' They simply let them get on with it. This was No. 10 after all – and they made the rules. Who were they to say otherwise? The next day, the Prime Minister announced that due to the spread of a highly contagious new Delta variant, tight restrictions would lead to Christmas being ruined for most people. Members of the press office had been working on the announcement while they partied and, hours after they'd all gone home, cleaners discovered red wine spilled up the walls and over photocopying paper.[3]

Was it the building that was at fault? I don't think so.

Back in the BBC studio, Tom said that people inside No. 10 were even thinking that the day-to-day running of government should be moved to the Treasury, the Foreign Office or even the Home Office. Jonathan Powell had considered the idea when he first entered No. 10 as Chief of Staff in 1997, and I recall that Tony Blair had thought of setting up his Office of the Prime Minister in the nearby QEII Conference Centre before he was in government. But such plans came to nothing. They couldn't afford the upheaval then, and people in No. 10 now are apparently weighing up the same issue. Doubtless they would come to the same conclusion.

Governing is different to campaigning, I said to Matt Chorley. No. 10 works well together when there's a clear vision and plan in place, not because the political staff can hear everyone else's conversation (which in some cases should not be overheard anyway, for national security or management reasons). Strong leadership, not the office configuration, gives everyone a sharp purpose so they can get on with their job rather than fighting each other.

But there is certainly a size issue, and No. 10 has become too big. Since Thatcher's and Major's day, it has grown exponentially, but has it actually become more effective? In Thatcher's time, there were only around 100 people working in the building, and that included cleaners who were only there at night and people like messengers who would not exist today. There were very few political staff: the Parliamentary Private Secretary and Political Secretary shared a room adjacent to the Cabinet Room and around a dozen people in the Policy Unit located at the front of the building occupied cramped rooms along a narrow corridor on the upper floors overlooking Downing Street. Under Tony Blair, the number of political advisers and civil servants ballooned, and this trend has continued under successive PMs, such that it is reported that there are now some 300 staff in No. 10, so many that they have spread into No. 11, No. 12 and even the Cabinet Office, all connected by corridors with No. 10 (so you can still enter through that famous door and maintain the illusion of small government as No. 10 spreads its tentacles ever wider). In Thatcher's day, there were only five Private Secretaries; when I told Theresa May this at a Downing Street party to celebrate the women who had worked in No. 10, she was amazed and said she had many more (thirteen, I think she said). And by March 2025, there were forty-two special advisers.[4]

Does bigger actually mean better? Whatever you think of Thatcher's policies, no one would say that she struggled to implement them. Trying to govern everything that happens in Britain from the centre will never work, whatever the size or design of the building, especially as the challenges become more complex and drift further outside their control.

Yet successive think tanks have recommended a beefing up of the centre: in 2024, for example, the Institute for Government called for a new 'Department of the Prime Minister' including much of the current Cabinet Office.[5] John Major, speaking at their launch event, lamented that No. 10 was now three and a half times bigger than in his day but no more effective, in his view. Major said, 'We are not a presidency and I do not wish to see an increase in the power of No. 10. The PM has many powers and with a large majority it can be almost unconstrained. I prefer effective Cabinet government to Prime Ministerial diktat.' Gordon Brown, speaking at the same event, also expressed shock at how big No. 10 and the centre had become, even since his day, and said that what was needed was not more people but better coordination and communication, specifically a National Economic Council staffed by the Treasury and the Cabinet Office, including relevant departments and agencies, and a Council of devolved nations. I agree with them both.

As I said to Matt Chorley, infighting inevitably happens inside No. 10, not because people aren't working in an open plan, but because their principal is weak and doesn't have a clear vision or inspire loyalty. Political advisers dominate when campaigning rather than governing is the key objective. It's government, not the building or even the composition of No. 10, that needs to change. No. 10 needs to look outwards to the rest of Whitehall and open its doors to wider social actors, like civil society and business, rather than constantly speaking to itself.

But let's get back to the building. Jack Brown, author of *No. 10: The Geography of Power at Downing Street*, joined our conversation on Matt Chorley's show. He said that Gordon Brown created a mini open plan around him in the shape of a horseshoe on which his closest aides sat, but the plan didn't really work. Everyone wanted to be in the horseshoe, of course; everyone in No. 10 wants to be as close as they can to the Prime Minister. Some things never change.

Privately, I think of the newspaper reports of Brown allegedly throwing a mobile phone or stapler at his team in an outburst of anger or frustration. Clearly, proximity has its dangers.

Jack explained that the building, which was constructed on a swamp, is really two buildings, one facing Downing Street and built in the seventeenth century, then connected in the eighteenth century to another, much larger one, where all the state rooms are housed. It has since been endlessly adapted to the needs of successive Prime Ministers, who each use different rooms in varying ways. Boris Johnson, I recall, worked in the room adjacent to the Cabinet Room, in my day occupied by the Principal Private Secretary, Andrew Turnbull, and the Foreign Affairs Private Secretary, Charles Powell, the two most senior of us five. Johnson worked there when he had Covid and had to be stopped from coming out and infecting everyone else; to this end, staff erected a 'puppy gate' of two chairs at the entrance to the office.[6]

Matt Chorley reminded us that the current PM likes to work in what has long been known as the study. Starmer chose to remove the portrait of Margaret Thatcher which had been hanging there, which had led to it being called 'the Thatcher room'. Gordon Brown had commissioned it after inviting Lady Thatcher to tea at No. 10 in September 2007. According to the artist, it is the first painting of a former Prime Minister ever to be commissioned by Downing Street.[7] Starmer rather awkwardly defended his decision to move it to another room by saying that he disliked being looked down upon when working and always had (even when he was a barrister, he hated being surrounded by pictures of judges – he prefers landscapes, apparently).[8] This decision to move Thatcher's portrait caused some outrage from political opponents, almost as much as Starmer received from Labour supporters when, in the run-up to the election, he praised her in a piece in *The Telegraph*, writing that she was a leader who effected 'meaningful change' and that she 'sought to drag Britain out of its stupor by setting loose our natural entrepreneurialism.' Later, he said it was not her politics but her 'sense of purpose' that he admired.[9] A hard act to follow, or indeed to be looked down upon by. Finding your own sense of purpose, judging by recent Prime Ministers, is even harder.

When Thatcher died in 2013, Tony Blair confessed, 'I always thought my job was to build on some of the things she had done rather than reverse them' and described her as 'a towering political figure.'[10] Her long shadow still hangs over recent politics, from Liz Truss's attempts to mimic her – that headscarf on top of a tank or that pussybow blouse during her leadership contest – and Rishi Sunak's decision to launch his leadership campaign at her birthplace of Grantham, to, perhaps most surprisingly, Rachel Reeves choosing to call herself 'the Iron Chancellor'.

In the radio interview, I was invited to reminisce about the study in Thatcher's day. The study is located at the bottom of the stairs to the No. 10 flat, so was a natural choice for her to work in as she could move seamlessly between the two places. It was where she wrote her speeches and where I and others used to pour her a scotch in the evening when we were helping her write them, opening the drinks cabinet hidden behind a door. I remember when she once nodded off briefly with a glass in her hand, in mid-sentence, which she completed perfectly when she woke up. It's also where she held bilateral meetings with her ministers and, as it happened, where she interviewed me one-to-one for the job of Private Secretary, a nerve-wracking experience about which I have written elsewhere.

The real reason why the staff are unlikely to move from No. 10, for all its faults, is that it's incredibly convenient for the Prime Minister to live above the shop (even if some Prime Ministers now live above No. 11, the principle is just the same). It makes their extremely demanding job easier, and it means their private life and their families suffer less under the pressure of their 24/7 workload, even if it is not ideal for their staff in terms of working conditions.

But there is a contrary view, held by former Cabinet Secretary Gus O'Donnell, who worked closely with four Prime Ministers, that this arrangement is bad for the health of PMs, adding to their stress, leading to an overly rich diet of official dinners, and reducing their ability to exercise.[11]

However, I think it is the case that the relationship between the Prime Minister and those who support them is closer because it takes place in their extended home, with a blurring of professional and personal relationships that can strengthen bonds. I had worked as a Private Secretary to two Secretaries of State for Employment before No. 10, not just Lord Young but also Norman Fowler, but never visited their homes (or wanted to), and was less attached to them as a consequence. When one was replaced by the other, I scarcely looked up from my desk. But when Margaret Thatcher left Downing Street, she'd left her personal stamp everywhere, and tears were shed, as we have seen. The state rooms still have the decorations she put in place (though one room has since changed colour) and the carpet that she had laid in the corridor leading to the Cabinet Room and up the stairs to the state rooms is still, mysteriously, in place. Few Prime Ministers have left such a legacy, but their personal choices do help make No. 10 feel like their own. I think of that portrait of Queen Elizabeth I hanging in the Pillared Room behind Theresa May when I met her there at a reception. Or the unsettling modern, apparently religious paintings by the Portuguese-born artist Dame Paula Rego, that I saw hanging in the same room in Keir Starmer's No. 10.

One of May's Private Secretaries referred to No. 10 as 'the House' when I was there, which I queried because we had always used that phrase to refer to the Commons. She said, since Tony Blair's day, everyone inside the building knew it as 'the House', which seemed presumptuous to me, but then that's what it is – a house and a home, and certainly not an office block.

Mrs Thatcher used to hold family celebrations in the state rooms and invite us to join in – I recall drinks with her son Mark and his then wife Diane in the Pillared Room when they were visiting. The public never normally observe this more informal side of No. 10, but it was there for all to see at that infamous Covid birthday party for Boris Johnson in the Cabinet Room, during which Carrie Symonds (Johnson's then partner, now wife) and the couple's interior designer Lulu Lytle came down from the flat and mixed with civil service and political staff, along with the Chancellor, Rishi Sunak (who maintained that he was only present because he had arrived early for a meeting). No big deal, normally, but on this day they were breaking the law, which is why we got to know about it, eventually. Three months earlier, Johnson had handwritten a note to a seven-year-old girl congratulating her for cancelling her birthday party, twice, and saying 'we've all got to do our bit to protect the NHS and save lives, and that is exactly what you are doing. Well done!'[12]

People were appalled by the double standards of Partygate but I think the public generally like the fact that it is also a home, not just an office, and would dislike the idea of moving people into a conventional building, which is another reason why the step contemplated by Starmer's people will very likely not happen. It's relatable, approachable even, unlike many parts of government: that relatively modest façade and famous front door in front of which journalists stand. The Prime Minister greets heads of state outside with a handshake, Cabinet ministers walk up to it during a reshuffle and sometimes we even see Larry the cat. People delivering petitions, or even just visiting, often get their photograph taken in front of the famous door.

Although I was quite often caught on television getting in and out of cars with the Prime Minister when I worked there, I only had my photograph specifically taken outside once, with my parents and my fiancé, now my husband, all of us looking just a little awkward. Everyone working inside No. 10 then, and probably now, was allowed one chance to take their close family around the building for a tour, typically at the weekend when the Prime Minister was not there. During the visit, my father, who died a year later, revealed that he'd been there once before, during the Second World War, but was not allowed to say anything about it. My mother, who at that point was long divorced from him and took a jaundiced view of everything he did, told me later that this was just a fantasy, and it did seem extremely unlikely. But I liked the idea, somehow, that I was not the first person in my very modest family to step inside No. 10. It made it seem like the people's house.

The most important thing to remember, I said on Matt Chorley's radio show, is that No. 10 is not just an office but the Prime Minister's home. But what if Prime Ministers become too comfortable in No. 10 and its echo chamber and start to cut themselves off from their MPs and the rest of the world? That way lies bad government…

• • •

The security takes me by surprise every time I return to No. 10, because with a staff pass you don't have to go through it, so you think nothing of it: the long, regimented queues snaking outside the gates, the presentation of ID to the police who consult their list, then taking off your coat and belt and removing anything metal in your pockets, the X-raying of bags, then walking through the metal detector arch. And then suddenly you are free to walk into that relatively normal-looking, entirely familiar but strangely quiet street protected by the gates from the bustle of tourists and sometimes chanting of demonstrators outside in Westminster.

Whenever I go there, it feels as if in some strange way I'm travelling back in time, such was the intensity of the experiences I had there, and I feel a strong connection with it still. It's like returning to *Doctor Who*'s TARDIS – a different Doctor and assistants in residence now, of course, but the Doctor, the TARDIS and the sense of peril are still essentially the same, as the inhabitants try to put the world to rights. When you live in the TARDIS, that world seems full of colour. It's never dull. Outside in the dreary streets of London, however, living as an ordinary person in an ordinary world, it seems black and white.

When I drove home at the end of a long working day in No. 10, behind the wheel of my little Peugeot 306, my journey took me from Westminster, through the glamour of the West End and the wealth of the City, then to Shoreditch and onwards to my one-bedroom flat in Stoke Newington in Hackney, fashionable now but then 'up and coming', with every tenth house or so derelict or in visible disrepair, and many of the people walking the streets evidently poor or unwell. Thinking about them was very far from a priority for the people inside No. 10.

I was living in two entirely different worlds. Only once did they come together, when I was in the Private Office, alone as I remember it, with the TV on mute in the corner, when I happened to glance up as the presenter walked down Evering Road, the road on which I lived. I turned on the sound and heard, 'It was on this very street, in this very house where the Kray twins murdered their victims, whose blood was papered over but is still there.' The house was three doors down from my flat. All in the past, of course, but now my present. Was that world in which I lived as a private person all a dream, or was it No. 10 that was in its own bubble, cut off from the world?

This otherworldly quality became even greater when permanent gates were erected at the end of Downing Street over the Christmas of 1989, in response to mounting security concerns, seven months after I started working there. Before that there were just flimsy steel barriers and police who nodded you in if you were a familiar face.

The wonder is that it took so long to step up protection in this way. After all, Margaret Thatcher and her Cabinet had been bombed by the IRA in 1984 in their hotel in Brighton, the night before the party conference; five people were killed and thirty-five seriously injured. She herself had only narrowly escaped harm when the bomb went off in the early hours of the morning, destroying her bathroom, at a time when she was still awake and working on her speech. The couple above them, the Tebbits, were seriously wounded, and Mrs Tebbit ended up in a wheelchair for the rest of her life. Robin Butler, the Cabinet Secretary, who was with Mrs Thatcher, led her and Denis both to safety.

Thatcher always seemed fearless to me, but in her private papers she once wrote, 'After that, you walk into a crowd – it's absolutely terrifying. Or if someone hands you something – look at Rajiv Gandhi [who was assassinated] – hidden in the flowers.'[13] Her close colleague, Airey Neave, had been killed in 1979 by an IRA bomb detonated as he was leaving the House of Commons carpark. While I worked in No. 10, every morning and night as I returned to my car I would check underneath for a bomb, as instructed by No. 10 security when I began my job. The car in which the Prime Minister travelled was strengthened to make it bomb-proof. In 1990, in her final months in office, another former close aide and now a government minister, Ian Gow, was blown up outside his home in the small Sussex village of Hankham. The bomb had been placed under his car by the Provisional Irish Republican Army (IRA) in the night.

The security around Thatcher was very tight, as it has remained for every Prime Minister since, and, although necessary for her safety, it led to visits outside No. 10 being stage-managed, effectively cutting her off from the public, and I suspect the same remains true for Prime Ministers today.

That also meant that there were no demonstrations to greet her and people, caught on the hop, had little time to get their thoughts in order to make even constructive criticisms. Sometimes, we would literally drop in from the sky in an army helicopter, as we did when we visited a disused mine in Wales, and leave less than an hour later. It was all smiles, despite the massive hostility mining communities felt toward her.

The gates were the idea of security professionals, not Margaret Thatcher, though she took an interest in the design. She wanted them to be in keeping with the plain style of the street. They were highly controversial because they were seen as denying the public access to the door of Downing Street and as a sign of retreat from the public by an increasingly unpopular PM.

As it turned out, the new gates only partially protected No. 10 from the IRA. On 7 February 1991, when John Major was Prime Minister, it was mortar bombed by the IRA from a van parked outside in Whitehall. I was in the Private Office facing the garden when the bomb fell, and I saw the windows blow in and then magically fall back into place, as if in a movie played back in reverse. I dived under the desk, not knowing what would happen next. It was the special bomb protection film that had been installed at the same time as the gates that saved members of the Cabinet, the intended target, who were in the Cabinet Room next door. Fortunately, the windows were closed: the specialists had advised that had they been open even by only six inches, lives could have been lost were a bomb to fall outside. The Cabinet were led to safety, again by Robin Butler, a veteran of the Brighton bomb. He put his head round our door to assure us that they were going – through the internal door – to a Cabinet Office safe room in the basement. We were left to face whatever might happen next and eventually ended up in what I think was then the post room, with no windows overlooking either the garden or the street. We set up a new office and carried on working. We were only allowed to leave in the evening after the area was declared safe.

The gates did provide full protection against another kind of physical threat, however. On Saturday 31 March 1990, eight months before Thatcher was forced out of Downing Street, I was working inside No. 10 while a demonstration against her deeply unpopular 'poll tax' was taking place in nearby Trafalgar Square. The tax, which was to be introduced nationwide the next day, would levy a charge on every individual of voting age regardless of whether they owned their own home or what it was worth, and many people were very angry. This included many Tory families in the home counties who found that they were paying far more than in the past, because the new tax was calculated by the number of adults in the household, not the home. I was watching the protest on the television in the corner of the office while I worked, as news came through that it was turning into a riot. I saw that a portable cabin had been set alight and the South African embassy attacked. The police were charging on horses in full riot gear and some protesters threw whatever came to hand in response.

And then I saw some of the protesters charging down Whitehall to the gates of No. 10 and trying to break through. It was certainly frightening, but the gates held them back, even after an hour of trying. The protesters gave up and went on to Soho, where they set cars alight and looted shops to vent their rage. Thatcher, the source of their ire, was not even in London at the time, but she saw the events on television and was characteristically defiant, digging in deeper to her entrenched position on the tax, not realising that the real threat to her at this point was not the demonstrators but her failure to listen to those who told her to change course.

• • •

No. 10 can feel like a sanctuary when you're under attack, both physically and politically. Essentially, it's the job of those appointed to No. 10 to remain loyal – but unwavering loyalty may result in it becoming an echo chamber, and even a bunker, when the Prime Minister is unwilling to listen to messages coming from outside its four walls and is increasingly on the defensive. A Prime Minister's very closeness to the home team can become the problem. Their ministers, infuriated, might resign. Before too long, the people who keep them in power – the very MPs who voted for them – might even ask them to step down. At least, this is what happened to Margaret Thatcher, creating a path which others have since trod.

Thatcher's No. 10 was in many ways high performing and had contributed greatly to her longevity and effectiveness. It was lean, focused and cohesive, powered by a decisive Prime Minister with a strong vision and sense of priorities. As Andrew Turnbull, her Principal Private Secretary, the head of No. 10, said in his valedictory speech at her leaving party:

> No. 10 is a collection of tribes, huddling in cubby holes up and down this extraordinary building. We know from accounts of previous administrations that it was not always a happy ship – indeed, a previous occupant of my room used to lock the door to the Cabinet to keep out previous occupants of John Whittingdale's [Thatcher's Political Secretary's] office. But under you, Prime Minister, we have all – civil servants, politicos, those with life sentences, those merely on remand – come together. And it has happened because you have generated loyalty. With that loyalty has come a bond that will remain as we go our separate ways.

That loyalty was both a strength – helping her achieve her objectives – and a weakness, because it drove a wedge between her and her ministers. The fault lines first started to show in what became known as the Westland affair in 1985–86, which involved two key No. 10 advisers: Charles Powell, her Private Secretary for Foreign Affairs (of two to three years standing at that time), and Bernard Ingham, her loyal Press Secretary who had served her since 1979.

The Westland affair was a protracted dispute over a helicopter contract between the PM and her archrival and then Defence Secretary, Michael Heseltine. Powell and Ingham were accused of arranging for documents to be leaked by others which cast Heseltine in a conveniently bad light. Eventually, he stomped out of Cabinet, his long hair flying, and resigned shortly after, bringing down another Cabinet minister, Leon Brittan, in his wake. Powell and Ingham denied that they had done this but the scandal ran so deep that Thatcher nearly had to step down and was only saved by a carefully worded 'independent' report on what happened by her Cabinet Secretary.

Whether she knew what was happening in her name, I don't know. As Powell explained years later, 'Please don't misunderstand this, but in a strange sense it was quite hard to tell what was me and what was her. I knew her way of doing things and what she wanted, so I could pretty much read her mind.'[14] He may not have ordered the leak but I know that he was prepared to step over boundaries that other civil servants might not. He later told me that he realised he was over-stepping traditional civil service norms in terms of taking on tasks and responsibilities well beyond his notional role. However, he said he was doing this not because he had become too politically close to the PM but for *institutional* reasons. In his words, 'She deserved to have champions fight for her point of view, make sure her decisions were in fact implemented and say things on our own responsibility because we knew they represented her mind.' He was conscious, despite appearances, of a great imbalance of power between her and her ministers. But then, as he pointed out, there were only around twenty frontline staff at No. 10, compared to the many thousands of staff working on those ministers' behalf in their different departments.[15]

It didn't surprise me that he saw part of his job as being to help the Prime Minister manage her relationships with ministers, relationships which – if they turned sour – had the potential to bring our 'first among equals' Prime Minister down. Which ultimately, they did. It is part of the job of every Private Secretary to do what they can to ensure good relationships with the rest of government, including ministers, because this is essential to good government. But it is certainly not our job to make already damaged relationships worse.

Likewise, Bernard Ingham felt he could act freely as her agent because he had her full trust. On a regular basis, he was briefing the press on her views without consulting her. He did so, he said in his autobiography, because he could reliably read her mind because he knew her views so well and she was so constant in the way she held them.[16] To be fair, I suspect others in a similar role today do the same.

Why do advisers become so powerful? There is so much *stuff* that comes a Prime Minister's way: not just the big decisions – which in reality require the processing of considerable detail and often the reconciliation of different departmental views – and the increasingly relentless media work, but also the unexpected crises, domestic and international, which can throw an entire schedule off course. And then there is the busy international diary; parliamentary business, including Prime Minister's Questions; managing ministers; all the handshaking and meeting with the public across the country that helps bring policies to life and wins votes; working on speeches; dealing with piles of correspondence and newspaper headlines; and the stuff most people would never have thought of, like ecclesiastical appointments and who gets honours. That's why a Prime Minister needs civil servants and political advisers – to stop them from drowning in detail, to help government join up and to make sure time is used wisely. Ministers can't run everything. They have to rely on the civil service and, increasingly, their political advisers.

Advisers are the eyes and ears. They digest for the Prime Minister the vast volume of material that comes their way, advising them on options, conveying their views to the rest of Whitehall, having conversations on their behalf and taking on the mantle of the Prime Minister to say, and even do, things they don't have time for. And this is why trust is important; they couldn't survive without it. No. 10 is partly there to be a filter, particularly against the impossibly large volume of correspondence and invitations that come in, much of which is from the public. Many of these are never seen by the Private Office, let alone by the Prime Minister. In my day, there was a special unit in the basement of No. 10 which sent the vast majority of such things off to officials in government departments to reply to. Generally, only letters forwarded by MPs or written by VIPs got through, though some particularly affecting personal letters from people would occasionally be sent 'upstairs' for a reply, leaving it to the discretion of the Private Secretaries whether to draft a reply for the Prime Minister's signature or, as was more often the case, reply themselves on their behalf. These would typically start with the phrase, 'The Prime Minister has asked me to reply on her behalf... ', even though she hadn't.

We would often know exactly what the PM *would* say, so many times had we had drafted words for them to sign or speak, and we had often successfully steered them towards the decisions we thought best, having read all the papers and outlined all the options. It's not such a big shift to start believing that you know what the PM thinks without consulting them or even to decide in your infinite wisdom that there are some important things or views they don't need to see. Charles Powell once wrote, 'CDP [i.e. him] to bury' on a request by the Foreign Secretary for her to make an unequivocal statement on apartheid in South Africa, in order to save the 1986 Commonwealth Games from a growing African boycott.[17] This was a highly charged issue. The Queen was so infuriated by the Prime Minister's failure to intervene she accused her of damaging her Commonwealth and even threatened to cancel her weekly audiences with her, official papers released thirty years later revealed.[18] Powell did in fact admit to Foreign Office officials that he had withheld the letter, on 'grounds of tact', fearing his boss would react badly.[19]

By the time I was in No. 10 in 1989, the then Foreign Secretary, Geoffrey Howe, and his top civil servant, along with the Cabinet Secretary, were trying (unsuccessfully) to remove Powell. There were even some who were calling him 'the real Foreign Secretary'. Howe was demoted to Lord President not long after, though he was also given the honorary title of Deputy Prime Minister – a term that was openly mocked by senior No. 10 staff in private, because they felt he was that in name only.

Later that year, Chancellor Nigel Lawson resigned. Two days before, he'd been barracked in the House of Commons by the shadow Chancellor, who said there were 'two Chancellors' and that only one of them was elected (a reference to Bernard Ingham, who had briefed the press that Thatcher believed 'You can't buck the markets' at a time when Lawson had been trying to keep the value of the pound fixed to the deutschmark). But it was the Prime Minister's Economics Adviser, Alan Walters, who finally made Lawson lose his rag. Walters had published an article expressly contradicting a course of action to which the Chancellor was entirely wedded – joining the European Exchange Mechanism – to which the Prime Minister at that time was implacably opposed. Lawson stomped into No. 10 while Thatcher was still in the flat, her hair in rollers. She kept him waiting until her hair was ready and she felt in a position to face him. When she came down to the study, Lawson told her Walters had to go or he would resign. She refused to sack him, and so Nigel Lawson went. Her justification has become famous: 'Advisers advise, ministers decide.'

An unsuccessful leadership challenge by Sir Anthony Meyer followed and, shortly after, George Younger, who had headed up her leadership campaign, met her in private over 'a scotch or two'. He told her that Bernard Ingham and Charles Powell must go, that she must be more positive about Europe and she should spend more time talking to MPs. The only change she made was the last.[20]

• • •

A year later, I was sitting in No. 10 watching TV as Geoffrey Howe delivered his resignation speech in Parliament, with Nigel Lawson at his side. Margaret Thatcher was sat immobile on the front benches, unable to turn round and look him in the eye. Howe later recounted in his biography that the night before he'd been watching her on TV at the Lord Mayor's annual Guildhall Banquet. She was wearing 'an enormous white collar and long black train, like an assertively self-confident Elizabethan monarch,' he wrote, before noting that in her speech she likened herself to a batsman, saying, 'The bowling's going to get hit all round the ground. That's my style.'[21]

Howe picked up the cricket metaphor in his speech and turned it against her, saying, 'It is rather like sending your opening batsmen to the crease only for them to find, the moment the first balls are bowled, that their bats have been broken before the game by the team captain.'

I instantly knew she was finished. It had been a long time since she had treated her longest-standing colleague and now Deputy Prime Minister as if he was on the same side.

Eight days later, members of her Cabinet were telling her one by one that they would support her but she should stand down, as she could not win the race for the leadership of her party. Next day, she informed her Cabinet that she was resigning. She sat in front of them around the coffin-shaped table, a powerful woman whose voice normally never failed her in times of crisis, suddenly becoming vulnerable, surrounded by men, struggling to read out her resignation statement because her voice broke down. She insisted on finishing it and then read it again, saying she feared they hadn't heard it the first time around. She did so with the same emotion. Others in the room, overcome by the raw sadness of it all, shed tears, myself included.

Nowadays, the defenestration of a Prime Minister seems almost commonplace, but back then it had seemed impossible. A taboo had been broken and the enormity of it made everyone suddenly look small. Over her eleven and a half years, she had reshaped the country – for better or worse – and been a commanding figure on the international stage. She knew how to use power to effect change but in the end her steamroller approach lost her the confidence of the country. No. 10 had become part of the problem: we were a mirror which only reflected her – and she had lost touch with political reality.

• • •

There's a pattern here that can still be seen years later: Prime Ministers too easily become remote from their backbenchers and the electorate. They promise to serve you but end up serving themselves. And then their troops, facing electoral oblivion, rebel. In the case of Thatcher's defenestration, the electoral strategy worked: they won the next election with a new leader at the helm. Emboldened by that example, the Tories have forced their Prime Minister out a further three times.

And Keir Starmer's premiership has been beset by similar challenges and may end in defenestration too.

First, they come for your advisers, and then they come for you. Is it the advisers who are at fault, or the person who appoints them?

Ultimately, Prime Ministers choose their key advisers and if they let them become too powerful, they are to blame. But over-centralisation of decision-making may play a part: Prime Ministers who feel vulnerable can draw more and more decisions into No. 10 to assert their authority but then, even more overloaded, they become further reliant on their advisers, who may then assert more and more control over the rest of government, to consolidate their own personal power. Eventually, it slows the whole of Whitehall down, as decisions from an overloaded No. 10 take longer and longer and delivery suffers.

Over decades, No. 10 has taken more power into itself, contributing to its considerable growth in size. In 2025, John Major commented that 'these days the amount of decisions that have to go up to the PM is outrageously high' and observed that the quality of decisions suffer because they lack the expertise held by Secretaries of State and individual departments. As Major also touched on, Prime Ministers have very little thinking time because the pressure is 'appalling' – and this has multiplied a hundredfold since his day, because of the media.[22]

Prime Ministers struggle under the weight of it all, especially if they find it hard to make up their mind. In his biography of Gordon Brown, who was famously indecisive as Prime Minister, Andrew Rawnsley wrote,

> Routine decisions took weeks to process. Cabinet ministers and their senior officials began to speak with extraordinary vehemence about what one called 'the sheer dysfunctionality' of No. 10. They did not know the half of it. On the account of one civil servant: 'However chaotic it looked from the outside, it was a billion times worse inside.'

According to one senior civil servant quoted by Rawnsley, confronted with difficult decisions, 'he just delays and delays, thinking he will get a better set of options later. But quite often the options just get worse.' And all this was exacerbated by Brown's distrust of his colleagues and his wish to give himself ever more power.[23]

This slow creep towards inefficiency may have begun slowly, but Brexit tipped it over into complete dysfunction. Who didn't feel sorry for Theresa May when David Cameron resigned after the Brexit referendum and left it to her, another Remainer, to resolve impossible contradictions, deliver on unfounded promises and sort out a divided country and Parliament? This was an enormous task on top of the already crippling day-to-day business of government. Her response was to take even more power into No. 10, rather than spending time building a consensus in her Cabinet, her party and across the country as a whole, perhaps because she concluded that was almost unattainable anyway.

The Brexit chief negotiator, Olly Robbins, who was nominally employed by the Department for Exiting the European Union, in fact reported directly to May. Decision-making became more and more centralised and other ministers were increasingly cut out, as the Deputy Cabinet Secretary Helen MacNamara has since made clear.[24]

This move towards a more presidential style of government first became apparent when May attempted to deny Parliament a vote on leaving the EU, a move which was overturned by the courts. The following year, in what turned out to be a disastrous election for her, she opted to make the campaign all about her, with the slogan 'Theresa May – For Britain.' Quite apart from the fact that UK elections are for governments, not presidents, she lacked the personal charisma or political skills to carry it off.[25] The result was the loss of a double-digit lead in the polls and an existing healthy majority, and she ended up relying on an agreement with a minority party to shore her up, as well as an almighty struggle to get her deal through Parliament.

Understandably, given her additional responsibilities, she became over-reliant on her Chiefs of Staff, Fiona Hill and Nick Timothy, whom she had brought in with her from the Home Office. They knew her style – and her style was already to micro-manage – and when she came to No. 10, a lot of other decisions were pulled into her gravity field, well beyond the priority that was Brexit.[26] Her joint Chiefs of Staff acquired a huge amount of power as a result, and MPs started complaining that they were behaving more like Deputy Prime Ministers than aides. They certainly had considerable influence over the 2017 general election campaign, including its highly unpopular social care policy that Theresa May had to disown (needless to say, they ended up carrying the can).

She was given an ultimatum: either they go, or she would face a leadership contest, and she was forced to choose the first. Two years after that, the 'men in suits' came for her and she was forced to go herself, because her strategy wasn't working, whoever she chose as Chief of Staff.

• • •

It was bad government, turbo-charged by Brexit, but what followed was on a much grander and wilder scale. Brexit merged into Covid, and people who were masters of performative politics delivered an expert lesson in how *not* to do government.

All the key ingredients were there. Campaigning, not governing. An indecisive Prime Minister. An overmighty adviser and a concentration of power in No. 10. And a disregard for democratic accountability and standards in public life, as well.

As a child, Boris Johnson had wanted to be king, so when he became Prime Minister it was unsurprising that he tried to sweep the usual checks and balances aside. There was the proroguing of Parliament in order to stop it getting in the way of what he wanted to do on Brexit. I and others thought that this was precisely why we had a monarchy – to protect us from this kind of tyranny – but no, the monarch only felt able to do as he wished, leaving it to another diminutive elderly woman, Baroness Hale, with a diamond spider broach on her black dress, to bring the power of the Supreme Court to the rescue and overturn the Queen's order.

There were those who thought that this was down to his chief adviser, Dominic Cummings, who appeared to be pulling Johnson's strings. If only he could be forced out, Johnson might prove to be alright, turning back into that affable, even lovable, figure that my teenage children used to find funny when he was regularly on the satirical TV show, *Have I Got News for You*, appearances which helped him get elected as Mayor of London. Always 'Boris', never 'Johnson' (and definitely not the same Boris Johnson who gave the address of a journalist to his old Eton pal Darius Guppy, so that he could arrange for heavies to give the journalist 'a couple of black eyes' and a 'cracked rib' for trying to expose Guppy's part in a jewellery heist – all caught on a secret tape, so even Johnson could not escape that truth). [27]

Who can forget the sight of Cummings, sitting behind a desk in the garden of No. 10 in front of rows of journalists (whom he kept waiting for no very clear reason), explaining why he hadn't broken lockdown rules imposed by his boss during Covid. At the first signs of the illness, he had driven to Durham. As he started to feel a bit better, he had driven his family to Barnard Castle to 'test his vision' so he could be sure he could drive back to London safely. I don't think any chief adviser before or after has been given such a platform in No. 10, let alone been allowed to get away with such nonsense.

Surely, many people speculated, Cummings had something on Johnson, or he would have been summarily sacked. Or perhaps Johnson feared to lose him, because Cummings had made him what he was. Cummings was credited by many as the real person who won the EU referendum, with its psychologically powerful slogan, 'Take Back Control', and its simple and mendacious advertising, most famously on the Brexit campaigning bus: 'We send the EU £350 million a week, let's fund our NHS instead'. Never mind factual accuracy, let's make it up. If it wins votes, it wins. Cummings repeated this EU referendum 'triumph' by masterminding Johnson's 2019 election success. But it was Boris Johnson whom he made to look mighty, even getting him to drive a bulldozer with the slogan Cummings had given him, 'Get Brexit Done', through a mock brick wall. The majority Johnson subsequently won was so large that people confidently predicted he would be Prime Minister for at least the next decade. Would he lose his magic touch without Cummings to do the heavy lifting?

Cummings also helped bring a kind of order out of – or at least to disguise – Johnson's chaos. Simon Case, the Cabinet Secretary, laid the scale of the problem out in a WhatsApp later released to the Covid inquiry:

> He changes strategic direction every day (Monday we were all about fear of virus returning as per Europe, March etc – today we're in 'let it rip' mode cos the UK is pathetic, needs a cold shower etc). He cannot lead and we cannot support him in leading with

> this approach. The team captain cannot change the call on the big plays every day. The team can't deliver anything under these circumstances.[28]

After leaving No. 10, Cummings wrote in one of his blogs that Johnson is 'hopeless at bureaucratic infighting, and routinely says and does things so foolish that people are open-mouthed'. He added he knew Johnson was 'in any objective sense, unfit to be PM' when he agreed to become his chief adviser at No. 10. But he and former members of the Vote Leave campaign decided to 'roll the dice' and join his No. 10 team anyway, believing his defects could be 'partly mitigated' in office. They thought that 'precisely because he doesn't know what he's doing, we may be able to get him to agree things "the system" will think are "extreme" but we think are necessary'.[29]

Cummings's strategy was to smash through the establishment but he had no real plan for what happened afterwards, being, like his boss, a natural campaigner without a clue how to govern. Instead, it was all about gaining – and abusing – power. In 2020, the Chancellor was forced to resign because Cummings had persuaded Johnson to require Sajid Javid to sack all his special advisers and share advisers with No. 10, after months of tension between Cummings and his team. Cummings also took over the appointment and management of all of Whitehall's special advisers, turning them into his eyes and ears in an unprecedented way.

In other ways, too, Cummings amplified Johnson's worst qualities. At the height of Covid, when the country needed harmonious, team-playing government focused on us, not them, No. 10 became a nest of vipers. Cummings, for example, was at war with the Cabinet Office instead of focusing exclusively on managing the crisis. Messages shared at the Covid inquiry showed that Cummings wanted to sack the Deputy Cabinet Secretary, Helen MacNamara, and said 'I'll personally handcuff her and escort her from the building', referring to her as a 'cunt'.[30] And he (and others) had an extremely low opinion of the Secretary of State for Health, Matt Hancock, with Johnson calling him 'fucking hopeless' in a WhatsApp message to his chief adviser.[31]

Centralising and reinventing became the main rules of the game, even when reinvention was entirely unrequired. This was seen most notably with the creation of a whole new 'test and trace' system led by Conservative peer and businesswoman Dido Harding, costing an eye-watering £37 billion, which Johnson promised would be 'world-beating' but which failed in its key objectives. This came at a time when local 'test and trace' teams already existed, could have been deployed earlier and were in a much better position to track down contagious people.[32]

Cummings may have had power over Johnson but that did not stop him being forced to leave when Johnson's partner Carrie pulled the strings, briefing against him in the media. In high dudgeon, he left Downing Street with his possessions in a box and the loud sound of 'The Winner Takes It All' by ABBA allegedly heard coming from the flat, as Carrie Symonds (now Johnson) and her friends partied during lockdown.[33] Live by the sword, die by it.

Eventually, of course, Johnson also had to fall on his sword, helped by the civil service, a story we'll look at more closely in the next chapter.

• • •

Liz Truss, the next Prime Minister to fall in this avalanche of fatal Prime Ministers, was in some ways even more centralising, power-crazed and presidential in her style of government. She sacked the Permanent Secretary at the Treasury because she did not want his advice and managed to sidestep the Office for Budget Responsibility (OBR) – set up in 2010 by the coalition government to ensure that governments couldn't mark their own homework on fiscal projections and rules – because she did not want that external accountability, either. However, she could not buck the markets, and their reaction quickly brought her down. But not before she sacrificed her closest colleague, Chancellor Kwasi Kwarteng, in an effort to save herself.

If Johnson torpedoed the Conservative Party's reputation for honesty and integrity, then Liz Truss did the same for sound financial management.

• • •

Did the cycle of bad government end there?

Liz Truss's successor Rishi Sunak said all the right things to put clear water between him and his predecessors when he took power, promising 'integrity, professionalism and accountability at every level' but then immediately appointed Suella Braverman as his Home Secretary, just days after she'd been forced to resign on account of breaking the Ministerial Code.

Many hoped for more grown-up government. After all, Sunak had said in his letter to Boris Johnson when he resigned from his administration that 'the country rightly expect government to be conducted properly, competently and seriously'. But electoral gravity pulled him in a different direction, and in a bid to recover his party's ailing fortunes he started chasing headlines. A notable example was his wild promise to 'Stop the Boats', an unattainable goal, especially when the main route to delivery was Johnson's crackpot, extremely expensive and almost certainly illegal Rwanda scheme, which sought to prevent asylum seekers from claiming asylum here and deporting them instead. In the end, at least £318 million was spent on it and only four volunteer asylum seekers were ever sent. Great headlines, poor long-term thinking.

Sunak also put off decisions that might have cost him the next general election but which were essential to the health of the country. In the last months and weeks before he called an election, our prisons were overflowing to the point where there was a risk new criminals could not be processed. The Prison Governors' Association was telling him the criminal justice system was on the 'precipice of failure' and – just days before the election – police chiefs asked Sunak to take 'immediate action to begin to address this crisis and mitigate its worse impacts', warning that 'simply waiting for a new government to be formed after the election means an unacceptable delay in mitigation'.[34]

It seems Sunak had learnt from his previous Prime Minister, Boris Johnson, about whom the MP Jesse Norman had written in his letter of no confidence, 'You are simply seeking to campaign, to keep changing the subject and to create political and cultural dividing lines mainly for your advantage, at a time when the economy is struggling.'[35] It's not surprising that the first thing Johnson reportedly did in the morning is look at the newspaper headlines, because a big measure of his success in his own eyes was whether he was dominating them. After all, he was formerly (and is now again) a newspaper columnist.

An iron focus on trying to control the news agenda and the messaging within government has been a feature of every No. 10 since Tony Blair's New Labour. We've become used to an army of political spin doctors, a grid of announcements planned months ahead, the daily minister out there on the airwaves repeating the same script robotically and MPs, briefed by the whips, sent out later in the day to echo the same points. And with this has come the regular use of political polling and focus groups to test out ideas and policies. Not a bad thing in a democracy, you might say, but sometimes the right thing to do is unpopular in the short run and needs a conversation with the public, not a reflection of their current views.

There comes a point where this becomes a substitute for government, and it's not made easier by the 24/7 news cycle and increasing dominance of social media. Governments are elected every five years for a reason – they are given time to deliver on the mandate of their manifesto – but government by opinion polling is inevitably more short-term. Photo opportunity and soundbite government also prevents grown up conversations with the public and ultimately contributes to the erosion of trust, as ministers cease to sound human or look like normal people.

When politics rather than country comes first, difficult, long-term decisions either become political footballs – we can think of action to achieve net zero, which Rishi Sunak turned into a culture wars issue to gain political advantage – or get kicked into the long grass, like social care. Every Prime Minister has to be good at the cut and thrust of politics, but if they want to deliver good government, they must keep it focused on the medium- to long-term, rather than on the day-to-day currents of the political world. They can't simply play to their political base at the expense of the interests of the whole country.

These practices have by now become so ingrained they have become the norm, and the general conception of No. 10 is that it's a control centre, rather than setting the direction for the rest of government, listening to and inspiring its people and creating a sense of common values, identity and purpose. It campaigns rather than governs, broadcasts rather than listens.

• • •

So, what does good government in No. 10 look like?

Part of the answer to an over-centralised, over-politicised No. 10 must be more decentralisation of power – something which started under New Labour with the creation of devolved administrations in Scotland, Wales and Northern Ireland, and then to their credit was extended under the Conservatives to combined local authorities in England led by mayors, which have increasingly been given more power, particularly to the established ones, like Greater Manchester.

When Andy Burnham, the Mayor of Greater Manchester, moved from national politics to this role, he found the change refreshing. In a lecture in 2025, he said, 'If you set a clear mission which everyone understands, everyone pulling in that direction, the power is immense. Mayors can reach the parts ministers never can.' He added, 'Recognising the primacy of place in the way the country is run opens up an opportunity to create a better politics … Unlike the divisions of party, place is a unifying force.'[36]

But this doesn't mean we don't need a Prime Minister or a No. 10; we just need a No. 10 that works differently. No. 10 should not become a black hole into which decisions better taken elsewhere are sucked, nor a bubble or a bunker which becomes ever more divorced from the people, nor simply a campaigning unit that chases the next day's headlines and delivers initiatives it thinks might shift its position in the opinion polls. Instead, the Prime Minister should establish a clear sense of purpose, direction and values, creating the clarity and trust that the rest of government and wider society need if they are to pull together. It should create strong relationships and shared vision by reaching out and working with others, not looking within. It should serve the whole country, not the party, first.

Good governments have a Prime Minister at the helm who does not try to drive all the vessels in the fleet and then become overwhelmed. If No. 10 becomes dysfunctional, it is very hard for the rest of government to thrive.

• • •

So why hasn't Keir Starmer's No. 10 ended this downward cycle and brought a new style of good government to bear?

Despite his commitment to 'a decade of renewal' on the steps of No. 10, Keir Starmer has failed to set out a clear vision and values for his premiership and has a technocratic, managerial style – his job is to 'clear up the mess', he told the journalist Tom McTague.[37] He has replaced these with missions and milestones that seem to chop and change frequently, as explored in Chapter 4. He has struggled to communicate a sense of purpose and seems to lurch from one announcement to another rather than telling a coherent story.

There were encouraging signs when Starmer came to power that he intended to work through others, not take more power unto himself, and run a more outward, decentralised form of government. He committed to further devolution and announced a new Council of Nations, including the Mayor of London and combined authorities, and set up a new Partnership Unit in No. 10 to build new relationships and partnerships with civil society, business, devolved administrations and combined authorities. But with each 'reset' in the face of tanking popularity, No. 10 seems to be taking on more power. In September 2025, he appointed a new Chief Secretary to the Prime Minister to better coordinate delivery and, in the face of catastrophic local election results in May 2026 and amid mounting calls for his resignation, he brought in former Prime Minister Gordon Brown as an adviser on global finance, along with former Deputy Prime Minister Harriet Harman as an adviser on tackling violence against women and girls.

And No. 10 has still felt like an institution that is too focused on the day-to-day news cycle and short-term political goals rather than government for the whole country. It has been prone to making rash decisions and announcements that do not stand the test of time. Such decisions include its early intention to abolish the Winter Fuel Payment and cut disability payments, both of which had to be overturned. Or the sudden announcement of a compulsory digital ID card in September 2025, in an apparent bid for popularity, which then had to be quietly downgraded to a voluntary scheme when it went down like a lead balloon.

Amid all this noise, what has been far from clear is the overarching sense of purpose, the values and the vision, which No. 10 and the rest of government needs to deliver.

At the time this book goes to print in May 2026, it looks like Starmer's premiership is following a similar path to many of his immediate predecessors and faces a premature end.

Like many of those others before him, he was forced to get rid of Chief of Staff Morgan McSweeney in February 2026, in order to save himself from internal coups. He had promised on entering No. 10 to restore trust in politics but this was undermined when revelations from the Epstein files about the deep corruption of Peter Mandelson emerged (as detailed in Chapter 7). Starmer had appointed Mandelson, on the advice of McSweeney, as Ambassador to the US. It was almost a terminal blow, but with McSweeney's departure he survived, at least for a while.

McSweeney, like Dominic Cummings, was seen as the kingmaker and genius behind the throne, having chosen Starmer as the best person to oust Jeremy Corbyn and the left of the party in opposition, as Patrick Maguire and Gabriel Pogrund have outlined in their book *Get In*. 'He thinks he's driving the train but we sat him in front of the Docklands Light Railway', is the killer quote in the book. DLR trains are automated, with a 'driver' at the front there only for safety.[38] However, No. 10 under McSweeney focused more on politics than clarity of vision and delivery, and, after his departure, Keir Starmer still appeared to be struggling to govern in a different way.

No. 10 under McSweeney did not come across as a united team. McSweeney became Chief of Staff only after protracted briefings against his predecessor Sue Gray, and negative briefings about others have continued since, including one that directly accused Wes Streeting of trying to unseat Keir Starmer and led to Streeting calling for resignations. In June 2025, Starmer gave an interview to Tom Baldwin in which he said that he regretted his highly controversial 'island of strangers' speech about immigration and should have looked at the words more closely. The perception has been that he simply reads what his advisers give him and, even though Baldwin did say that Starmer had put his foot down about negative briefings, they continued.[39]

As Starmer came ever closer to his likely end, he did not look in control of No. 10 or events and, despite McSweeney's departure, the Mandelson affair came back to haunt him again in April 2026, this time with a huge row over whether he had unfairly sacked Olly Robbins, the Head of the Foreign and Commonwealth Office, for apparently failing to inform him that Mandelson had not passed his vetting. When Robbins had the chance to tell his side of the story, it began to look more like it was he who had actually followed due process and, far from overturning the vetting decision, he had taken a pragmatic decision to put mitigations in place to deal with the problems that were likely already known to the Prime Minister when he precipitously decided to appoint Mandelson as Ambassador to the US, before allowing time for extensive vetting. This was a process which his own National Security Adviser Jonathan Powell described as 'weirdly rushed'. Surely Robbins was just doing his best in difficult circumstances to execute the decision of his political master, rather than serving himself?

At that point many were beginning to notice that Starmer had sacrificed far more people than you might expect in a steady and happy ship. Quite apart from losing two Chiefs of Staff in his first eighteen months, along with a number of other key staff, there had been four different Directors of Communications and a new Head of the Policy Unit by February 2026. As part of the changes to restore confidence after the Mandelson affair broke, the Cabinet Secretary whom Starmer had personally chosen, Sir Chris Wormald, had also by this point been sacked, after months of backstabbing about him in the media.

There comes a point when a Prime Minister gets rid of so many around them that the finger of blame can only point to them. And, when the loyalty of those around them is not repaid, trust begins to crumble and ever more things start to go wrong, as the machine of government starts to fall apart.

• • •

When I left No. 10 in 1991, tears welled up in my eyes as I walked down Downing Street. I loved working there – partly because the power you enjoy in the name of the Prime Minister is addictive – and it's a hard place to leave. But there is a great deal more to government than No. 10, central though it is, as I was about to discover.

But all of this is still to come in my story. The next chapter starts at the beginning, before my No. 10 years, with me joining the civil service. It looks at the role of the civil service in ensuring good government and considers just how essential trust between ministers and civil servants really is.

Chapter 3

THE CIVIL SERVICE AND MINISTERS

'Integrity, professionalism and accountability at every level.'

RISHI SUNAK ON THE STEPS OF NO. 10

'A return of politics to public service.'

KEIR STARMER ON THE STEPS OF NO. 10

Bad government: *serving yourself, not the public, and waging war on those who serve you.*

Good government: *mutual trust and respect between ministers and civil servants, with both upholding standards in public life.*

Who does the civil service serve?

Immediately, the government of the day. But ultimately, I'd say, the people and the constitution, unwritten though most of it is. If ministers go rogue and let standards in public life slip, or if they start serving themselves, not the public good, can civil servants stop them? Or are they simply in thrall to their political masters?

Over many years, a war between civil servants and ministers about ethical standards has been on increasingly public display, ending largely with the civil servants resigning rather than ministers. Ministers have had the whip hand – with some notable exceptions.

A narrative has also taken hold that the civil service, at its worst, is stopping ministers from exercising the democratic will and delivering for the people. Such a view is not new, but it has become increasingly poisonous. Is the institution I devoted much of my professional life to really just 'the Blob'?

• • •

It's 1983 and I'm sitting in a classroom at the Civil Service College on Belgrave Road in Victoria, a short walk from Whitehall, listening to an official from the Department of Trade and Industry talking about the relationship of government to business and the economy. It's one of a number of courses designed for people like me, recruited for fast-stream promotion to the top of the civil service. I'd joined the year before, aged twenty-six, and I was working in the Department of Employment, which was undergoing a dramatic sea change in its mission to serve the relatively new Conservative government. Before 1979, it had been pro-trade union and workers' rights, but was now busy sailing in the opposite direction under the steely direction of Margaret Thatcher and the Secretary of State for Employment, Norman Tebbit (who in the popular *Spitting Image* puppet show was portrayed as a skinhead with bovver boots and knuckle dusters). He had famously told the rising number of unemployed due to Thatcher's economic policies to get 'on yer bike' – like his father – and look for work.

The Department of Trade and Industry civil servant who is

talking to me and my fellow trainees is saying that projections of the UK's growth over the next decade put us on a path of relative decline, with an expectation that we will have the same GDP as Portugal eventually. This is inevitable, he implies, and our job is to help ministers to manage this process.

I'm listening with interest – and disbelief. Is this really *our* job? And is it really the case that ministers, however hard they try, however much they promise, can have no impact on long-term trends? I remember Margaret Thatcher's famous words during the 1979 general election campaign: 'I can't bear Britain in decline. I just can't.' We're all working for her now in the civil service; she has other ideas, and it's our job to implement them. Or at least that's how I see it. We're in a democracy, after all, and even though I didn't vote for her, that's how democracy works.

• • •

Fast forward some forty years to December 2024, and I am watching the current Prime Minister on my laptop, streamed live from Pinewood Studios where he is delivering a speech about his 'Plan for Change'. It's a theatrical scene, set with no deliberate irony in a venue where movies and television shows are made, not real-life changes. Starmer's seated Cabinet are lined up in front of him, mostly in dark suits, just like his, but with the occasional splash of colour – a red dress from Bridget Phillipson and an orange trouser suit from Angela Rayner, all seemingly (but maybe entirely coincidentally) coordinated with the Prime Minister's backdrop of his 'five missions'. They all appear to be listening attentively, although they're probably thinking of the many pressing issues waiting for them back in London and wondering why they've been instructed to come here instead. This is a performance – this is how politicians communicate with the public nowadays – and they know the cameras are on them. Starmer is setting out new targets for the government's mission for the next five years. But then he suddenly turns on the civil service in a way that takes me back to that moment forty years earlier.

'I don't think there's a swamp to be drained here,' the Prime Minister says. 'But I do think that too many people in Whitehall are comfortable in the tepid bath of managed decline.'

I understand the point, but these words are a disaster. All those high hopes I and many others had had when Labour came to power of a reset in the relationship between ministers and their civil servants and an end to the attacks by the last government are now apparently dashed. One reason for my optimism had been that Starmer had been a civil servant himself when he was Director of Public Prosecutions and had chosen a former civil servant, Sue Gray, as his Chief of Staff. I thought it was great when, in his first few days, he had put out a video to the civil service in which he said, 'From the get go I want you to know that you have my confidence, my support and, importantly, my respect.'[1] And I was relieved when the Culture Secretary, Lisa Nandy, promised that the new government would put an end to culture war attacks. I thought it was an excellent sign that their new version of the Ministerial Code urged ministers to remember that they share a 'common duty of public service' with their civil servants and to 'demand and welcome candid advice'.[2]

And yet here is Starmer, characterising the civil service as a block to his government rather than being at its service, all against the backdrop of a right-wing conspiracy, turbo-charged by Trump's America, suggesting that the so-called 'liberal elite' in the civil service and elsewhere – what Trump calls 'the swamp' – are blocking attempts to bring about change.

As mentioned earlier, the equivalent phrase to 'the swamp' in the UK is 'the Blob', first used by Dominic Cummings about the civil service when he was in Downing Street. Many others in government and beyond echoed his disdain under Boris Johnson, Liz Truss and Rishi Sunak. It got to the point where then Home Secretary Suella Braverman signed off an email to political supporters which claimed 'an activist blob of left-wing lawyers, civil servants and the Labour Party' blocked the Conservatives from stopping migrant boats crossing the channel. In response to intense criticism from the civil service unions, she said she had not authorised the email. But proof that this mindset was present in at least some members of the Sunak government came a month later, when the Deputy Prime Minister Dominic Raab claimed in an interview with the BBC that a 'very small minority of very activist civil servants' were effectively trying to block reforms they did not like; he cited Brexit, prisoner parole and human rights. 'That's not on. That's not democratic,' he said, adding, 'If, actually, they block reforms or changes through a rather passive aggressive approach, we can't deliver for the British people.'[3]

Quite right, but was this really what was happening, or were civil servants just pointing out the genuine obstacles that stood in the way – like the law, or practicalities that simply can't be ignored? Raab at this point had been forced to resign, having been found guilty of bullying his staff by an inquiry led by senior lawyer Adam Tolley KC. The eight complaints were made not just when he was Justice Secretary but also Brexit and then Foreign Secretary. Tolley concluded that his conduct involved 'an abuse or misuse of power', and that he 'acted in a manner which was intimidating' and 'persistently aggressive' towards officials.[4] Rishi Sunak may have sacked him in response but he also allowed Raab to put out a lengthy statement attacking not just the civil service but also the inquiry itself:

> This precedent sets the playbook for a small number of officials to target ministers, who negotiate robustly on behalf of the country, pursue bold reforms and persevere in holding civil servants to account. If that is now the threshold for bullying in government, it is the people of this country who will pay the price.[5]

Civil servants who work closely with ministers are used to outbursts and temper tantrums. They know that ministers are under huge pressure and will sometimes lash out or become angry and frustrated when things get in their way. As such, they have a high tolerance of this kind of behaviour. They are there to serve, and sometimes that means taking a few knocks for the team. Complaining about them can only be a very last resort, as that is likely to end the relationship and damage a career. If you can't stand the heat, get out of the kitchen.

It's striking, therefore, that under the last Conservative government, civil servants had taken to making such formal complaints. The most public of these was from Philip Rutnam, the Permanent Secretary at the Home Office – its most senior official – in 2020.

• • •

Standing underneath an umbrella held by an anonymous hand out of camera shot and dressed in a sombre suit and tie with no coat in the February cold, Philip Rutnam is reading a statement, the paper shaking slightly in his hands. The media are there, of course: a man used to being in the shadows is in the limelight and is looking utterly miserable about it.

He says that he will be taking a legal case against the Home Office for constructive dismissal and that he had been the 'target of a vicious and orchestrated briefing campaign'. That sounds bad enough, but then he points out that the Home Secretary, Priti Patel, had denied any involvement to the Cabinet Office. And then the punchline: 'I regret I do not believe her.'

And that's not all. This, he claims, is all 'part of a wider pattern of behaviour'. He has received allegations from staff, whom it was his duty as their boss to protect, and you could see that he took his responsibility of service to them seriously. He says that Patel's 'conduct has included shouting and swearing, belittling people, making unreasonable and repeated demands – behaviour that created fear and that needed some bravery to call out'. He had encouraged her to change these behaviours, he says, but it seems that had had no effect. He concludes, 'This has been a very difficult decision but I hope that my stand may help in maintaining the quality of government in our country, which includes hundreds of thousands of civil servants, loyally dedicated to delivering this government's agenda.'[6]

Wow! I never expected to see anything like this in my lifetime. A civil servant, in public, calling his minister to account and appealing to the public to be on his side. I knew Philip Rutnam when I was in the Treasury and could never have anticipated his career would end like this. The man I knew was no lion, but he had just roared.

• • •

The Ministerial Code expressly states that 'Ministers should be courteous and professional in all their dealings and treat all those with whom they come into contact with consideration and respect ... Harassing, bullying or other inappropriate or discriminatory behaviour wherever it takes place is not consistent with the Ministerial Code and will not be tolerated.'

A subsequent investigation found that Priti Patel had been in breach of the Ministerial Code – although 'unintentionally,' as she said she was unaware that 'shouting and swearing' might be seen as bullying. Notwithstanding the account given by Philip Rutnam, she said she had received no feedback. The report also noted that the Home Office was 'not as flexible as it could have been' and that Ms Patel had 'not always felt supported' by the department.[7]

The investigation was undertaken by the Prime Minister's independent ethics adviser, former senior civil servant Sir Alex Allan, and it was said that he was strongly encouraged to make the report as sympathetic as possible. He showed his independence, however, as he promptly resigned when Boris Johnson decided to ignore his conclusion and stand by his Home Secretary, with the Prime Minister declaring that he did 'not believe that Priti Patel is a bully' and ordering his colleagues to 'form a square around the Prittster'.[8]

Allan's resignation letter only included two short sentences to the effect that he recognised it was for the Prime Minister to decide on a breach of the Code and he felt this was now the right moment for him to resign. This was a man who in the past had been Principal Private Secretary to Chancellors and Prime Ministers and had been around the block in working with ministers. He was well equipped to distinguish bullying from normal impatience. He'd also once windsurfed along the Thames to work during a train strike, wearing a suit and bowler hat and holding a briefcase, so he knew about the value of symbolic (if slightly futile) gestures – and resigning in this case was one of them. Advisers advise, ministers decide: Priti Patel and the Prime Minister remained, and a new independent adviser was duly appointed.

But you can be sure that the civil service was watching and taking note.

The temperature between civil servants and ministers was already high at this point, with the resignation that summer of the most senior civil servant in government, the Cabinet Secretary Mark Sedwill, after numerous briefings to the media against him and amid allegations that he was forced out.

Ill-feeling between the government and civil servants had come to a head over Brexit and the prolonged attempts to try to reconcile high-sounding promises made during the referendum with getting a good deal with the EU and making it work for the UK, especially for Northern Ireland. David Davis had said during the Brexit campaign that this would 'be the easiest deal in human history' but was subsequently jeered in Parliament in 2017 when, as Brexit Secretary, he said 'nobody thought Brexit would be easy'.

The word was that Johnson was frustrated by what he thought was civil service opposition to his plans and wanted a 'Brexit' Cabinet Secretary instead of Mark Sedwill.[9] His choice was Simon Case, a young and relatively inexperienced candidate who had previously worked closely with the Prime Minister as his Permanent Secretary at No. 10 and had also worked as Private Secretary to Prince William.

The narrative of the civil service blocking ministers took root and was then carried forward through Liz Truss's brief premiership and then Rishi Sunak's. The same notion, albeit in a relatively minor form, re-emerged in Keir Starmer's speech on his 'Plan for Change'. Starmer also added grist to the mill by removing Chris Wormald, the Cabinet Secretary that he had appointed himself, in February 2026. Media briefings from No. 10 had said over many months that Wormald had been guilty of 'hand wringing' and had failed to deliver reform.[10] He heard he was sacked via the media. The summary dismissal of Olly Robbins for his part in the Mandelson affair, as mentioned in the previous chapter, followed not long after, adding to a growing narrative that civil servants were being thrown under the bus.

Performative politics likes nothing better than to pick a fight and find a scapegoat, and civil servants, bound by a duty of confidentiality, are sitting targets who cannot normally fight back. For this reason, they make ideal whipping boys and girls.

• • •

This situation is a far cry from that depicted in *Yes Minister* and its sequel *Yes, Prime Minister*, both of which were extremely popular television programmes from 1980 to 1988, or even from the far more brutal *The Thick of It*, which followed in the Blair years.

I started watching *Yes Minister* two years before I joined the civil service and I still loved it when I became a Private Secretary to two Secretaries of State for Employment, first Lord Young and then Norman Fowler. I continued to watch it when it became *Yes, Prime Minister*, just before I entered Downing Street in May 1989. Reality might have been very different but for me it portrayed something of the balance of power between ministers and civil servants and the creative tension between them. And it made me laugh. It still does.

For those of you who have never seen it, *Yes Minister* is about an ongoing battle between an inexperienced and hesitant minister in the Department of Administrative Affairs, Jim Hacker, who wants to make his political mark, and his Permanent Secretary, Sir Humphrey Appleby. Appleby appears to go along with Hacker's wishes but runs rings around the minister in an attempt to stop him doing things he thinks are unwise. Hacker's Private Secretary, Bernard Woolley, who has divided loyalties but ultimately knows where his career prospects lie – with Sir Humphrey, not ministers who come and go – mediates between the two in an attempt to keep the peace. As Hacker becomes more experienced and eventually becomes Prime Minister, he frequently outwits the wily civil servant, but in every case the game is good-humoured, fostering a sense that the state is in relatively good hands, with the civil service an effective ballast to political whims or ill-considered plans. Ministers who are sure what they are doing are still able to get the upper hand.

The writers of the series, Antony Jay and Jonathan Lynn, said that the idea for the show came into their heads when they read about the case of Sir Frank Soskice, a lawyer and Labour Party politician who had passionately demanded that the Home Secretary hold an inquiry into an injustice. When he became Home Secretary himself, Soskice said equally firmly that there were no grounds for the very same inquiry, presumably swayed by advice from his civil servants to change his mind. Whether rightly, I don't know. But I do know that, for ministers, getting control of the machine rather than simply becoming its mouthpiece is one thing that distinguishes a good minister from a bad one, and I am sure every civil servant I know would agree.

To bring the whole thing to life, the authors of *Yes Minister* drew on many factual sources, most notably Richard Crossman's *The Diaries of a Cabinet Minister* (1975–77) and Marcia Williams's *Inside Number 10* (1972), as well as speaking to many politicians and serving and former civil servants.[11] Bizarrely, this included my own husband, John Nightingale, who came across Jonathan Lynn when John sent him a play he had written about a civil servant who was unable to get out of bed, a dilemma that does not feature in *Yes, Prime Minister*. After some initial interest, Lynn declined to put John's play on the stage, however.

Margaret Thatcher was a great fan of the political satire. Giving out an award to the show in 1984, she said it was her favourite programme and that 'its clearly observed portrayal of what goes on in the corridors of power has given me hours of pure joy'.

As if to demonstrate the point, she then took part in a short, mocked up version of the show in front of the award ceremony audience, playing (with some aplomb) herself, alongside the actors of Jim Hacker and Sir Humphrey. She had reportedly written the script herself with the help of Bernard Ingham and, by some accounts, Charles Powell – both civil servants, of course. In her episode, the Prime Minister inevitably gains the upper hand over Sir Humphrey by getting him and his minister to agree to abolish economists and then forcing Sir Humphrey to admit that he had a degree in politics and economics, and so had to abolish himself.[12]

Her enthusiasm was not as surprising as it might seem. She was a Prime Minister who had won the *Yes, Prime Minister* game. It hadn't been easy, but she'd made the civil service work for her and had been tough when she felt that wasn't happening. In 1981, in her first few years in the job, she got rid of the Head of the Civil Service, Sir Ian Bancroft, by abolishing his department and merging his role with that of Cabinet Secretary.[13] This was the man who, after Thatcher had proposed cuts of 20 per cent to the civil service, suggested that she send a Christmas message to the civil service to repair its damaged morale. Her handwritten reply said, 'I just don't think this is a very good idea.'[14] Chemistry was lacking.

But she also formed deep and lasting partnerships with her civil servants. Her Cabinet Secretary, Sir Robert Armstrong, served her faithfully from 1979 to his retirement in 1987, and Sir Robin Butler, who was once her Principal Private Secretary at No. 10, replaced him.

Indeed, it was Bernard Ingham and Charles Powell, not her Cabinet colleagues, who came to her on the morning of her resignation and offered their support. According to Ingham, she was worrying about their futures, not hers, and they told her to stop being silly and think about herself for a change. The night before, as she was pondering whether to resign, Ingham went up to the flat to see her privately and told her that, whatever others felt, 'We in No. 10 are with you.'[15]

In her final years, Charles Powell was a regular visitor, often singing along to hymns with her during the televised Church of England service, *Songs of Praise*. The night before she died, he sat by her bedside and read from her favourite book, a compendium of brief lives of British Prime Ministers, and as he left, she kissed him goodbye.[16]

No wonder she loved *Yes, Prime Minister*.

In an interview many years later about the Thatcher administration's relationship with the civil service, former Cabinet minister and Conservative Party chair Cecil Parkinson said:

> I look back now – I did in the early days when the coalition was saying that it was finding it difficult to get things done. Well, there never was a more radical Conservative government than the Thatcher government, but the civil service never stopped us from doing any of the things we wanted. The civil service had lots of opportunities to be obstructive but they weren't … I hope

> they won't be offended if I describe them as mercenaries. They make it quite clear to you: 'Minister, it's your policy – all we do is implement it and try to help you form it.'

And he said that Margaret Thatcher 'never, ever sought to take the civil service on and to reform it from top to bottom. She sought to make sure that it could do what we wanted.'

He was speaking at a time when Francis Maude, a Cabinet Office minister under the coalition government which served between 2010 and 2015, was openly claiming that civil servants were blocking him from putting reforms in place.[17]

Yes Minister was followed in 2005 by *The Thick of It*, a very different take on the relationship between ministers and those who work for them, reflective of the Blair Labour government, during which political appointees gained significantly more power. The central character, the one who often gets the better of the minister, is no longer a powerful civil servant but the foul-mouthed No. 10 spin doctor, Malcolm Tucker. The harried minister no longer fights back but stumbles through one crisis after another, with his young political aide, not a Private Secretary, at his side and civil servants as largely passive bystanders. *Yes Minister*'s Department of Administrative Affairs is replaced by the Department of Social Affairs and Citizenship, set up by the Prime Minister to 'join up' government but sounding rather similar to parts of the Cabinet Office.

The progression from *Yes Minister* to *The Thick of It* isn't just a change in satirical tastes to the darker end of the spectrum. Government has changed since Thatcher's day – there's more spin, more politics and much greater No. 10 control, along with a far less powerful civil service. *Yes Minister* and *The Thick of It* both seem so innocent compared to where we are today. Indeed, Armando Iannucci, writer of *The Thick of It*, has said many times that he thinks modern politics has moved beyond satire.

• • •

So, who do civil servants really serve and what makes them tick?

Few people think themselves into the heads of civil servants – they are faceless bureaucrats to most people. If they try, they may feel baffled by how civil servants can work for any master, regardless of their personal belief. So let me present myself to you as an example.

Joining the civil service was not an easy or natural thing for me. When I applied for the civil service, I initially regarded it as a last resort. I had been studying for a PhD and had been hoping for an academic career, but due to Margaret Thatcher's cuts to funding for arts departments in universities (compounded by my choice of a specialism, American literature, that was only taught in some English departments), there were no jobs to apply for. The only ones that were advertised were either abroad or were for a few hours a week only, and on a temporary basis. That didn't stop me from trying, but I wasn't getting anywhere by the time my funding came to an end. I'd been fully funded by the state for the first three years of my PhD – both tuition fees and living expenses – as I had been throughout my higher education, because I came from a poor family and that was what happened in those distant days. But as the clock started ticking for my grant to come to an end, I started looking elsewhere, beyond my beloved academia.

Before I knew it, I was unemployed and was becoming ever more despairing. Going home was not an option, as my mother with whom I had lived before university didn't have the funds to support me and I needed to be in London to continue with my research, in the hope of completing my PhD and maximising my chances of getting employment.

The isolated life of a PhD student didn't really fit my temperament, and when I did eventually get a job I realised how much I enjoyed working with other people. Back then, I was living in a cramped and squalid bedsit in the red-light district of King's Cross, which was cheap and close to University College London where I was studying. I would escape most days to the wonderful circular Reading Room of the British Museum (now closed, with the books relocated to the purpose-built British Library at St Pancras), with its ethereal acoustics created by its domed ceiling, which turned the few voices that were speaking in low tones into what seemed like a collective whisper, broken only by the occasional thud of a falling book. There were many days when I spoke to no one – you called up your books by filling in a slip and they would be silently delivered to your desk a few minutes later. I only met my PhD supervisor every few months and the only other teaching at UCL took the form of a small number of postgraduate seminars.

I confided about my despair in finding a job to my supervisor, Steve Fender, who suggested I apply for the fast-stream civil service. He thought I was in with a chance, graduating with the only First in my year, and would be good at the work. This option had never occurred to me. The fast-stream civil service was intended for those who would reach the very top of the profession and was known for only accepting the best and the brightest, which in those days seemed to be only people from Oxbridge and mostly men. It was also a much smaller scheme than the one in place today. It seemed out of reach. The civil service also had a stuffy, bowler hat, pinstripe suit and umbrella type of image and I couldn't see myself fitting in. This was the elite establishment and nothing in my background made me feel I could be part of that.

Neither of my parents had been to university – my father was a self-employed printer who built up a small business in Wimborne, Dorset, the rural market town in which I grew up. He left school at fourteen without any qualifications, and I don't think he ever worked for anyone but himself, nor would he have felt remotely comfortable doing so. Rules and conventions were for other people. If he saw a 'No Entry' sign, he would want to step over the fence and take a look. I think I only saw him in a suit once, at my wedding, a year before he died. He wore his shirtsleeves rolled up, even in winter, as they were too short for his long, burly arms. He was six foot four inches tall and over twenty stone – and the polar opposite of my image of a civil servant in every respect.

My mother was very different but was no establishment figure, either. She had grown up in Canada on the family farm. She did well at school but never got the opportunity to go to university, even though she had secured a place in Canada, because her parents lost their money in the Great Recession and came back to Dorset. She ended up working in a dairy and, when my parents got married, she joined my father in the printing business until their marriage fell apart. She had to find alternative employment working as a secretary, and it was hard to make ends meet, bringing up five children on her own. Even though my father worked non-stop, the business always seemed to be on the edge of bankruptcy and there was little or no money for any of us. I remember her crying when household bills arrived, and I lived in fear of services being cut off. I grew up wearing second-hand clothes because we couldn't afford anything else.

What did connect me to government was my strong interest in

politics, which led me to choose 'American Fiction of the Vietnam War' as my PhD topic. I didn't want to write about something only of interest to a handful of academics, and the Vietnam War was the most vivid political event of my teenage years. It had divided the US and entered everyone's home in the UK through vivid pictures and film shown daily on the television.

Once seen, who could forget the photograph of a nine-year-old girl, Kim Phuc, her skin covered in napalm, which sticks and burns into the flesh, running in terror away from the planes that were dropping this noxious substance on her village, her open mouth and terrified eyes saying it all.

Apart from the terrible horror and futility of that war for everyone involved, the thing that stayed with me from the novels and autobiographies I read in my research was the underlying sense of service, in the broadest sense, that kept the American conscripts going even when they felt the war was unjust and that the politicians who sent them there were wrong. On the whole, they did their best in appalling circumstances, particularly for those they served beside and, despite the atrocities committed by some of their fellow servicemen, most tried to do a job they never wanted with integrity, all for the greater good. There was something noble in that.

Maybe that was somewhere in the back of my mind as I contemplated applying for the civil service. I did think a lot about why I should want to work directly for a government, led by Margaret Thatcher, that I thought was doing great damage to the country. Most of my friends couldn't understand how I could do this. I had a particular animosity to Mrs Thatcher and I would never have imagined then that in less than a decade I would end up working directly for her at No. 10.

I decided that government could be done well, or badly, whoever was in power, and it was important that it be done ethically. I would be serving a higher cause – democracy. Although an elected government might not pursue policies that I personally agreed with, executing them was executing the will of the people, and hopefully in the most beneficial way.

And I knew first-hand that there were things government could do better. My experience of claiming unemployment benefits was an unhappy one – incomprehensible letters from unnamed bureaucrats referring to opaque rules and visits to unemployment benefit offices to talk to people behind screens who were as unhelpful and incomprehensible as the people who sent the letters. Eventually, through a lot of persistence, I got what I was entitled to, but I felt things shouldn't be that way and that the faceless system was designed to put off all but the most determined.

Many months after putting in my civil service application and a set of exams later, I found myself at something called the 'Final Civil Service Selection Board', which took place over a couple of days and involved practical exercises such as summarising a complex bundle of evidence into options and making a recommendation on the way forward, as well as group exercises where we had to show we could work together to solve problems, taking turns to chair meetings. The whole process ended in a one-to-one interview with the chair of the three-person selection board, which included an exercise for which we'd been asked to prepare a proposition of our choice. We would have to argue, either for or against.

I chose one of the hottest political topics of the time, the sinking of the *Belgrano* in the Falklands War, which was still raging at the time. As it turned out, a few years later this issue would become the subject of a landmark criminal case about who the civil service served – ministers or the public good.

The ARA *General Belgrano*, the Argentine Navy's only cruise ship, was sunk by a torpedo from a British nuclear submarine on 2 May 1982, killing 323 of the thousand sailors on board, mostly young conscripts. *The Sun* celebrated the event with the headline 'GOTCHA!', but the sinking became controversial because it took place outside the 200-mile exclusion zone the UK had put in place to protect the Falklands after the Argentinians invaded. It was therefore argued by some at the time that it may have broken international law. The Falklands had been a British territory since 1833 and was home to nearly two thousand British citizens at the time. The British government claimed that the *Belgrano* was 'closing on elements of our task force' despite being outside the zone (and some evidence suggested it was actually going in the opposite direction).

The precise framing of my final selection board discussion topic was 'the sinking of the *Belgrano* was wrong' and, as requested, I was ready to argue the case either way. I knew from my Vietnam War studies that the first casualty of war is truth, and I thought the evidence pointed to a cover-up. However, I discovered through the exercise that I was perfectly capable of arguing against the proposition equally well, as the facts were inconclusive and, having heard me out one way, the chair of the board asked me to do the reverse straight after.

It was the perfect exercise to demonstrate the mental flexibility required of civil servants who work very closely with ministers, as fast-stream civil servants need to do. You must be able to put yourself in their shoes, understand and execute their priorities, literally put words in their mouth – writing their speeches and lines to use in the media – while remaining objective, impartial and open to all sides. This means that when the next minister comes along, or indeed a different government, you can do the same for them.

I passed the test and got through. The civil service embraced me and I devoted myself heart and soul to public service for the next twenty-five years of my life.

When I showed a draft of my first book, *People Like Us: Margaret Thatcher and Me*, to Lord Turnbull, who was the Principal Private Secretary when we both worked in No. 10 and subsequently became Cabinet Secretary and Head of the Civil Service, he said that the story I told there proved the civil service model worked, i.e. that we could serve any minister faithfully, even if our personal politics pointed in another direction. That was true of me, but what about Margaret Thatcher, who it is said only wanted civil servants around her who were 'one of us'? You'll need to read my first book to find out how that turned out.

But we don't just serve ministers. As I said before, I firmly believe the civil service serves a higher cause. That proposition was put to the test when Clive Ponting, a senior civil servant in the Ministry of Defence, leaked a copy of a secret submission about the sinking of the *Belgrano* he had written to his Secretary of State, Michael Heseltine, sending it to the MP who had most doggedly pursued the case against them, Tam Dalyell. This made it clear that, far from 'closing in on' the British fleet, the *Belgrano* was indeed sailing away and had been retreating for several hours before the torpedo was fired. Ponting had advised ministers to correct the record, which they chose not to do, even though it is a fundamental requirement for ministers to tell the truth to Parliament and to correct false statements if they have been made. Indeed, claims that he had lied to Parliament were the very thing that brought Boris Johnson down. If the truth is not told, Parliament is hindered in its constitutional role of holding the executive to account, which is precisely what Tam Dalyell had been trying to do.

The British government was furious about the leak and launched an investigation which resulted in Ponting being brought to trial for a breach of the Official Secrets Act in 1985. This was despite the fact that he had been something of a favourite with Margaret Thatcher in the past. He had presented his plans to reduce military waste to the Prime Minister in 1979, and she was so impressed she asked him to repeat it to the full Cabinet, for which he was awarded an OBE. According to his obituary in *The Guardian*, she personally ensured that his salary was restored after his arrest in 1984, saying of his treatment, 'I think it is a bit rough. He and his family have to live on something.'[18]

To the government's consternation, Ponting was acquitted by the jury, on the grounds that he had acted in the public interest. The Act had allowed for the release of classified government information if it was in the 'interests of the state' to do so. The judge in this case argued that the 'interests of the state' were the same thing as the interests of the government of the day. The jury did not agree.

In response, the government removed that defence from the Official Secrets Act in 1989, the same year I started working in No. 10. Civil servants no longer had a defence if they chose to call out bad behaviour by their ministers by leaking documents. Not that this stopped leaks. For the record, I never did (nor ever would have) leaked documents while I was a civil servant, as I thought this kind of behaviour undermined trust. Thankfully, I never had call to. In more recent years, particularly under the last Tory government, I noticed an avalanche of leaks, some clearly from politicians but some also likely from civil servants who couldn't find any other way to highlight wrongdoing. If politicians are doing it, it is harder for them to point the finger at their servants, and although there have been investigations no prosecutions have followed.

There have been calls for the Official Secrets Act to be updated to give a public interest defence, most notably in 2020 from the statutory body, the Law Commission, to bring the UK in line with other countries. But this has not been put in place.[19]

Our system therefore mainly relies on self-policing by ministers, particularly the Prime Minister, and we've already seen what happens when a Prime Minister is not, to use the historian Peter Hennessy's phrase, 'a good chap'. Hennessy maintains that our largely unwritten constitution relies on the 'good chaps' theory of government – that those in charge will play by the rules.

The rules for ministers are set out in what is now called the Ministerial Code, partly enforced by the Prime Minister's independent ethics adviser, though neither of these are on a statutory footing and the 'independent' adviser is appointed by the Prime Minister, not independently at all. It is the Prime Minister of the day who determines ultimately what the Code says, when it is broken and if resignation is required. That process has become more transparent and stronger since the time of Clive Ponting, when a confidential 'Questions of Procedure for Ministers' was in place – confidential meaning that it was hard for journalists, the public or even civil servants to use it to point out when breaches occurred. Following various scandals, John Major as Prime Minister first published the Questions of Procedure in 1992, and three years later established the so-called Nolan Principles, named after the judge who set them out: selflessness, integrity, objectivity, accountability, openness, honesty and leadership – or in common shorthand, integrity – and these are now enshrined in the Code.

A 'Code for the Civil Service', first issued in 1996, requires civil servants to act with integrity, honesty, objectivity and impartiality at all times and includes a specific requirement to 'set out the facts and relevant issues truthfully, and correct any errors as soon as possible'. If required to do things by ministers that break this Code, civil servants can raise the issue up the chain of command and ultimately to the Civil Service Commission. But, if that fails, it advises they should resign.

Resignation was the option taken by Boris Johnson's chief legal adviser, Jonathan Jones, who stood down after the government announced plans to override a legally binding EU exit agreement, the Northern Ireland Protocol. The government's decision to break international law, which is against the Ministerial Code, put him in an invidious position and he felt he could not continue to serve, as the Civil Service Code requires civil servants to comply with the law at all times.[20]

But it was leaks from civil servants and special advisers that ultimately brought misbehaviour to light following the most prominent breach of the Ministerial Code under Johnson's administration: Partygate.

• • •

I am watching ITV's *News at Ten* on Friday 10 December 2021, open-mouthed. Boris Johnson's spokesperson, Allegra Stratton, is standing at a podium between two Union Jacks, taking questions from her colleagues in a mock press conference. The video of this has been leaked, and it's blowing a hole in denials by the PM, senior ministers and No. 10 over the previous week that there had been a Christmas party during lockdown on 18 December the year before.

'I've just seen reports on Twitter that there was a Downing Street Christmas party on Friday night, do you recognise those reports?' says one adviser on the video, pretending to be a journalist.

'I went home,' replies Stratton, laughing, before composing herself, telling colleagues to 'hold on,' as she looks around the room for a better response.

The next question also floors her.

'Would the Prime Minister condone having a Christmas party?'

She laughs and says, 'What's the answer?'

'It wasn't a party, it was cheese and wine,' replies one.

'It was a business meeting … this fictional party was a business meeting, and it was not socially distanced,' she replies, laughing even more.

The next day, Allegra Stratton was forced to resign for making light of such a serious matter, and she did so with tears running down her cheeks, in front of the cameras outside her house. She was the only person to take accountability for lockdown parties in No. 10, even though, as she said, she didn't attend the party in question and went home instead.

In response, the Prime Minister, who had previously flatly denied in Parliament that there had been any law-breaking in No. 10, told the House of Commons that he was 'furious' about the video and commissioned a Cabinet Office investigation into the allegations, eventually led by Sue Gray, which continued to grow as more leaks pointed to multiple lockdown parties involving not just his staff but the Prime Minister himself.

Years later, Dominic Cummings claimed it was he who brought Johnson down by leaking details of Partygate – but he did this only because he thought him unfit to rule, not out of any moral outrage. After all, he had broken lockdown rules himself.

Would the scandal have come to light if he and others hadn't leaked it? I doubt it. Some journalists attended at least one of those parties, according to Cummings,[21] and *The Times* had even mentioned the Johnson birthday party during lockdown without any hint of opprobrium, and no exposure or scandal followed.[22] Like the policemen who came to the lockdown party in the press office or the cleaners who cleaned up the mess afterwards, they just accepted that it was none of their business. The actual 'establishment' that Johnson and Cummings presided over had the license to make its own rules.

Johnson repeatedly referred to Sue Gray's investigation as independent, which cut to the heart of the question of who civil servants really serve: the government (and in this case the Prime Minister of the day) or the Crown and the wider public, as Clive Ponting had thought? Unlike the Prime Minister's ethics adviser, Gray was a serving civil servant and any public statement she made was likely to be vetted by, or at least discussed with, her political masters. Even if not, it put her in a very public and invidious position. To be fair, Sue Gray had earned herself a formidable reputation as a troubleshooter and enforcer with regard to allegations of ministerial misconduct, most notably writing a report that led to Theresa May sacking her Deputy Prime Minister, Damian Green, for misconduct. But here it was the Prime Minister himself who was under investigation, even though Johnson himself professed innocence. She knew her report could destroy his, and quite possibly her, career.

She put off the day of her final report by bringing in the police midway to undertake their own investigations. Fixed penalty notices and fines were served, including on the Prime Minister and the Chancellor, taking some of the pressure off her. In the end, her report, which was published in May 2022, was largely factual, like a police record of events, and its conclusions were generalised.

'The senior leadership at the centre, both political and official, must bear responsibility for this culture,' she wrote, adding that the public have 'a right to expect the very highest standards of behaviour' in Downing Street and 'clearly what happened fell well short of this.'

Artfully, she still failed to name the prime target: the man who set the culture inside No. 10. Accountability shared is accountability blurred. The Prime Minister was wounded but not down. Responding to the report in the House of Commons, he said he took 'full responsibility for everything that took place on my watch', having previously said 'the rules and guidance had been followed at all times'.

A trickle of resignations followed in June, including from his anti-corruption tsar, John Penrose, and his independent ethics adviser, Lord Geidt. A no-confidence vote in the Commons was won, but 41 per cent of his own MPs had tried to oust him. The House of Commons Privileges Committee started investigating whether he had lied to Parliament on Partygate, a clear resigning offence, at the end of that month. By-election after by-election in hitherto safe seats were catastrophically lost.

But still he survived.

What finally brought Boris Johnson down was a lie about his Deputy Chief Whip, Chris Pincher, who resigned a month after Sue Gray's report, on the last day of June, after a story in *The Sun* about him groping two men in the Carlton Club. It emerged that there had been allegations against him before, when he was a Foreign Office minister, but No. 10 categorically denied that the Prime Minister knew about this before appointing him as a whip. Doubt was cast on this when stories emerged that Johnson joked about Pincher being 'handsy' and said of him, 'Pincher by name, pincher by nature.' But the denials from No. 10 continued. A series of ministers were sent out on the airwaves to say that they had been assured by No. 10 that the Prime Minister knew nothing about the previous case.

And then…

• • •

It's the morning of 5 July 2022 at 8.10 a.m. and I'm listening to the ex-Permanent Secretary of the Foreign and Commonwealth Office Simon McDonald on Radio 4's *Today* programme delivering the closest thing I have ever heard to a Prime Ministerial 'assassination'.

Lord McDonald is saying that in the summer of 2019, when he was the most senior civil servant in the Foreign Office, a group of officials had 'complained to me about Mr Pincher's behaviour … In substance, the allegations were similar to those made about his behaviour at the Carlton Club … Mr Pincher apologised and promised not to repeat the inappropriate behaviour.'

And then the killer blow: 'Mr Johnson was briefed in person about the initiation and outcome of the investigation.'[23] In other words, Johnson had knowingly appointed someone with a track record of sexual abuse in charge of the welfare of his MPs – Pincher by name, pincher by nature – and no amount of obfuscation, including his claim in the Commons that day that he had simply forgotten it, was going to get past this fact.

This was not like the behind-closed-doors conversations that forced Margaret Thatcher to resign. It happened in broad daylight and the stiletto blow was given not by the Cabinet but by a former civil servant giving his account of events to the public at large, delivered in a quiet, factual and impersonal way.

As I listened to him, I felt proud to have been a civil servant and I, and I suspect many others in the country, breathed a sigh of relief. It was as if a window had been opened, and the air had begun to clear.

He had betrayed a confidence, but he had done so in the name of a higher cause. The civil service, which had been bullied and abused by Johnson's government, struck back in the name of integrity.

Shortly after, the entire edifice came tumbling down. Most of Johnson's Cabinet, his ministers and their Parliamentary bag-carriers were furious. They had been marched up to the top of the hill and then down, but they weren't going to be led by him anymore. Boris Johnson saying he would 'stand and fight' and all but promising to barricade himself inside No. 10 rather than be dragged out was not going to stop them. First, Health Secretary Sajid Javid resigned and then a few minutes later the Chancellor, Rishi Sunak, did too. They were swiftly replaced, but then others stepped down – more than fifty on the ministerial and government payroll in total by the end – and Johnson began to run out of people to appoint.

By midday on 7 July 2022, Boris Johnson resigned as Prime Minister, and nearly a year later, after the Parliamentary Standards Committee reported, he resigned as an MP as well.

• • •

But should it ever have come to this?

You might say that the checks and balances of our unwritten constitution, of which the civil service is a part, worked. Loyalty in politics is an extremely powerful thing, and what this story illustrates to me is just how much it takes to get rid of a politician who clearly doesn't care about breaking rules. While these tortuous and lengthy events unfolded, good government went out of the window and trust in politics was seriously undermined.

So, what needs to happen? First, the machinery for enforcing standards needs to be strengthened. This would mean putting it on a statutory basis, so that there is a legal obligation on the Prime Minister of the day to have a Ministerial Code, which would also give it more constitutional status. Advisers should be given more genuine independence and power.

The incoming Labour government did tighten the Ministerial Code, giving the Prime Minister's independent adviser the power to commission their own investigations, rather than wait for the Prime Minister to ask for them, but fell short of implementing all the recommendations of the independent Committee on Standards in Public Life that had been set up to advise Prime Ministers. It had also recommended that the adviser be appointed through an independent process and that he or she should have the right to determine a breach of the Code, rather than merely giving advice to the PM and leaving the final decision to them.

Starmer's government also established a new Ethics and Integrity Commission which incorporates the former Committee on Standards in Public Life, and like its predecessor it will also make recommendations to the Prime Minister about changes to the standards system. However, these recommendations can also be disregarded, as we have seen so often in the past, although there is a new requirement for him or her to respond promptly. The new Commission subsumes various bodies, including the Advisory Committee on Business Appointments, and new rules and penalties on business appointments have been introduced, hopefully making them more enforceable, as they have often been ignored, most notably by Boris Johnson. In response to the Mandelson scandal exposed by the Epstein files, of which more is written in Chapter 7, the government promised 'to work with the Ethics and Integrity Commission to ensure it achieves its aim of the highest standards' as part of a package of strengthening safeguards.[24]

Critically, the whole system still relies on the discretion of the Prime Minister of the day and, as we saw with Boris Johnson, it is painful and hard, though not impossible, to bring him or her to account through Parliament.

Could such breaches of integrity happen again? Stronger enforcement of standards is important, but ultimately the public need to ensure that they elect people of the highest integrity and values, not people like Boris Johnson or Donald Trump who are good at theatre, ruthless in politics and ultimately divorced from the truth.

Can the civil service be a thorn in the side of government? It is there to serve and has expertise and knowledge it should be able to share without fear or favour, as no minister has all the answers or knows all the issues. A policy should be tested to make sure that it will work or is compliant with the law. If, as happened under Brexit, the civil service is cast unfairly as a block and attacked in public by ministers, then the relationship of trust and mutual respect that is essential to good government will break down.

And that relationship is showing real strain once again at the time of writing, starting with the sacking by Starmer of his Cabinet Secretary in February 2026. The issue was not his right to remove a Cabinet Secretary in whom he had lost confidence, but the manner in which it happened. The former Cabinet Secretary Lord O'Donnell spoke out on the *Today* programme about what he called 'shabby' briefings against Chris Wormald and others, including Sue Gray, which he said were damaging relationships. He called on the Prime Minister to stop them.[25] The General Secretary of the union for top civil servants, the First Division Association, wrote that this habit of negative briefings to the media was undermining 'effective government', saying lessons had not been learnt from 'the chaos of the Johnson-Cummings years'.[26] And that veteran of the

Johnson government's war with the civil service, Philip Rutnam, told *Newsnight* that 'an end to this kind of corrosive negative briefing … would be the single biggest thing this government could do to improve the effectiveness of the civil service in the short run and the long run'.[27]

But that was nothing compared to the comments that followed the sacking of Olly Robbins. Former Cabinet Secretary Lord Butler said that the sacking was a 'grave injustice'[28] and Lord O'Donnell called it 'one of the worst crises of modern times' in the relationship between the civil service and ministers.[29]

Lord Butler reflected a few days later that the political climate had changed over a number of years, and the relationship between civil servants and politicians, which used to be a 'we', had turned into more of a 'them and us'.[30] In that message Starmer sent civil servants in his first few days in Downing Street, he promised that the new government and the civil service would work 'together, as one team', signalling a break with that past.[31] A few days after sacking Olly Robbins, with all the damage to his relationship with the civil service that this caused, he delivered a similar message to the civil service, repeating the 'one team' sentiment in an attempt to repair the damage.[32] But actions speak louder than words, and it won't have escaped their notice that this was issued a few hours before a critical set of local elections – elections Labour then heavily lost.

Governments struggle to deliver their agenda when they undermine those who work for them. Trust and relationships matter, as they do in all forms of management, and when they deteriorate it gums up the works. But it's also understandable that ministers can feel frustrated by the pace of change. What can ministers do (or not do) to make government work better? It is to these questions that I turn in the next chapter.

Chapter 4

MAKING GOVERNMENT WORK

'I think we are absolutely fucked.'

THE DEPUTY CABINET SECRETARY, HELEN MACNAMARA, TELLING DOMINIC CUMMINGS IN NO. 10 ON FRIDAY 13 MARCH 2020 THAT THERE WAS NO COVID PLAN.[1]

***Bad government**: randomly axing or reorganising the state; micro-management and 'megaphone' government.*

***Good government**: being clear about the job and giving people the freedom to get on with it; orchestrating government rather than seeking to control it from the centre.*

Most Prime Ministers want to drive the ship of state in a fresh direction, whether it's to deliver better-performing public services, Brexit or higher growth. But politicians increasingly say the state itself is getting in their way, rather than being the vehicle to get them there. It's too big, it's too slow and it's hard to get the results they want to see.

Their recipe for delivering more efficiently? Top-down cuts and ministers making ever more decisions themselves, while shouting targets at the front line to get results – what I call 'megaphone government'. All this, when clarity of purpose, shared outcomes and autonomy with clear principles would work far better.

The incoming Labour government promised a fresh approach based on missions, not targets, and a 'decade of renewal'. But has such an intention stuck?

• • •

It's February 2025 and I'm watching a news clip of Elon Musk being handed a huge chainsaw by the populist Argentinian President Javier Milei, who had famously used the symbol during his election campaign to show what he would do to the state. They are on the stage of the Conservative Political Action Conference in the US, and Musk struts around in black sunglasses, a black MAGA baseball hat, a long black jacket and jeans, with a gold chain over his black-and-white T-shirt. He holds the blood-red chainsaw high above his head, bellowing like a wild animal, 'This is the chainsaw for bureaucracy!' Milei, in a conventional suit and tie, looks very pleased with himself. The message is clear: this is an international movement, and they are going to slash the hell out of those bloated bureaucrats who stop countries from being 'great again'.

Musk was leading the Department of Government Efficiency, known as DOGE, at the time, sending his storm-trooper software engineers and associates to – as Trump had put it – 'restore competence and effectiveness'. The initial target for savings was $2 trillion but, as fantasy hit reality, Musk eventually downgraded this to $150 billion, without taking into account the additional redundancy and other costs incurred.[2] Tens of thousands of federal employees were fired, spending on international aid agencies and medical research was slashed and over 10,000 government contracts were terminated, which they claimed were worth $52.8 billion (but some estimate that only 5 per cent of that was actually saved).[3] Many of DOGE's cuts were in the Government Services Administration which managed government office leases, many of which Musk terminated, often incurring higher costs as a consequence, and many of its employees were sacked – only to be eventually asked back, having had in effect a seven-month paid holiday.[4]

By the end of May, Musk himself stepped away from DOGE and a few days later fell out spectacularly with Trump. For his part, Milei did make massive cuts in public services and reduced sky-rocketing inflation, but the real-life consequences of his chainsaw also massively haemorrhaged public support, which spooked the markets and forced an unconditional bailout by the Trump government by the autumn of 2025, which then threatened to withdraw its support if Milei were not re-elected. Unsurprisingly given these circumstances, he was.[5]

Nigel Farage raved about Milei in June 2025, calling him 'Margaret Thatcher on steroids' and introduced his own DOGE for councils where Reform had won control.[6] A few months later, one of those councils, Kent, despite its best efforts to find cuts, concluded that the local council tax would probably still have to rise or vital services would fail, and other Reform-led councils have since followed. Governing is so much harder than campaigning.

The real Margaret Thatcher worked in less spectacular and altogether more methodical ways. 'The cock crows but the hen lays the egg,' she used to say. Elected in 1979 on a mandate to reduce taxation and create a smaller state, she quickly set about reforming the civil service and the wider public sector to make it more efficient, bringing in private sector expertise to help her, including the boss of Marks & Spencer, Derek Rayner, and later Sir Robin Ibbs from Imperial Chemical Industries (ICI). I played a direct part in those reforms, of which more later, and have seen over my lifetime that their legacy has been long-lasting.

Despite Thatcher's ambition to cut the size of the state, the cost of the state actually rose by an average of one per cent per year (after taking account of inflation) during her administration, though the number of civil servants did fall significantly.[7] This was despite the privatisation and contracting out of many services that up until then had formed a core part of it. She did succeed in reducing the size of the state as a proportion of GDP, but only due to economic growth. And she did make the state run differently – so that it was more aware of its costs and was run more like a business.

Much of this thinking has continued to this day – but it is starting to be increasingly challenged.

• • •

It's 13 March 2025, a month after Musk's and Milei's theatrical performance – which I suspect is no coincidence – and Keir Starmer, shirtsleeves half rolled up and one button open at the neck, is revealing his own plans for 'a fundamental reform of the state' to a small audience of staff at a research and development facility for health products in Hull. He is pacing around, speaking with no notes as the staff stand motionless behind him with studied expressions of neutrality, as the nation's news cameras record every movement. Did they expect to be a bit part in this understated British 'chainsaw' moment when they got up that morning? Probably not. But they have been carefully selected, I am sure, and the key thing is they all work for the private sector, not the state, so they don't have to take it personally.

I'm watching him closely from my desk in London to see what he has to say. I'm in favour of fundamental reform, so I'm hoping for something fundamental today. Starmer says,

> At the moment the state employs more people than it has in decades. And yet – look around the country. Do you see good value everywhere? Because I don't. I actually think it's weaker than it's ever been.
>
> Overstretched ... Unfocused ... Trying to do too much ... Doing it badly ... Unable to deliver the security that people need.

I agree – but that word 'security' flummoxes me. Is that what politicians used to call 'service'? When I go to a GP, am I looking for security? Is that what bin workers are providing when they empty my bins, or HMRC when they take my taxes?

> I believe that working people want active government – they don't want a weak state. They want it to secure our future. They want it to take the big decisions so they can get on with their lives. We don't want bigger state, or an intrusive state, an ever-expanding state.

Yes, we want a state that works, and one that works for all of us, not just for 'working people' but for children, carers, pensioners, the unemployed and those unable to work due to disability. And why shouldn't that be the product of a bigger state, as in Scandinavia, with properly funded public services that work? One of the reasons the electorate rejected the Tories at the last election was austerity and the cuts that decimated services. It was a Labour government that created the welfare state. We like the welfare state, don't we? We are not America. Chainsaws are not for us.

And then Starmer lays into the regulators, those who 'see their job as blocking the government from doing the very things it was elected to do. You can't justify it. And it's a pattern.' Hang on, I thought the regulators were there for *our* security – stopping financial crashes, ensuring our health and safety, protecting our environment? But he's talking tough, and he's the new sheriff in town: 'We've created a watchdog state – completely out of whack with the priorities of the British people … Well that's got to end, no more. We were elected to take on blockers and deliver change and that is what we'll do.'

Then here it comes, the big announcement: abolishing NHS England.

> I don't see why decisions about £200 billion of taxpayer money should be spent by an arms-length body, NHS England, on something as fundamental to our security as the NHS, and can't in all honesty explain to the British people why we should spend their money on two layers of bureaucracy. That money could and should be spent on nurses, doctors, operations and GP appointments. So today I can announce we're going to cut bureaucracy across the state, focus government on the priorities of working people and shift money to the front line. So, I am bringing management of the NHS back into democratic control – by abolishing the arms-length body NHS England. That will put the NHS back at the heart of government, back where it belongs – freeing it to focus on patients, less bureaucracy, with more money for nurses. An NHS refocused on cutting waiting times at your hospital.

My heart sinks. If there's duplication, why not stop ministers second-guessing, cut down the department and let the experts get on with it, rather than implementing more centralisation and ministerial micro-management, slowing decisions down. Worst of all, this is yet another NHS reorganisation that will take everyone's eye off the ball.

Do they have any idea how much energy and time these things take and how distracting it will be? 13,500 public servants, until this moment focused on delivering the government's ambitious agenda for the NHS – the number one issue in the last election – will be immediately wondering if they have a job, with the best applying for other jobs and getting out as soon as they can, not to mention how much time and energy will now have to be devoted to making this reorganisation happen.

I know because I'd been through it all before. My last public sector role was as CEO of the Equal Opportunities Commission, the body charged with enforcing gender equality which the then Labour government decided to fold into a new Commission for Equalities and Human Rights, along with the other relevant disability and race statutory bodies. Preparation for this involved huge amounts of management and staff time and disruption for probably two years, taking us away from the real work we had to do, and many experienced and effective staff left. The new body, established in 2007, is still finding its way nearly twenty years later.

The highly paid man who was appointed to project manage the whole thing had come from the NHS and spent his whole career reorganising it, one reorganisation after another. It's all he knew how to do.

Governments often turn to administrative reform when they want to show the public they mean business but the immediate impact is to slow things down. As Starmer reminded us at the beginning of the speech, Labour had promised 'Change', but fundamental change is hard to deliver and can take years, even decades. Reorganising the organisational deck chairs is something ministers can make happen at the stroke a speechwriter's pen, even if it is much harder for the institutions to put their plans in place. And it all starts to look pretty futile when that change is simply reversed or replaced by the next administration.

Take a trip with me on the NHS merry-go-round for a few minutes.

In 1991 under John Major, an 'internal market' was set up in which new hospital trusts were created. These competed to provide care commissioned by new health authorities. New 'GP fundholding' gave some family doctors budgets to buy care on their patients' behalf. Less than a decade later, New Labour shifted the institutions again, creating new primary care trusts in 2000 to purchase healthcare on behalf of GPs.

A decade after that, the coalition government gave spending power back to GPs, setting up new Clinical Commissioning Groups (CCGs), sidelining primary care trusts and dismantling much of the regulation and the targets introduced by Labour. It also created NHS England. These reforms were not mentioned in either the Conservative or Lib Dem manifestos but were so big that one head of the NHS said they could be seen from outer space.

In 2019, CCGs were replaced with Integrated Care Systems and Boards. These were designed to bring local authorities in charge of social care and public health together with the NHS and voluntary bodies, so that there would be a much-needed integrated approach to health. Collaboration, not competition, was the name of this new game.

And in 2025, as we have seen, Starmer announced the abolition of NHS England and cut the budget of Integrated Care Boards in half.

Feeling dizzy? Imagine how health staff must feel. But all this would be OK, wouldn't it, if these reforms actually made government work better for us?

Three years after the coalition's 2012 reforms, the Chief Executive of the King's Fund, an independent think tank specialising in the NHS, wrote that 'the first three years were wasted on major organisational changes when the NHS should have been concentrating on growing financial and services pressures. This was a strategic error.' Which, to translate, means no, restructuring doesn't improve our services.

Lord Darzi in his 2024 report on the NHS commissioned by the incoming government put it far more bluntly:

> The Health and Social Care Act of 2012 was a calamity without international precedent. It proved disastrous. By dissolving the NHS management line, it took a 'scorched earth' approach to health reform, the effects of which are still felt to this day. It has taken more than ten years to get back to a sensible structure. And management capability is still behind where it was in 2011.

He added that

> while a top-down reorganisation of NHS England and integrated care boards is *neither necessary nor desirable* [my italics], there is more work to be done to clarify roles and accountabilities, ensure the right balance of management resources in different parts of the structure, and strengthen key processes such as capital approvals.

> Change will only be successful if the NHS can recover its capacity to deliver plans and strategies as well as to make them.[8]

As with the NHS and reorganisations, so it is with quangos (otherwise known as non-departmental public bodies or NDPBs). Ministers love to announce they are going to abolish them. Some quangos may overstay their welcome (and it is true that Lord Darzi thought the NHS had too many regulatory bodies) but a 'bonfire of the quangos' seems to happen with suspicious regularity. We first heard that phrase under the coalition government, which cut the number of UK public bodies by more than a third. Fast forward a few years to 2022 and Jacob Rees-Mogg ordered another review and, yes, another bonfire. And now Starmer's government is at it again.

And with NHS England, if duplication is the problem, centralisation is not the answer. Ministers getting involved in the day-to-day running of services is a recipe for disaster. When my husband was being treated for cancer during the pandemic, his oncologist explained to him in despair that ministers were now setting the amount of time he had to talk to patients in order to make him more 'efficient'. It was now half of what it used to be and what he judged to be needed. And that was why he was ringing him at eight o'clock at night, four hours after the scheduled appointment. Because, whatever ministers thought about it, he had to treat people, and they deserved the time that they needed to get well.

Consider for a moment the impact on the minister's red box, which may now dictate decisions with a direct impact on your life. Ministers are already overloaded, and there is almost nothing more likely to slow things down in government than a department waiting around, sometimes for months, for decisions ministers have not found time to make. I will never forget the sight of Norman Fowler arriving as the new Secretary of State for Employment with a trolley behind him filled with a backlog of unfinished ministerial red boxes from his previous department, the Department of Health and Social Security. And ministers who have their noses stuck in boxes have less time to think strategically about the change they want to see.

Just as No. 10 has become larger and larger over my professional life, so more and more decisions seem to have been sucked into ministerial red boxes, or so I hear from current civil servants. This pattern has got worse over the last fifteen years, partly because ministers don't trust others to take decisions for which they might be held accountable and partly because civil servants in response have become increasingly risk averse, pushing often trivial things upwards for decision. Imagine the impact, now, of the summary dismissal of Olly Robbins by Starmer, as civil servants worry even more about protecting themselves from being blamed for taking decisions without reference to ministers.

That's not just bad for government delivery; it's also damaging the ability of ministers and their departments to connect up the dots. Acting rather like No. 10 for government as a whole, the Private Office of a Secretary of State is a central nerve centre that can see across different issues right across the department, join things up and present the bigger picture. When a Private Office is small, that is easier, but as it grows in order to process all those decisions, this becomes much harder. I know of one Private Office for a Secretary of State in a major department that has grown from four Private Secretaries in 2006 to ten in 2025, mirroring what has also been happening in No. 10.

Mixing politics with operational decisions can also end badly. I think of Robert Jenrick's planning decision as Secretary of State for Housing, Communities and Local Government: shortly after sitting next to the property developer and former owner of the *Daily Express*, Richmond Desmond, at a Tory fundraising event, he overturned a decision made by both a local council and the government's planning inspectorate in order to approve one of Desmond's developments. Jenrick did this a day before the introduction of a community infrastructure levy (which would have been used to fund local education and health projects), saving Desmond's company at least £40 million. Shortly after Jenrick did this, Desmond donated £12,000 to the Conservative Party. When challenged, Jenrick accepted his action had been unlawful and was forced to reverse his own ruling.[9]

Ministerial control does not always lead to enhanced efficiency, either, because politics plays a role. To placate the angry constituents of Conservative MPs over the environmental impact of HS2, Tory ministers agreed to additional expensive tunnelling, driving up costs. In the end there were plans for tunnels for thirty-four miles of the 140-mile track,[10] and that political pressure will have contributed far more significantly to the spiralling costs than Keir Starmer's much vaunted 'bat tunnel'.[11]

Abolishing quangos can also be counterproductive. At least one quango terminated under the last government, the Audit Commission, was there to reduce the cost of local government and drive up performance, and by all accounts it was very good at it. At a time when the current Labour government is committing to giving patients more of a voice in frontline services, it has decided to abolish Healthwatch England, whose job it was to amplify their voices both nationally and locally.

Perverse effects often follow when arbitrary cuts are made to the public sector. It's true that when left to their own devices bureaucracies can become bloated, and it's tempting to think that top-down 'efficiency' targets, a common practice in the past, are a painless way to force them to slim down, rather than identifying functions that should be abolished or finding new ways of doing things. Rachel Reeves's Treasury is also doing this now, with ambitious departmental cuts and efficiency targets set in her first Budget and Spending Review. In March 2025 she promised to cut the civil service by 15 per cent, amounting to £2 billion a year at that point, with 10,000 civil service job losses.

To achieve these top-down 'efficiencies', organisations often resort to arbitrary and damaging measures rather than having difficult conversations with ministers about what the priorities should be and what might be dropped. Senior civil servants, intent on proving to ministers that they can deliver, have poor incentives to volunteer their own staff for redundancy. And redundancies cost money, too. In the face of this, they often impose recruitment freezes – keeping vacancies unfilled when someone leaves. Recruitment freezes are now being used in the NHS to balance budgets, for example. As well as being entirely random, this also creates pressures on other staff which may force them to move on, and the service to the public further suffers.

Head count targets have been repeatedly used over the decades but these can often lead to higher costs, as expensive management consultants are brought in to replace public servants. Freezing pay, as the last administration did, led to over-promotion to give staff pay rises, otherwise known as 'grade inflation', and to the departure of some of the best staff, leading to a damaging loss of competence and, it seems, no lowering of staff costs overall.[12] It has also meant staff move jobs more frequently in order to get the range of experience to be promoted, causing vacancies and a loss of stability.

They call it 'false economy'. When I was working in the Department of Employment as one of Lord Young's Private Secretaries, I saw what so-called 'efficiency' and staffing cuts could do. Lord Young, formerly a businessman and now Secretary of State, was intent on trying to manage the unemployment statistics which stood at historically high levels due to the government's economic policies. He wanted to avoid the politically damaging level of three million unemployed and was looking at every way to avoid it, including putting more people on disability benefits. As a man who knew how businesses actually work, he saw that recent reductions in staffing levels in Benefit Offices and Jobcentres in line with Thatcherite 'efficiency thinking' were hampering his efforts, leading to higher levels of benefit fraud and fewer people getting jobs, and he argued for more money, received it and invested in more staff – and his efforts paid off.

Similar arguments apply to reductions over many years in staffing levels at HMRC, leading to lower tax intake due to lack of enforcement, or reducing immigration case workers, creating more expensive backlogs and undermining any savings from the cuts, not to mention the political damage. AI and automation may enable some cuts without a loss of effectiveness but that requires investment, not just arbitrary upfront cuts. Recently, things have been moving in the opposite direction: austerity led not just to reductions in manpower but to cuts in planned capital investment, reducing productivity.

Indeed, Lord Darzi, in his report on the NHS, concluded that cuts to capital budgets and systemic underinvestment in equipment, buildings and digital technology were a key cause of low productivity in hospitals. Another was lack of action to tackle the crisis in social care, which the government has essentially parked until the next election by commissioning yet another review, this time from Louise Casey.

And, of course, as noted earlier, Lord Darzi did not recommend the abolition of NHS England.[13]

• • •

How do you speed the state up and make it nimbler and more flexible?

When my children were young, they loved Babar the Elephant, and so did I. The moment I first heard the 'Committee' song in *Babar: The Movie*, it struck a chord, and I've never entirely got the words out of my mind.

Picture the scene. There's a war in the jungle and King Babar wants to stop it. He turns to his experienced civil servants to help him do it. They have a plan, or rather they have a process, and they are excited about it.

> There's work to do, we'll call in all the experts
> To hear just what they say, is there general agreement and
> consensus today?
> And then we'll take a survey to get the public point of view
> With colour chart projector, and graphics too
> And then duplicate it, and it never will never do
> Then send it to committee for review.
> Then we'll circulate a memo to all the staff concerned
> Discussing all the options and note what we have learned
> And then submit the matter to a democratic thorough debate
> It'll be glorious, glorious!

Consulting the public and staff, bringing people across departments together to look at every angle and thrash out differences, thinking before you act – what's wrong with that? Nothing. This is all part of good government, and we need more of it.

But what if the process becomes the objective, not the means to an end? A substitute for leadership and a means of avoiding difficult decisions. We've all seen it in those endless inquiries that are set up, sometimes one after the other, taking years to complete and then producing reports that are simply ignored by ministers, because they and the wider machine have moved on. Knocking it into the long grass, we used to call it in the civil service, using a golfing analogy. We've seen it in the processes that are established to resolve longstanding disputes and deliver compensation – like the Post Office or the Windrush scandal – that take for ever and never work. It's like wading through sludge.

If you're on the receiving end of such obfuscation, marked by a lack of accountability and indeed humanity, it can be hell. It's the experience of what Bishop James Jones in his Hillsborough inquiry calls 'the patronising disposition of unaccountable power' – institutions close ranks, refuse to disclose information, use public money to defend their interests and act in a way that is both intimidating and oppressive when victims of malpractice ask questions with the aim of finding out what went wrong. This applies not just to the Hillsborough families but, as Jones notes, to many other victims across many decades.[14] The government's commitment to a new Hillsborough Law – requiring public servants to be honest in these circumstances and giving victims access to independent advocates to pursue their case – is a great step forward. The culture is ingrained, however, and a single law will not necessarily change it.

Some of the lack of accountability within the civil service is structural: because civil servants move so frequently in a constant 'pass the parcel' of responsibilities, they rarely see the longer-term impact of their decisions or are held accountable for their mistakes. Working with the civil service from outside as I do nowadays, I can see how the frequent change of roles also means that officials often lack the deep knowledge and experience that would help them do a good job, or the depth of relationships with external experts that might have helped compensate for this. When you are inside the civil service, moving jobs frequently, facing fresh challenges, it can feel exhilarating. I loved it. And you feel, wrongly, that you can master any topic within a few months.

The public sector is also better at listening to ministers and to itself than it is at listening to people outside its institutions. It can be very good at internal consultation, involving an often-lengthy process to gather and reflect views from different departments, and then funnelling them through layers of ministers. But it is often very poor at engaging with people and institutions outside of government, bringing in the perspective of those who are at the sharp end of what it does, who often know more than it does about what is working well and what is not. Interaction too often focuses on process, rather than substance, with box-ticking meetings with external stakeholders rather than genuine dialogue. Public servants often spend ages perfecting documents internally and then give outsiders almost no time at all to comment, often dumping formal consultations at the last minute just before Christmas or at the end of July when they go on holiday, expecting everyone else to still be in place.

At the same time, I've rarely met a civil servant I didn't like and admire personally – for their flexibility in meeting ministerial demands, their calmness under fire, their intelligence and professionalism and desire to do a good job and their politeness and impartiality. The same holds true for other public sector officials.

What I have found – both from working in a number of different departments and working through them from No. 10 or the Treasury – is that some departments are much more flexible than others. The Department of Employment, for example, before it was abolished, had an enterprising culture. The Treasury moved quickly to engage with new ideas. The Home Office was the worst – slow and inflexible, with entrenched views.

Making things happen in government can be hard, whether you are someone outside trying to get redress or inside trying to make services and policies work better for the public. There are so many layers and aspects of government, so many hierarchies you must go through, so many different bodies with separate management, creating silos, blind spots and revolving doors. I know from A Better Way, the leadership group I co-founded and convened for many years, that there are many good people in the public sector and elsewhere trying to get through this maze to achieve fundamental change but so many local pilots fizzle out or fail to take off, partly because the wider machine works against them.

Despite all this, Covid proved that a fundamental shift could be achieved, and quickly.

• • •

Things most people would have thought were impossible were done at amazing speed during Covid, particularly by the NHS. NHS staff were redeployed within days to the Covid front line. Later on, it worked seamlessly with pharmacies and others, including an army of volunteers, to set up and run a hugely ambitious vaccination programme for the whole population. It was easy to book, there were no queues and it all worked extraordinarily well.

A brand new and complex real time data dashboard was put in place extraordinarily fast by Public Health England, working alongside private sector expertise. Up-to-date data was collected locally on the number of cases and assembled nationally by public health officials and communicated to us as we sat, waiting anxiously in front of our screens, dazzled by the graphs and updates in the daily ministerial press conferences. At least we knew what was happening across the country as a whole and in each region, which helped us judge the level of risk in the place we lived. I know one of the people involved who was working regionally for Public Health England. He was called to take part while he was abroad and, like James Bond, was essentially parachuted into the crack squad that did this.

The energy unlocked at the front line by the pandemic was extraordinary. People running services flocked to A Better Way's online leadership network meetings to hear from others about how they were managing to work during the crisis – and a surprising message came back. We heard that things that in the past would have faced huge obstacles were being achieved, almost overnight. Services and sectors put their lanyards at the door, worked out what needed to be done, agreed roles and just got on with it.

A shared, clear purpose was the key reason: saving lives and protecting the NHS. People saw what the situation required and did it, stepping over organisational boundaries as they did so. A lack of interference from bosses and entanglement from bureaucratic rules, like procurement – which in normal times required lengthy competitive processes, which were temporarily suspended – also helped.

The message from members of the network doing it on the ground was that we can collaborate, we can work differently, we can 'build back better' – a slogan that was first coined by our group and others but which was eventually adopted, through a process of osmosis, by Boris Johnson. It became just words, covering the fact that the public sector returned to the status quo once the threat from Covid subsided just as quickly as it had changed during Covid. Johnson broadcast a bizarre video on Twitter of him tucking into fish and chips, then drinking a pint, and finally buttering some toast in front of a copy of *The Telegraph* and *The Sun*, saying 'Build Back Batter, Build Back Bitter, Build Back Butter' with a common caption of 'Build Back Better'.[15] The gimmick did not take off and the slogan died.

It wasn't surprising, either, that Covid did not lead to a fundamental shift toward decentralisation, collaboration and empowerment of the front line. That might have been happening locally during the pandemic but at the centre of government the very reverse was true. One of the most centralised governments in Europe became even more so – centralisation on steroids – even as people working closer to the front line momentarily felt the chains of central government loosen, to good effect.

Although every government would have struggled to find their feet in that crisis, it sorely tested the quality of political leadership – which was found lacking. We could all see that decisions on whether to lock down before the NHS was overwhelmed seemed to come too slowly and too late, long after many people and organisations had started to voluntarily lock down. But the full scale of the failure started to become clear during the Covid inquiry, which later reinforced these points and concluded that Johnson oversaw a 'toxic and chaotic' culture within government that led to poor Covid decision-making.[16]

'No. 10 and the Cabinet Office operated as a separate island from the rest of Whitehall,' wrote Helen MacNamara, the Deputy Cabinet

Secretary at the time, in her evidence to the inquiry. 'Departments were not brought into the full thinking and time and again had to respond to late and partial information about what was about to happen.' She added that there was 'a failure to understand that there was a much bigger machine outside No. 10 and the Cabinet Office that we could use and direct'. The political centre was unaware, for example, that there were local public health officials who knew their patch and could have been rapidly deployed for test and trace.

There was a 'prevailing governing mindset in No. 10 … that everything had to be built from scratch and controlled centrally,' she said. This mindset led to NHS Test and Trace being established centrally and emergency Nightingale hospitals being created without thinking about whether there were enough staff to run them (which there weren't).[17] The VIP commissioning lane for equipment, which allowed ministers' contacts and friends to get priority status, ended up wasting billions of pounds on unusable goods.

Public Health England, which was so key to the handling of the pandemic, was abolished in August 2020, right in the middle of the crisis, and replaced with a new National Institute for Health Protection, which also included Test and Trace, creating damaging uncertainty for its staff and attracting widespread criticism from experts at the time.[18] That person I mentioned earlier from Public Health England who put together the new data dashboard on Covid? He left, in exhaustion and disgust.

Ministers and officials were unclear about their roles and responsibilities. According to MacNamara, this had begun during Brexit and left the government hamstrung during Covid, leading to more and more decisions being sucked into the centre and ministers being left out in the cold.

So it was that the Department for Education had no plan for

closing schools in 2020 and had to make arrangements literally overnight to lock them down after No. 10 decided to announce their closure the next day, in March. The Secretary of State for Education at the time, Gavin Williamson, told the Covid inquiry he thought he 'probably' had no authority to have made any plans. All decisions were being taken by No. 10 and he felt powerless, it appears.[19] In fact, no one from the department was in the room when the crucial decisions were made in Downing Street to lock schools down in 2020 and 2021.[20] Despite this, Boris Johnson, in his evidence to the inquiry, insisted that he had assumed someone was on top of it.[21]

Government looked, and was, in complete disarray. In 2021, parents, children, teachers and schools were blindsided by the decision to close schools a day after they had just opened after Christmas, and it seemed the worst of all worlds, as the virus, which had been spreading within families over Christmas, was brought back into the schools and into the wider community before they closed. By this point, the Department for Education had put in place a different plan to roll out testing in every school, and tests had been delivered (heroically) to 97 per cent of them before they were then closed by a sudden decision in No. 10. The Permanent Secretary at the time, Susan Acland-Hood, told the inquiry she remains convinced to this day that this would have worked and that lockdown was unnecessary.[22] But neither she nor her boss had any say in the decision.

In contrast, the Treasury and HMRC stepped in very quickly with furlough payments and business support to stabilise the economy and ensure people had the money they needed to continue to live. MacNamara said they had less interference and more autonomy than other departments.[23]

• • •

What can we learn from Covid that might inform successful 'fundamental reform' today?

Clarity of purpose is a critical first step but in government things are often far from clear. Purpose can be complex, fuzzy, and can shift as ministers change or change their minds. Civil servants who work around ministers prize their ability to handle complexity and hack their way through a host of mixed signals to deliver a result, and tend to see this as normal rather than a failing of the system. However, if a minister has a clear purpose and can communicate it successfully so that the end goal and the philosophy behind it is clear, as during the Covid crisis, the machine can be very impressive, fast and inventive in helping the minister achieve those goals, often in ways they would never have never thought of.

I enjoyed working with ministers who could do this, and I was lucky enough to have worked closely with quite a few. I loved the way that ministers had the power – if they knew how to use it and had the vision to use it well – to cut through the bureaucracy and inertia of the civil service at its worst and deploy its considerable resources to help them do what they'd been elected to do.

I felt that way when I was working with Margaret Hodge in the Department for Education and Employment, when I was in charge of childcare policy. She had introduced childcare centres in Islington and wanted to do so across the country, but she was hated by many civil servants whom she gave a hard time when, as she saw it, they weren't delivering what she wanted. But I loved working with her because of her clarity of purpose and energy in seeking to secure it. We were a team, I felt.

Likewise, I liked working with special advisers because they could speed things up enormously due to their direct route to ministers and their ability to reach deep into the department in ways that ministers lack the time to do. I have particularly fond memories of Ed Miliband, when he was working for Gordon Brown in the Treasury. He was a highly effective special adviser with a particular passion, like his boss, for reducing child poverty. When I moved from the Treasury to the Department for Education, I was able to work through him to make Margaret Hodge's case for an expansion of childcare, working under the radar of my new department's finance department, which had other priorities.

Proximity to ministers allows civil servants to really understand their fundamental purpose, which day-to-day events can sometimes obscure. It builds up trust which makes genuine communication easier and enables civil servants to act on their behalf, even when circumstances change, because they know their mind. Trust also allows civil servants to have honest conversations about the genuine barriers that may exist and create a shared understanding of the problem to be solved, which makes it easier for them to design effective solutions for ministers.

Brexit damaged that trust and set up a difficult dynamic that undermined any sense of shared purpose. Helen MacNamara confirmed Lord Butler's observation, mentioned in the previous chapter, that under Boris Johnson there was 'a them and us mindset' between, on the one side, ministers and political advisers and civil servants on the other, as well as a view that civil servants needed 'driving' and 'pushing'. She thought that this was a 'cost of the overall outcomes because of the productive hours lost to the friction that this created'.[24]

A shared sense of clear purpose is essential, and most especially where fundamental reform or a major shift in direction is the end goal. A senior policeman I once knew told me that the thing that most stood in the way of trying to change the way his officers worked was their fixed idea about what their job was. He was attempting to introduce a different, preventative approach, which involved officers referring young offenders for help to other parts of the public sector, rather than charging them with an offence. Studies had shown this was more likely to reduce crime and re-offending. But many police officers had a fixed idea that their job was to lock people up, he said, and he had to change that first. When his police force started to work in the preventative way he wanted, it was highly effective.

I can personally testify that changing any institution is hard, having tried to change the Treasury's culture after the spectacular failure of Black Wednesday on 16 September 1992 – I had moved to the Treasury after leaving No. 10 the year before. This was the infamous day when the pound fell out of the European Exchange Rate Mechanism, because it had been fixed at too high a rate. The Chancellor, Norman Lamont, had to hike interest rates to 15 per cent and spend billions of pounds to keep the value of the pound from plummeting. On that day, I remember passing a gaggle of journalists and a film crew around Norman Lamont as I left the building to go to a meeting, wondering what was happening (this was in the days before mobile phones and 24-hour news). I was heavily pregnant and, slipping on some wet leaves a few minutes later, I fell flat onto my front, unbalanced by the weight of the pregnancy. I was worried for my unborn child, and I also felt like a fool. But that was nothing compared to how the Treasury was feeling. My baby, Elizabeth, who was born seven weeks later, was OK, but the Treasury was not.

In response, Terry Burns, the Permanent Secretary, decided to change the Treasury's culture and make it more outward-looking, more professional, especially in terms of economic expertise, and better at working with others. As the new Head of Personnel, after my return from three months' maternity leave, it was my job to change *how* the Treasury worked to deliver this culture change. I introduced a new set of standards for judging civil servants' performance – known as competencies – which embodied these objectives and, for the first time, I introduced performance pay linked to each annual performance assessment.

Did it work? The Treasury's cultural problems ran deep and senior people in leadership roles had built careers on them. We wanted the Treasury to take a more collegiate approach to the rest of government rather than seeing them as an opposing team they had to defeat, but as one very senior person told me, what he thought was needed were 'sharp elbows' (a term which I assume derives from rugby and which embodied everything we were trying to change). At the time I was presenting the new competencies to his senior management team, and he might as well have responded with 'Bollocks' (but his face said it all). Some years later, after I and many of the other senior women in the Treasury had left because we found the culture of the department inimical, a staff survey revealed that the Treasury had a major problem with bullying.

The steamroller approach to the rest of government is still apparent today. There is something about the balance of power between the Treasury and the rest of government – it holds the purse strings, after all – that makes it poor at listening and consulting, as the humiliating reversal of decisions pushed through by the Treasury under a Labour government to end Winter Fuel Payments and to cut disability benefits has demonstrated.

Back in the 1980s, just before I went to No. 10, I had helped put

Thatcher's reform of the civil service, the Next Steps initiative, into effect, which aimed to create much greater clarity about roles, bring about decentralisation and foster a much sharper focus on delivery. This was to prove more successful, but it was fiercely opposed by the Treasury at the time, because they feared loss of control and thought that public expenditure would rise. The idea was to create semi-autonomous business units out of government functions, like the Passport Office, the Driver Vehicle Licensing Authority and the Benefits Service, and let them get on with the job without day-to-day interference from ministers or their senior civil servants. These new executive agencies would operate within a framework agreement negotiated between the chief executives and their ministers, including agreed objectives, priorities, performance measures and resources.

Ultimately, it was hoped that the public would receive a better service and public money would be spent more efficiently, as agency chief executives, who were often recruited from outside, were freed to focus on the job in hand and given flexibility and autonomy to deliver it. It would also allow ministers to be more strategic, setting the overall direction of travel but not micro-managing how to get there. The scale of this was enormous, with a target that 75 per cent of the civil service would eventually work in these agencies.

Treasury opposition delayed the initiative by a year but eventually Thatcher pushed her reforms through. By 1997, when Labour came to power, the target for the proportion of civil servants in these agencies had been achieved.[25]

It all started in 1988 with the setting up of a tiny 'Next Steps Team', of which I was a part. You can see a picture of me and the other three people in the team in Peter Hennessy's book *Whitehall*, with the caption 'Wave of the Future?' Back then, these ideas were dynamite and we were insurgents, but after I left the team in 1989 to go to No. 10, and later went to the Treasury, the Next Steps Team became a Next Steps Unit, grew much larger and was eventually closed down in 1997, because Next Steps Agencies had become the new norm and its work was done.

• • •

It's 1988 and I'm in my early thirties, sitting in the Cabinet Office at my desk in a room with high ornate ceilings, big windows and a leafy view of St James's Park. It's the most impressive room I've ever called an office, having recently been seconded from the Department of Employment where I was working in Caxton House, a modern building that speaks to its modern roots and its 'let's get things done' culture, and which was largely open plan. The grand building of the Cabinet Office, in contrast, is redolent of a bygone era of colonial power, and shouts hierarchy, tradition and inhibition. I remember writing to my erstwhile colleagues in the Department of Employment at my shock at discovering that the nearest loo was not just old-fashioned – flushed by pulling a chain and with a wooden seat – but also included a wall-mounted container of disposable toilet seat covers, which I had never seen before and have never seen since.

I'm sharing this office with another older colleague, Diana Goldsworthy, who was at the same relatively junior level in the civil service hierarchy as me, Grade 7, and we are grappling with the question of how to go about reforming the civil service. We are part of a four-person team led by the very much more senior Peter Kemp, a former Treasury Second Permanent Secretary (so a poacher turned gamekeeper), who is now reporting direct to the Prime Minister, Margaret Thatcher, on how we are going to reshape the corridors of power into her preferred image, despite resistance from the Treasury and much of Whitehall. We've been charged with implementing Next Steps, which had been recommended by her then Efficiency Adviser, Sir Robin Ibbs, a former senior director of ICI, so part of our exam question has already been answered. We know what we have to do: our job is to take on Whitehall, change its business as usual and set up new Next Steps Agencies – but where do you start?

Thatcher believes that the civil service, which at the time was seen as the best in the world, is too focused on serving ministers and not enough on serving the consumers of its services, the public. It is too dominated by a mandarin culture of policymakers, rather than policy deliverers. Although I don't agree personally with much of what she is trying to do, I believe she is right in this, based on my own dire experience before becoming a civil servant.

Part of her vision is to make the civil service leaner, more efficient and more accountable. A chief executive would be appointed for each Next Steps Agency and his or her pay would be linked to the delivery of that performance. If something went wrong, then their head would roll, not ministers'. Or at least that is the theory.

In her world, business is king and the civil service must learn from it. A year or so later, I would visit Ely Cathedral with her to see the stained glass windows with inscriptions from the business world, including John Lewis, Tesco and NatWest. Money talked, especially if it was not taxpayers' money.

So how could four people, three of them relatively junior, take on the whole of Whitehall and make this happen? Answer: by using the Prime Minister's authority and providing regular progress reports to her. Even if they didn't think it would work or had doubts about the plan, Permanent Secretaries would sit up and listen, even when a humble Grade 7 is speaking to them. Because we had the Prime Minister's backing.

So that is what we did, and it worked. We carved up Whitehall between us, established relationships, set up plans and ensured they were executed. When I say we established relationships, this is also how I met my husband, John. I fell in love with him over the telephone and engineered an in-person meeting with him at Ernst and Young on the other side of the river facing St Thomas' Hospital where, a few years later, as it happened, our daughters were born. Our mutual subject: setting up the Benefits Agency. He was in the Department of Health and Social Security making it happen, liaising closely with me. Both the agency and our marriage have endured over thirty-five years.

There was another relationship taking form, though I didn't know about it at the time. The other Grade 7 in the team, Diana Goldsworthy, was having a secret affair with our boss, Peter Kemp, who later left his wife for her, but the relationship did not stand the test of time, sadly. Looking back, I can now see there was something a little too cosy about the meetings we had with Peter in his comfortable office, the starlings forming murmurations over St James's Park outside, Diana curled up on one of his sofas (Permanent Secretary's offices are typically luxurious), strategising together, as the night drew in. Somehow, I was always the first to go home.

We all felt passionate about our work, and it was that passion which helped me get the job, a year later, working for Margaret Thatcher as the first female Private Secretary at No. 10, having been nominated for that role by the Permanent Secretary in my home department. I had proved that I could take on the establishment and win.

The thing which most frustrated me about the civil service

then was its entrenched hierarchical structure, or what we called 'gradism' – deferring to those above you rather than giving power to those who were closest to the consumer or had the real expertise. And with this, its 'drafting culture', where getting the words right was often more important than getting the right result, with endless circulation of drafts for comments from more senior staff and other policy areas with an interest. This slowed everything down.

Peter Kemp was the perfect fusion of the old and the new. He relished leading a small team, had no regard for grade, just competence, and sliced through Whitehall like a knife. At the same time, he spent many hours over drafting and redrafting minutes, especially to the Prime Minister, and when I told him that another senior civil servant had praised the skill of his drafting his face shone with pleasure. It was the ultimate mandarin compliment back then, but really was the least important of his skills in that job.

Clarity of purpose and accountability for delivering it – these were qualities we were trying to introduce through Next Steps. But these qualities were not in strong supply in Whitehall, where the focus was more on managing ministers and delivering their agenda, if they had one, in the short term rather than on delivering long-term change for the good of the country. Next Steps was anti-mandarin, pro-public service.

But could it work?

• • •

Do you remember the accusation that Michael Howard had 'something of the night about him'? This comment was made in 1997 by his political colleague, Ann Widdecombe, while he was standing to be leader of the Conservative Party, and it killed off his chances of getting the top job. I suspect there are very few who will remember the context for her remarks – a row about the Prison Service, which had been established as a Next Steps executive agency in 1993, and specifically whether its CEO had autonomy or not.

Here was a drama that had everything in it. In November 1994, six dangerous convicts – including five IRA members – broke out of a top security facility, Whitemoor prison, and shot a guard during their escape. A few months later, in January 1995, another three high-risk prisoners escaped from Parkhurst on the Isle of Wight. Michael Howard, the Home Secretary, was under intense pressure to resign but he said that as this was an executive agency it was therefore an operational matter, so not his fault. He commissioned investigations which concluded that there had been serious operational failings, which Howard refused to take responsibility for. Up until that point, it was understood that ministers would resign for serious failings under their watch. Instead, he sacked the man who had been appointed as its Chief Executive, Derek Lewis. Lewis subsequently sued him and won £280,000 in damages in an out-of-court settlement. He had had no experience of the public sector, let alone the Prison Service, but was improbably chosen for his track record in turning around ailing media companies. Possibly because of that, he was not going to go quietly.

When Michael Howard decided to stand as Tory leader a few years later, Widdecombe, who had been the Prisons Minister at the time of the sacking of Lewis, decided to put the knife in. She said Howard had misled Parliament three times – a cardinal offence – by refusing to admit that he had personally intervened heavily in prison operations. Howard had told Parliament that

> the Leader of the Opposition made three allegations: that I

> personally told Mr Lewis that the governor of Parkhurst should be suspended immediately; that when Mr Lewis objected as it was an operational matter, I threatened to instruct him to do it; and when Mr Lewis further objected, I told the operational director of the Prison Service, by fax, that I would announce it in the House of Commons that day. Each and every one of the allegations is untrue.

But these claims weren't untrue, Widdecombe insisted, adding that he was unfit to lead his party or the country.[26] All seemed lost for Michael Howard's career, though he was eventually able to recover and did become the leader of his party some years later – and with Ann Widdecombe's support.

Although this incident led many commentators at the time to doubt the viability of the Next Steps Agency model, most executive agencies have somehow survived to this very day. The principle of operational autonomy, although inevitably breached in some high-profile areas because of ministers' ultimate accountability for public agencies to Parliament, has been largely honoured. This is perhaps because it actually makes a huge amount of sense for both ministers, who no longer feel they have to resign for failings over which they genuinely have no influence, and agencies, who generally do better if they are left to get on with a clearly defined job.[27]

As with executive agencies, so also with non-departmental public bodies (NDPBs) which, unlike Next Steps Agencies, are generally set up by statute and have their own governing bodies in place. My first job in the civil service, in the Department of Employment, was 'shadowing' one such body, the Health and Safety Executive (HSE), which was led then as it is now by the Health and Safety Commission. There was only a tiny team liaising between the NDPB and the minister ultimately responsible for it, at that time Peter Bottomley, and there were regularly high-profile cases of deaths or injuries at fairgrounds and theme parks due to faulty equipment that had not been properly maintained or – some argued – inspected regularly enough by HSE. I used to inform him of the tragedies, often at antisocial times, and provide some words for him to put out as a statement. What he didn't do, generally, was interfere. He saw his role as being to ensure that the NDPB was properly resourced to do the job set for it and to make sure that it was performing that job satisfactorily. If he had taken a different view, our little unit would have ballooned.

To come back to NHS England, also an NDPB, which Keir Starmer announced the abolition of in March 2025, there are thousands of things it did which ministers either should not or could not be involved in due to sheer impracticality, unless they set up whole teams of people to advise them inside the Department of Health and Social Care. This seems to be what happened long before Starmer came to power, a bad case of bureaucracy gone mad. Will ministers be able to do as good a job as NHS England? We shall see, but I suspect the next government will decide the situation is managerially unsustainable and politically undesirable and put something similar in place again.

• • •

Alongside introducing executive agencies, Thatcher also privatised or contracted out many activities that at that time were run by the state. Her philosophy was that the market knows best and competition was the route to efficiency.

Many of the industries she privatised, like the railways, water and what is now known as BT, had been badly run, partly because of ministerial interference, and had been starved of public investment.

At first these decisions were popular and the proceeds helped reduce the cost of the state. Increasingly, however, the problems with setting up monopolies that serve shareholders, not the public, have become apparent and railway companies are being unprivatised and water companies are failing.

Likewise, cracks have begun to emerge in the growing practice, over successive administrations, of contracting out public services. People are questioning why, for example, children's care homes should be run by private equity firms which are making excessive profits and often remove children to locations far away from their original homes because it is cheaper for them. Some services, like probation, have been contracted out but then brought back into direct state control, because the service failed due to high staff turnover and poor performance. The management of contracts by civil servants has been criticised, including by the Home Affairs Commons Select Committee in 2025, which said that billions had been squandered on asylum accommodation because the Home Office failed to pick up on bad performance or reclaim excess profits.[28]

As a result of these and other changes initiated by Thatcher and continued by her successors, the state has become increasingly atomised. For example, the setting up of academy schools (first put in place by New Labour, after the seed was planted through City Technology Colleges by Thatcher, and continued by later governments) has led to 65 per cent of secondary schools and 26 per cent of primary schools being taken out of the hands of local authorities and placed in private hands, even though they remain public services.[29] This has paradoxically led to more centralisation of the state, as the Department for Education now oversees the management of these schools, rather than local authorities, and is ultimately accountable for them instead of locally elected officials. Likewise, social housing, which used to be predominantly funded and managed directly by local authorities, is now primarily run by housing associations, which are nominally entirely independent from the state and not subject to democratic accountability at all.

This has made radical reform of the state increasingly difficult, as managerial silos make it hard to work across services, to find new and better ways to address the needs of the people the state serves. Collaboration across these institutional boundaries, which often makes sense if you look at government from the perspective of those served, rather than institutions, becomes much harder. Telling the state what to do becomes almost impossible in these circumstances, but ministers still act as if they can, as Helen MacNamara wrote in her evidence to the Covid inquiry, explaining that the state is in fact 'more of a constellation of institutions and different and sometimes conflicting centres of power'. This has been compounded by increasing devolution, not just to the devolved countries but also to new combined local authorities in England.

The answer? The New Labour government introduced what I call 'megaphone government' – the imposition of countless targets by the top of government on a front line over which in reality it has little control – and that way of operating has pretty much stuck, to this day. At one point in my nine years in the Treasury, I played a key role in bringing such a state of affairs about, but experience inside and particularly outside government has since persuaded me that this is the wrong approach.

• • •

In 1996, I was sitting in the big wood-lined conference room of the Treasury, at one of the lunchtime events introduced as part of the change management programme under Terry Burns. The idea was to open our closed doors and bring in speakers from outside to challenge our assumptions and welcome fresh thinking. I was up for it, as were many others in the room. I was listening to someone from the Institute for Fiscal Studies presenting a series of graphs about public spending on health services in this and other similar countries, and the penny had begun to drop.

There was a reason why the public were increasingly disenchanted with John Major's government: the Conservatives had been seriously underfunding the NHS and other services compared to our competitors. It was obvious to me, at least, and I dare say to others in the room, that the Conservatives were going to lose the forthcoming election, and that Labour's promise to invest in public services was going to win the day. Because that was what was needed.

At this point in my career, I had moved to a new job in the Treasury, having recently returned from three months' maternity leave after the birth of my second child, Victoria, that April, and I had moved on from change management as the Head of Personnel and was now working in the General Expenditure Division (GEP). GEP is the bit of the Treasury concerned with public expenditure, coordinating the work of all the teams in the Treasury that 'manage' the expenditure of different departments and advising ministers on their decisions on where and how to spend taxpayers' money. GEP is also in charge of the 'spending rules'. My job title, Senior Adviser on Public Expenditure, gave me licence to roam and my focus was on fundamental reform of various kinds.

The day after the May 1997 general election, I made the spontaneous decision to go to the front hall and welcome Gordon Brown and his team in. When I arrived at the top of the stairs to the grand hallway, I saw that I was not alone, and a crowd of Treasury staff had gathered – and we all clapped as Brown entered the building. 'Things Can Only Get Better' was the song playing in Downing Street when Tony Blair arrived, and that was the mood in the Treasury now too, despite our political neutrality. The last government had been in power too long, had run out of steam and ideas and this government was going to be different.

• • •

Labour, however, had made a promise in its manifesto that it would stick to the previous government's spending limits for the first two years, trying to fight back against the accusation, originally made by Thatcher, that 'the problem with socialism is that you eventually run out of other people's money'. They wanted to demonstrate that they would not 'splash the cash', even though more investment in public services was what the public actually wanted. They later regretted this decision, just as I believe the current Labour government probably came to regret their manifesto commitments not to raise taxes. But they thought that, without it, they would not get elected.

New Labour also wanted to show they could deliver tangible changes that people would feel, in return for new investment, so they also made five pledges to demonstrate that they would deliver change – such as class sizes of no more than thirty and cutting hospital waiting lists by treating an extra 100,000 patients. It was what came to be known as 'retail politics', where voters pick and choose off the supermarket shelves of politics a 'deliverable' that they like, rather than judging parties by their values, vision and beliefs. Under this school of thought, it wasn't 'Thatcherism' that won Mrs Thatcher three elections but the promise of being able to buy your own council house or own shares in British Telecom. But, of course, both things can be true and proponents of retail politics, like Starmer's former political Svengali, Morgan McSweeney, often forget about the importance of values, vision and beliefs which give a government a sense of purpose and direction.

When Gordon Brown entered the Treasury in May 1997, I was closely involved in a fundamental reform of the way public expenditure was accounted for, which was designed to stop the systemic underinvestment in capital infrastructure which had contributed to many services not working very well. The idea was to introduce commercial accounting, which spreads or 'depreciates' the costs over the lifetime of the asset, thereby avoiding having to cut back on day-to-day spending to meet the upfront costs of capital in one year, which was a big disincentive to invest. This major modernisation was known as Resource Accounting and Budgeting, or RAB, and was a huge bureaucratic shift, involving all government departments and public bodies. It took years to put fully in place and it had lots of repercussions across the Treasury, particularly in my area.

One element of this reform involved trying to get different departments to be much clearer about their purpose and what they were trying to achieve through what were called Output and Performance Analyses (OPAs), and then matching resources to their objectives. OPAs were rather like the framework agreements for executive agencies, and I thought they were a good thing.

I had always worried that the Treasury was only concerned with controlling public expenditure, not how that money was spent. Before I joined the Treasury, I wasn't really sure I wanted to be there but Andrew Turnbull, a Treasury official, had encouraged me to go. While I was still at No. 10, I asked John Major what he thought about this. He said, disarmingly, that he had felt the same way before he was sent in to become Chief Secretary and later Chancellor. I saw OPAs as an attempt to change all that.

After much to-ing and fro-ing, the OPAs had finally been agreed, and then in 1998, three days before they were due to be announced at the start of the new government's first Comprehensive Spending Review, the Chancellor's special adviser, Ed Balls, suddenly announced that the new spending plans would be linked to new Public Service Agreements, modelled around and including the targets set out in their pledge card.

It was my job to do what the government wanted and blend the broadbrush OPA concept which focused on long-term aspirations with the far more specific and immediate pledge card approach. The first Public Service Agreements were published in June 2000, which included departmental and some cross-cutting objectives as well as supporting targets, most of which (like the pledge card) were inputs (we'll recruit *x* number of people, or deliver *y* amount of additional services) rather than outcome driven (we'll reduce crime or improve health), so that they would be tangible to the public and easily monitored.

Targets were very much imposed from above and subject to little discussion or scrutiny. It later became clear to me that most of them were plucked from the air by the different finance divisions within the spending departments, and the people in the agencies or on the front line who had to deliver them were not consulted about what the right targets should be or what level they should be set at. In other words, most of the targets were telling the rest of government and the wider public sector, including contractors, what they should do, rather than giving them flexibility over how to meet their ultimate goal. And the people setting the targets knew nothing about the job when they set them.

This is what I mean by 'megaphone government', with the Chancellor and Prime Minister in the control centre of government, the Treasury and No. 10, shouting precise and sharp instructions, expecting the long, often diffuse and semi-autonomous 'chain of command' to hear and deliver. Enormous focus was eventually brought to bear and, after I left the Treasury, a new Prime Minister's Delivery Unit was set up outside the Treasury in the Cabinet Office, led by Michael Barber. The Prime Minister held regular meetings – lasting between one to three hours – with key departments to review progress in delivering the most important political targets. As one former Permanent Secretary put it, 'I saw it as defining my job'.[30]

Unsurprisingly, given this degree of political pressure, the front line did hear and, up to a point, delivered – or at least they appeared to. Successive expert reports have pointed to perverse effects, such as neglect of other priorities and gaming, where data is manipulated to look like a target is met. It also began to dawn on politicians that targets could backfire if they weren't delivered. Some reform of PSAs was made, including fewer and more cross-cutting targets, with more engagement of the front line, but the basic megaphone design remained. PSAs were abolished by the incoming coalition government, but targets continued to be used.[31]

Take Matt Hancock's target to achieve 100,000 Covid tests, which he made the focus of his efforts during the Covid crisis, showing progress in daily No. 10 press conferences to demonstrate that the government had the situation under control. Originally, it was thought this meant the number of people tested but, according to informed reports cited in the press but denied by his department, a change in how it was measured was made in order to ensure it was delivered. By the time Hancock announced that the target was 'met', a third of those included in the figure were tests only ordered or just posted and many of those taken were retests by the same people.[32]

Behind the megaphone was a concept of government which cast politicians as managers of 'UK plc', and in particular of public services, working on behalf of their shareholders, the electorate, to make things better for them. They were in the Head Office, looking across multiple subsidiaries, seeking to ensure that the taxpayer got a real bang for their buck. And all this fitted very well with an increasingly commercialised public sector, much of it delivered through the private and voluntary sectors with tightly defined contracts based on delivering targets, too. Targets were the equivalent of the bottom line of profit in business.

However, meeting a target doesn't necessarily mean providing a good service. Government gets what it asks for – a shorter waiting list for that first referral to hospital, say, because that is what the government ordered, but not necessarily the rest of the treatment following in good time. And if there had been more opportunity to explore your symptoms before that appointment was booked, then maybe the treatment you received would have been different, and better, saving everyone time and money in the end. A political focus on targets in one area may also lead to neglect in another: an improvement in appointments for physical health conditions, say, while funds for mental health services or social care dramatically decline. But if a target is met, job done.

Can a target define a job, as that Permanent Secretary suggested? I don't think so. It can lead to a narrowing down of perspective so that one very precise thing is delivered but the bigger prize of good government is lost.

• • •

While all this was happening, another more personal drama was unfolding around me in the Treasury. Resource Accounting and Budgeting will, I am sure, sound rather dry, and it was, although it was extremely important and challenging to implement. The two senior people I was working with very closely were passionate about it, so much so that they would see any criticism of the detail of their approach as opposition and they ganged up together against the world – despite working in different parts of the Treasury where different perspectives, not a single combined view, were to be expected. I found them prickly and hard to work with and thought something was wrong, but I couldn't put my finger on it.

It never occurred to me that they might be having an affair, not least because both seemed to be entirely obsessed with their work. That was until one morning in November 1988 when I turned on the radio and heard that a senior Treasury official had been arrested, after his wife had been found bludgeoned to death. No name was given but when I got to the office I quickly discovered, to my horror, that it was one of these two colleagues, Mike Parsonage, an economist. Mike was an intellectually arrogant man whom I didn't particularly like, but he was otherwise quiet and unassuming, and I thought him quite incapable of murder. Then the story quickly came out through the rumour mill of the Treasury. Worried about his mental health, his wife had taken him to A&E and told them that he was delusional and she thought he would kill her. An inexperienced junior doctor told her to take him home and give him some tranquillisers.[33] Five hours later, he attacked her, delivering multiple blows with a claw hammer and leaving her body on the doorstep of their home before walking in front of a milk float in his pyjamas in an attempt at suicide.[34] It emerged in the trial that he had confessed his affair to his wife and thought his lover's husband, who'd been informed of the relationship, would be coming after him. He told police he was in a 'highly charged state of anxiety, panic and not in control of myself on the day of the attack … I felt a lot of guilt. I felt I betrayed her, I was leading a double life. I was fed up with the job.'

He was found guilty of manslaughter and incarcerated in a secure psychiatric hospital indefinitely.[35] Resource Accounting and Budgeting, his apparent work passion, came into force and Mike was never there to see it. This tragedy was another piece in the jigsaw of what increasingly became my firm view that the Treasury was not at that time a very healthy place in which to work (though it took me a few more years before I left).

• • •

What is a government's job?

Labour, in its 2024 manifesto, said, 'To rebuild Britain, we need to change how Britain is governed. For too long, Britain has been held back by governments that, because they lack a relentless focus on long-term ends, are buffeted about by events.' Too true. The manifesto went on to say, 'politics has enormous potential to change lives for the better, but too often different parts of the government have pursued their own narrow goals rather than working together.' Quite right. Narrow targets deepen institutional silos, when many of the issues people face can only be addressed by different agencies working together.

The manifesto added, 'Government is at its best when working in partnership with business, trade unions, civil society, faith groups and communities. But without a shared project those partnerships barely get off the ground.' Absolutely, government isn't just about the operation of public agencies. The things we care about, like good health or giving our children the best start in life, involve us all, and marshalling the resources of the whole of society around a common cause makes perfect sense.

To answer these broad questions, the manifesto outlined five missions. These were first launched in February 2024 and set out overall outcomes, not inputs or outputs, in stark contrast to New Labour's 1997 pledge card and, much more recently, Sunak's five pledges – to halve inflation, grow the economy, get debt falling, cut NHS waiting lists and stop the boats – which had been a last-ditch attempt to steady the sinking Tory ship but instead helped hole it beneath the waterline.

Labour's missions promised to 'kickstart economic growth', 'make Britain a clean energy superpower', 'create safer streets', 'break down barriers to opportunity' and 'build an NHS fit for the future', including reducing 'deaths from major killers'. For those of us who care about good government, this was big – a new government firmly set on the 'decade of renewal', not just the day-to-day shocks or political cross-currents that can lead to governments losing their way.

However, in the same Plan for Change speech in which the Prime Minister announced the abolition of NHS England, his five missions suddenly became six milestones for the first five years, which started to look a lot more like New Labour's pledge card. They committed to:

- Putting more money in the pockets of working people.
- Building 1.5 million homes and fast-tracking planning decisions on at least 150 major infrastructure projects.
- Treating 92 per cent of NHS patients within eighteen weeks.

- Recruiting 13,000 more police officers, special constables and Police Community Support Officers in neighbourhood roles.
- Making sure three-quarters of five-year-olds are school-ready.
- Attaining 95 per cent clean power by 2030.

These might have been measurable and ambitious but were definitely not missions, and mostly focused on the work of single departments, not even working across central government, let alone local government, the multitude of agencies and public bodies or forces beyond government.

By the party conference speech in September 2025, another priority had been added, 'securing our borders', in response to the party's sharp decline in popularity and the dominance of the Reform Party in the polls. So they were not unbuffeted by political pressures, as the manifesto had claimed, either. We were back to megaphone government, with mixed messaging about what the government is about, to boot.

Is the Department of Health and Social Care's job to deliver health and wellbeing or to lower hospital waiting lists by 2030? The government would likely say both, but the department will know that their top priority now is to treat 92 per cent of NHS patients within eighteen weeks, and the abolition of NHS England seemingly makes them think that nothing will stand in their way. Since then, ministers have given a green light to trusts facing budget constraints to impose *minimum* waiting lists of twelve to eighteen weeks for procedures such as hip replacements and cataract operations.[36] As long as people don't wait more than eighteen weeks, it won't affect the target. However, the patients, and the electorate, may notice, because a single target is not what their experience is about – and for many the wait may be longer. I hear from sources inside government that the NHS is very reluctant to work with other departments on common goals, so focused is it on delivering its targets.

What the public *really* want to see are the services they depend upon getting better, and evidence of a credible plan to get there.

• • •

What if there is no plan?

It's Friday 13 March 2020, at the height of Covid, and No. 10 is about to get some very bad news. According to Dominic Cummings, Helen MacNamara rushed into No. 10 and interrupted a meeting in the study to tell them that she had just been informed that 'there is no plan'. This was in spite of repeated assurances from the Department of Health and Matt Hancock, the Secretary of State, that there was indeed an operational plan for Covid. To be precise (albeit as related by Cummings but confirmed in substance by MacNamara), she said: 'I have come through here to the Prime Minister's office to tell you all that I think we are absolutely fucked. I think this country is heading for a disaster. I think we are going to kill thousands of people.'[37]

And she was correct. The contingency planning that had gone into the wrong sort of epidemic – flu – was not right for Covid, and the centre had not been flexible enough to realise their mistake and put in place a strategy to deal with the actual crisis in front of them, so that the many parts of government could kick into action in a coordinated way.

Likewise, no prior planning was done for Brexit, causing incalculable damage (though in that case the civil service had been instructed by David Cameron and George Osborne not to create one), and so it was with the incoming Labour government in July 2024.

Numerous briefings to the media suggested that Labour was disappointed that the civil service didn't present them with a plan on their arrival. Anonymous briefings from the civil service also found their way into the media, suggesting they were disappointed that Labour hadn't made any before they arrived. They knew about the missions but there was no strategy for delivering them. And then more anonymous briefings blamed Starmer's first Chief of Staff, former civil servant Sue Gray. People around Starmer let it be known that they had thought she was producing a plan in opposition but she hadn't. A few months after she entered Downing Street, she was ignominiously fired.

Now people close to Starmer have fallen out of love with the missions, I have heard from various sources. A year on, the missions' way of working had had little obvious influence, particularly on the Spending Review process and decisions, and the new missions style of government seemed to boil down to an all-too-familiar model of Cabinet Committee working, with the only real difference being that committees were chaired by two, not one, Secretaries of State, adding to the bureaucracy of it all.[38]

Why hadn't the civil service prepared a plan? You can be sure that they had studied every word of the manifesto, as well as every speech, and would have prepared options for ministers to consider from day one. But an 'all singing, all dancing' plan might have set alarm bells ringing for those who believe, or half-believe, in a deep state that really runs the government, not ministers. I gather from a conversation with a former Permanent Secretary that Jeremy Heywood, who was by temperament more of a fixer than a strategist, once did start a series of long-term scenario-planning events with

Permanent Secretaries but got the jitters because ministers might think they had overstepped their remit. It seems that civil servants can only await instructions from ministers on what to scenario-plan, and increasingly those instructions have been about initiatives and targets, not about missions.

In fairness, civil servants can be great at coming up with options and plans, if the trust and communication are there, but trust and communication take time to build and every time a minister or Permanent Secretary changes, that process must start again. In July 2025, half of all Cabinet ministers were either moved or lost their jobs in a major reshuffle intended to 'revitalise' government. By the end of 2025, half of the heads of departments were set to change as well.[39] The new Cabinet Secretary, Chris Wormald, whom Keir Starmer appointed in December 2024, was by October 2025 being briefed against in the media and tipped to be replaced by the end of the year.

One of the functions of the civil service used to be to ensure continuity when ministers moved on, but there has been an erosion of expertise and stability inside the civil service since my day which undermines its ability to do this. Constantly moving jobs has become the mark not just of fast-stream civil servants but increasingly of most civil servants, I hear from contacts in the civil service, partly to secure higher pay through promotion in order to get round pay freezes. Movement between departments has also become more common. Constant civil service 'transformations' create perpetual uncertainty. I've heard of one civil servant who has had to apply for her own job three times in the last four years. When Covid struck, almost all the people in the six Director General roles in the bit of the Cabinet Office that coordinates the rest of government had less than one year's experience.[40] All this makes the process of government tired. Fresh blood can be a good thing, but constant churn doesn't energise government. It's incapacitating.

However, it's worse than that – the institutional distrust between ministers and civil servants that started under Boris Johnson seems to have persisted. It is normal in my experience when a new administration first enters government, or a new minister comes into a department, for only the most senior civil servants initially to have contact with ministers. They need to gain their trust. But I understand that this habit has persisted under the new government, leaving more junior civil servants (who often have the expertise) out in the cold and often in the dark about what ministers really want. The setting up of complicated Cabinet Committee structures to run the cross-cutting missions of the new government has made things worse, as Cabinet ministers now have very limited time to spend in meetings in their own department. I'm told by one insider that the Cabinet Office's Economic and Domestic Affairs Secretariat, which is supposed to help resolve issues that cut across departments, is now so overloaded and weak that ministers have started talking directly to each other to reach decisions.

We have got to the situation where some senior civil servants rarely see their ministers, and civil servants have dress rehearsals for those meetings when they do take place. That's not how you create a team or build rapport.

What's the answer? Go where the energy is, for one thing. At the moment, that's mostly local. Many of the new devolved combined authorities, particularly Greater Manchester, find it easier to escape the sludge, to forge relationships within government and beyond and to innovate, and there are countless local examples of exciting new ways of working that, if adopted nationally, could be transformative in a way that cutting a few agencies here and there would not. This is the approach being adopted by the Labour government's Test, Learn and Grow programme, which is supporting innovation locally and seeking to identify the systemic barriers within government and fix those at the centre to smooth the way and make innovations stick. It's a way of driving change from the bottom, not the top.

Even better would be for central government to change how it views its job and to see itself as a facilitator, not a manager, of results, orchestrating the 'constellation' of government and wider social actors, rather than micro-managing it, working with others to build a clear vision of the change it wants to see, inspiring others at the front line through a sense of common purpose to find innovative ways to get there and removing the things that get in the way – for example, commissioning practices that foster competition rather than collaboration.

The centre should focus on what only it can do, such as foreign policy, defence, setting the overall direction of government and ensuring the resources and the right strategies are in place to deliver it. Good government would focus less on the 'what' and more on the principles of how the public sector should work; foremost among these is the idea that prevention is better than cure, though much of government currently offers a masterclass in the opposite. Precisely what I mean by the 'opposite', and how to correct it, is the subject of my next chapter.

Chapter 5

REWIRING THE TREASURY

'What is striking is that there has been so much written often covering similar ground and apparently sound, setting out the well-known major determinants of health, but rigorous implementation of identified solutions has often been sadly lacking.'

Derek Wanless in a report to the Chancellor, Gordon Brown, *Securing Good Health for the Whole Population*, in 2002[1]

Bad government: *short-termism and a vicious cycle of cutting back things that will save money in the longer term, only to splurge money when a crisis occurs.*

Good government: *an enabler, not a controller, investing in prevention, with services that focus on people and get things first right time.*

What is the Treasury for?

If you cornered a Treasury official over the last forty-five years or so and forced them to sum up the Treasury's job in one phrase, most likely they would say 'controlling public expenditure'. Or if they worked in that bit of the Treasury that specialises in tax and economic policy, they might say 'maintaining economic stability' and possibly 'promoting growth'.

Nowadays a simple Google search of the Treasury will send you to the government's website where it will tell you right up front what it's about: 'maintaining control over public spending, setting the direction of the UK's economic policy and working to achieve strong and sustainable economic growth'. Or at least that is what the website stated in May 2026.[2] Pretty clear. But is it right?

Control comes first, and I completely understand why it is so firmly lodged in the psyche of the Treasury. If you've ever worked there, as I did for nine years, you see a lot of evidence that departments only want to spend more and never want to stop doing anything. It can easily feel like only the Treasury has its eye on affordability.

In fact, the view that the Treasury is primarily there to control public expenditure was very much a Thatcherite idea, based on her 'household management' view of public expenditure. Before she came into power, government planned in terms of what it needed to deliver, rather than imposing a cash limit, and increased budgets routinely to follow inflation. But she thought you shouldn't spend more than you can afford on day-to-day expenses and started to control the cash, not the activities, and because in her view the state was too big, it became the Treasury's job not just to keep a lid on spending but also to cut it back. Before Thatcher's day, planning and controlling expenditure were said in the same breath, but she made *control* paramount.

New Labour continued with this idea of cash control but put a more sophisticated spin on it – a focus not just on how much was spent but on what was delivered, using targets to exercise a secondary form of control over the rest of government, as covered in the last chapter.

In the Starmer government, Rachel Reeves styled herself, after Thatcher, as the Iron Chancellor, and maintained her fiscal rules were paramount. These rules promised that, over the medium term, first, day-to-day spending is financed through taxation and, second, borrowing decreases as a proportion of GDP, which means that controlling public expenditure came a very big first for her.

But what if more investment in *prevention* might reduce spending over time, boost growth and make public services work much better, but the Treasury's obsession with bean-counting and top-down targets is getting in the way? By prevention, which is sometimes called early action in this chapter, I mean anything that stops problems happening altogether or prevents them from getting worse, from early years through to old age and including the environment and administrative processes.

• • •

Let's take Sure Start as an example. Over a decade or more, I watched the hollowing out of the programme, a highly successful initiative announced in 1998 to give children the best start in life, and the bean-counting regime enforced by the Treasury has to bear a big share of the responsibility. Bad government.

Ironically, it was the Treasury that put Sure Start in place in the first place, against all the odds, a brilliant example of how it can be a force for good and a case study that points the way for how it could be better in the future.

I had a tiny role in its inception because, among other things, I was advising the Chancellor, Gordon Brown, about child poverty when I was Senior Adviser on Expenditure. I was working on this with the wonderful Norman Glass, the Treasury's chief micro-economist at the time, and the author of the Sure Start initiative. Witty, warm and good with people, Norman did an unusual Treasury thing: he created an alliance of officials, academics, ministers and charities, based on an American programme called Headstart, which for some years had been working successfully with pre-school children and their parents to give them a better start in school. No 'sharp elbows' for him. He cared about the ultimate results, not Treasury quick wins against the rest of the world. Glass made a convincing economic and financial case for investing in this programme to Gordon Brown but I suspect what finally won Treasury ministers over was hearing first-hand from young mothers from deprived backgrounds who talked about the vital, practical impact on them and their children of similar forms of support provided by charities. They were speaking at an event which Norman had arranged.[3]

People forget that politicians are people, and Gordon Brown was then, and still is, passionate about tackling child poverty and social deprivation. These young mothers spoke to his heart, not just his head. Glass cleverly made sure he appealed to both.

Sure Start was unusual because as well as providing childcare and early education it also helped children and their families in lots of other ways, including offering information and advice, health services, family support, access to Jobcentre services and activities for parents. The first Sure Start centres were set up in the poorest 20 per cent of wards in England where the returns were greatest but eventually there were 3,500 right across the country. Throughout, the concept was to attract and support all families in an area, not just those who might be struggling, so that there was no element of stigma attached to coming through the door.[4]

When I moved from the Treasury in 2000 to what later became

the Department for Education and Employment, I helped set up what were then called Neighbourhood Nurseries in the most deprived areas for similar reasons, and these eventually became Sure Start centres too.

The financial case for Sure Start was a difficult one for any spending department to make, as setting it up would be very costly, the full financial and economic benefits would take years to be delivered and would fall to more than one department – better health, stronger educational performance, less crime and social exclusion, less dependency on benefits for parents and their children, to name but a few. It is hard for any one department to cut back on other things when the benefits would mostly not fall to them. It was also risky because it may not even have worked. A sharp-elbowed Treasury might say 'we can't fund it until you can prove to us that it'll work', but without funding they will never find out. Instead, Norman Glass's Treasury said, 'Let's take a risk and give it a go', knowing we would have to wait for those children to grow up before we could be sure of its effects. Finally, in 2023, the evidence from longitudinal studies made it clear: investment in Sure Start generated twice the amount of benefit it cost the taxpayer, bringing 'remarkably lasting' and widespread health, educational and social improvements to those it supported. By that time, it was too late, as nearly 1,500 of them had closed.[5]

So Norman Glass, Gordon Brown and the Treasury – with its overview of all public expenditure and its ability to appreciate the long-term impact on how much is spent over time across many different programmes, including on the benefits budget it directly manages – were ideally, and perhaps uniquely, placed to see that case, take that risk and to provide the additional funds required.

Gordon Brown was keen for the Treasury to take a longer-term view more systematically, and so he extended the period of Treasury spending plans from one to three years, so that public services could better plan ahead. It was my job as jack-of-all-trades in General Expenditure Policy to design how this would work. The answer was a new Comprehensive Spending Review that happened every two years, instead of every year as in the past. Three-year plans were set but the third year was provisional and formed the first year of the next review. The idea was to give public services greater financial stability, and perhaps in some cases it worked. But when I became the Chief Executive of an NDPB, the Equal Opportunities Commission (EOC), in 2002, I discovered that spending departments were not passing on budgets for years two and three but were keeping this back, so they had maximum flexibility to change priorities when and how they wanted. In the EOC, we generally started each financial year without a budget and only got confirmation of how much we had for that year by around May, so we were just as much in the dark as before. I heard similar stories from other parts of the public sector.

At the same time, Brown allowed departments to carry over unspent funding from one year to the next, stopping the wasteful spending sprees at year end on things that were not priorities. Again, that flexibility was not necessarily passed on to the front line, sadly.

I was also asked to redesign the public expenditure system, and the system created then remains to this day. The main idea was to protect public services from unexpected shocks, and this meant isolating spending on public services from demand-led expenditure, like benefits or interest payments on debt, that could otherwise lead to sudden, unexpected cuts in services, if, for example, a recession hit or the cost of borrowing went up. These demand-led items were put in a separate budget monitored and managed annually by the

Treasury – hence the name we gave to them, Annually Managed Expenditure, or AME (pronounced Amy). Though some have since argued that the change allowed those budgets to let rip, the original intention was that they should, as the name suggests, be managed annually. Spending on public services was held within what we named Departmental Expenditure Limits, or DEL, which were managed by departments and planned in the Comprehensive Spending Review, every two years. DEL and AME were added together to make Total Managed Expenditure, which had to be financed by either taxation or borrowing.

Within DEL, capital expenditure was ring-fenced in what was called CDEL, or Capital Departmental Expenditure Limits, and this had a one-way valve. That meant you could take money out of day-to-day running costs to top it up, but you couldn't reduce planned capital spending to fund that unexpected pay increase, or day-to-day public services. Ring-fencing was also used to protect preventative programmes like Sure Start and public health budgets from being raided to meet similar day-to-day pressures, in recognition of the fact that they were investments that would bring longer-term benefits well beyond the local authority budget in which they were held. Both Sure Start and public health could reduce benefit expenditure in AME, for example, which the Treasury controlled.

But then George Osborne in the 2010 coalition government introduced the policy of austerity, which led to that protective ring-fence on Sure Start and public health budgets being taken away, at the same time as large cuts to most public services. He also removed the 'one-way valve' for capital budgets. The pressure on councils to take money out of those budgets to reduce the cuts on services was enormous. In a deft political move, Osborne placed a disproportionate amount of the burden for reducing the size of the state on local government, and even larger cuts fell on those areas with the greatest social deprivation (which happened to be mostly Labour authorities), engineered through adjustments to the funding formulas. Central government funding of local authorities in England fell on average by 46 per cent per person over the decade of austerity. This was partially offset by councils putting up their own taxes to try and close the gap, but funding per person still fell by 26 per cent on average – and by 35 per cent in the most deprived areas.[6]

The so-called Graph of Doom, which I first saw in 2011, showed how dire the situation was for local government, even before austerity hit. This was prepared for the London Borough of Barnet but presented a picture that applied elsewhere – within twenty years, demand-led services, like adult social care and children's services which local government has to provide by law, would consume the authority's entire budget, if funding and demographic trends continued unchanged. Non-statutory services, such as libraries, parks, leisure centres, non-essential waste collection, road maintenance and youth services would be squeezed out. And once the ring-fence had gone, the same was true of Sure Start. Austerity brought that scenario forward, massively.

So, what did happen to Sure Start? In short, it was butchered. Its budget, which in 2009–10 was £1.8 billion, was cut by two-thirds by 2017–18.[7] Nearly half of the centres were closed, and others were scaled back.[8] At the same time, other preventative facilities were cut that promote health and wellbeing and provide the social support that stops problems getting worse, like youth clubs, leisure centres and daycare centres for older people. These are things that would save the Exchequer money over the longer term and contribute in many cases to economic growth, because more people would be able to contribute fully to society.[9]

Cuts to benefits and other services, including mental health and addiction rehabilitation programmes, helped to pour oil on the fire of social and health problems, especially in the most deprived areas, that preventative services like Sure Start were there to reduce.[10] Schools and hospitals, starved of maintenance because capital budgets had been plundered, started to become dangerous, especially when dodgy RAAC concrete, which is prone to collapsing, had been used in their construction. A lack of investment in diagnostic equipment in the NHS led to more deaths and longer delays. And all that affects growth and leads to higher costs long-term, as well as causing much misery.

Year on year totals for spending might have been achieved but the country's future and its long-term finances lost out because if growth slows, public expenditure becomes ever more unaffordable. If controlling public expenditure in the short run is the only goal, that doesn't matter. However, as the inception of Sure Start shows, it doesn't have to be like this. Contrary to those who rail against 'Treasury orthodoxy', Treasury ministers *can* take the Treasury in an altogether different direction.

There's a pattern of short-termism here that could be broken. Money can always be found for an emergency, as it was after the 2008 financial crash and later in Covid, but afterwards investment in the longer term is cut back and consequently the next crisis, when it comes, can be even more expensive. The personal, societal and Exchequer costs of the Covid pandemic were all the greater because of austerity.[11] Britain lacked resilience due to the growth in poverty and deprivation, underfunded social care and a weakened NHS, which had far fewer beds and doctors per person, higher acute bed dependency and less capital investment compared to similar countries. To make matters worse, billions of pounds which could otherwise have been invested in prevention were also wasted through lack of control on grants and dodgy deals through the VIP procurement track.

Then the cycle begins again, with new and often tentative investments in prevention after a period of cutting back. Enter the new Best Start family hubs, providing parent support from pregnancy to early childhood alongside a range of other services designed to extend that support for children to early adulthood. These were first set up as pilots in seventy-five local authorities at the tail end of the last government, with the first opening in 2024. Thankfully, the programme has now been given a major boost by the Labour government, who are committed to 1,000 of them – one for every local authority – by 2028, still below the 1,500 Sure Start centres that were shut down due to austerity, disproportionately affecting the most deprived communities.[12]

Will family hubs survive the next crisis? Only if the Treasury makes prevention a priority.

• • •

What if the Treasury changed its spending rules and practices again, this time to protect preventative spending, as with Sure Start?

This is what I am suggesting in 2011 at a meeting of the Early Action Task Force, and I am saying this with confidence because, as I explain, I've done it before and know that Treasury rules are not set in stone. We can build on the changes Gordon Brown brought in, I say.

The meeting is being chaired by David Robinson, the co-founder of Community Links, a charity working in Newham in East London, who set up and then chaired the Task Force. A charismatic and visionary man, David has a rare combination of grassroots knowledge – having worked in a community for decades – and big picture thinking, along with powerful communication skills. He also had the ears of government, having advised the Prime Minister, Gordon Brown, through the Council on Social Action, which David set up in 2007 and chaired. He's brought together an impressive cast list of experts in the Task Force, and the most committed of them are in the room with us now, including Professor Anne Power from the London School of Economics, an expert on housing and communities; Dan Corry, CEO of New Philanthropy Capital and formerly Head of the No. 10 Policy Unit when Gordon Brown was Prime Minister; Ben Jupp, seconded from the Cabinet Office when this work started, where he was Director of Efficiency and Reform; Anna Coute from the New Economics Foundation; and Nick Wright from the City bank, UBS. We're sitting in a room just off Aldwych in London at the Barrow Cadbury Trust, a charitable foundation that is supporting the initiative along with the Big Lottery, and Debbie Pippard from the Trust is there too. She knows a lot about what works and what doesn't, from the many organisations they fund.

Like others round the table, I am deeply committed to the Task Force's mission, based on my experience in a number of roles inside and outside government which sought to put early action into practice. The objective of my think tank, Civil Exchange, which I founded earlier that year, is to improve the way civil society and government work together, and this Task Force is a prime example.

The Task Force had been set up because Community Links had too often witnessed first-hand the vicious merry-go-round about to be experienced by Sure Start – preventative programmes funded by the government, often as a pilot, being cast aside because they could no longer be 'afforded' despite evidence that they were working well. The same pilots would then often reappear under a different administration with a different name, being piloted in new areas, so things would start all over again rather than building on what went before. For example, Total Place, which pooled local budgets to enable local collaboration and boost prevention, were launched in 2009 as pilots under Labour, but were scrapped when the coalition came into power a year later, only for them to launch Whole-Place Community Budgets to do pretty much the same thing by another name. By 2012 these were replaced by Neighbourhood Community Budgets and Our Place pilots, all sadly lost now despite their successes, as the short attention span and systemic underfunding of prevention which characterise bad government strike again. (However, the good news is that the Labour government announced in its 2025 Budget that pooled budgets are to be resurrected again in some of the mayoralties, and on a bigger scale.)

The challenge David Robinson gave us was to stop that merry-go-round and make sure early action was not just common sense but common practice; this was just at the point when austerity and the Graph of Doom were about to kick in, making our task even more daunting. By early action, he means all forms of prevention, not just investment in children's early years but also prevention across all life stages, and getting things right first time, when people present to a service. Most things that are called 'early action', or prevention, are not really early at all, we reflect in the meeting, but only kick in once serious problems have occurred, like the Troubled Family initiative, later renamed the Supporting Families programme, which works with families already facing serious problems to stop them from getting worse and recurring across the generations.

David likens this kind of programme to the cliff edge where people could all too easily fall down, at which point the 'ambulance service' side of services kick in – like your elderly parents ending up in A&E, your children being excluded from school or taken into care or the police locking you up. Our goal was to reduce the need for 'ambulance services' of all kinds and to increase government spending on actions that are as early as possible, ideally stopping a problem from happening at all. Generally, the later the intervention the more costly it is.

But bad government keeps on getting in the way. Top of the list is short-termism to suit electoral and Treasury planning cycles. Then there are organisations working in silos, without joining up, which often means pushing people with complex problems from one service to another, without ever resolving their issues, making things worse for them and adding to the demands on services and the cost of government. Another major barrier is lack of funding for preventative work because short-term pressures always come first.[13]

Could we change the incentives to correct for these problems and re-engineer the wiring of government? That's what the Task Force is discussing today. I and others are throwing out a lot of propositions. What if the Treasury treated prevention like capital investment and ring-fenced it, like CDEL, Sure Start and public health? What if, over time, the Treasury set itself the challenge of shifting total spending more towards prevention? A starting point would be to have a single, consistent definition of early action across government and to measure it.

To bring new money in, what if an investment fund could be set up and independently managed, which could be topped up locally by businesses and local philanthropists who have a vested interest in seeing their communities thrive? To tackle short-termism, where future benefits never count, what if public service expenditure were planned every three or indeed five years, rather than two, pencilling in ten-year plans. And what if individual spending decisions were also subject to a 'ten year rule', which meant that you had a longer horizon to judge its positive (or negative) impact? To break down silos, what if funding could be pooled between services, with savings from early action shared between them? And what if the Treasury took on responsibility for promoting prevention, just as Gordon Brown did in relation to child poverty and Sure Start?

Over many meetings and discussions, we knocked these ideas into shape and published a series of reports which began to seed more ideas, some of which are now being taken forward by other champions and think tanks today, after the Task Force came to an end in 2021. Demos is recommending the creation of what is now called PDEL, i.e. Preventative Departmental Expenditure Limits, a ring-fenced budget for spending on prevention.[14] The Chartered Institute of Public Finance and Accountability, with whom the Task Force worked back then, has produced a 2025 guide to defining, mapping and measuring preventative investment to support better decision-making and a shift towards prevention.[15]

At one point, I suggested to Margaret Hodge – with whom, you will recall, I had worked closely when I was at the Department for Education and Employment, who was a great champion of investment in children's early years and who by then was chair of the Public Accounts Committee (PAC) – that she might initiate a PAC investigation into investment in prevention, which she did. We briefed her on our ideas, and I also talked at length with the National Audit Office (NAO). Their reports were published in 2013 and 2014.

Their diagnosis was very similar to ours. The NAO did some

calculations and concluded that only around 4 per cent of public expenditure on the relevant programmes was being spent on early action. As we had suggested, they proposed that a single definition of early action be adopted throughout government, so that a proper audit of such spending could be made and action taken to increase that proportion over time, and the PAC backed them up.[16]

The PAC called specifically for ten-year impact assessments of all spending proposals in the Spending Review,[17] which the Treasury sidestepped, saying departments were required through their 'Green Book' to evaluate all new plans. This was true, but the requirement was almost entirely ignored at the time. Crucially, the Public Accounts Committee said the Treasury should explicitly take the lead on prevention across government, a role which it declined.

A later insight from the Early Action Task Force was that the quality of the places in which people live can also be preventative through its 'social infrastructure', much of it community-led. I like to think that I was one of the first people to start using the term 'social infrastructure' but, whether I was or not, it has increasingly taken off. By giving it a name, I hoped that it would become more visible to the Treasury, and by aligning it to capital infrastructure, I sought to underline that there was a sound case for investment.

For us, social infrastructure was broadly defined, starting with an affordable and good-quality home which is well connected to the local services that people need – the doctor, the pharmacy, the nursery and the school, the food shops and the hairdressers. It includes the green spaces, sports fields and leisure centres in which people exercise, play and socialise and build good health and well-being, as well as the youth clubs and day centres, cafes and pubs where people meet and enjoy each other's company or give each other mutual support. Also important are the sports clubs, choirs and community hubs that create connection and deepen social capital and integration, along with those other charities and institutions that help bind people together, connect up services and ensure everyone is heard and their needs are met.[18]

Public spending doesn't create all that, and it doesn't need to, but loss of critical public funding due to austerity has contributed to a hollowing out of many of our more deprived communities, and Treasury targets to sell off state assets to plug holes in current expenditure have depleted things with significant preventative benefits, like a school playing field, a community centre or social housing.[19] In some cases, these resources also provide a steady stream of income into the future that can be ploughed back into the community.

These and other ideas were things I discussed regularly for around a decade with Treasury officials, and generally received a positive and high-level hearing, but the problem was that ministers at the time were not interested in changing the wiring of the Treasury or investing more in prevention. Reducing expenditure was what they were about.

• • •

Ministers did know that there was a strong case for investing in prevention because they commissioned reports that told them so. Their problem was acting on it. Over the decade I worked with the Task Force, I reviewed the information available to ministers and was shocked to discover the existence of report after report which had been requested by the government which called for more investment in prevention. These received a fair hearing, but good recommendations were not followed through in the end, partly because the Treasury's mind was elsewhere and its incentives worked against it.

Just before the savage cuts to Sure Start began, there were a number of reports which contained overwhelming evidence for investing in the early years. Three government-commissioned ones – the Frank Field Review into poverty and life chances,[20] published in December 2010, and two reviews by Graham Allen of early intervention in the following year[21] – all showed that the benefits of investing in early action significantly outweighed the alternatives of doing nothing at all or continuing with existing policies. The coalition government accepted the economic and social case for investment in a white paper, 'Supporting Families in the Foundation Years'. But that did not stop the wholesale damage to Sure Start and other preventative problems that followed not long after.

Then there was social care, which, as the population has aged, has struggled to cope. During austerity, it became increasingly rationed and less preventative. The Dilnot Commission report in 2011 made recommendations for how to deliver a fair, affordable and sustainable funding system for social care in England, which successive Conservative administrations committed to take forward – but eventually abandoned.[22] There was a huge collective groan when, in 2024, the incoming Labour government announced yet another social care review, led by Louise Casey, which will report just before the next election, kicking the can further along the road, even though a significant contribution to the crisis facing the NHS is bed-blocking by older people unable to leave hospital because of lack of provision for them in the community, and a fair proportion of those in hospital are probably there because social care is often only available when older people reach a critical point.

That is not the only crisis facing the NHS. Derek Wanless, who advised the Labour government on health and social care, wrote two reports in 2002 and then 2004 about 'securing our future health' which concluded that around half of NHS expenditure could have been saved through improvements in public health and greater efficiency and effectiveness. He also pointed out in his 2004 report that 'rigorous implementation of identified solutions has often been sadly lacking', and the same unfortunately proved true for his two reports.[23]

Michael Marmot published 'Fair Society, Healthy Lives' in 2010, which had been commissioned by the previous Labour government, and advised on the most effective evidence-based strategies for reducing health inequalities – a goal for the NHS then and now. He recommended action on six policy objectives, including giving every child the best start in life, creating and developing healthy and sustainable places and communities and strengthening the role and impact of ill-health prevention.[24]

To the credit of the incoming coalition, it did commit to a cross-cutting strategy in 'Healthy Lives, Healthy People: our strategy for public health in England' in November 2010. New, ring-fenced public health budgets were launched with some fanfare. As you likely know, the ring fences were eventually removed and the budgets were cut back per capita by 24 per cent between 2015–16 and 2020–21, and by considerably more in some areas with the highest health inequalities and the greatest needs.[25]

A decade later, in 2020, Marmot produced a second report, 'The Marmot Review Ten Years On', which found that over the previous decade things had only got worse overall, with a decrease in life expectancy and an increase in the amount of time people spent in poor health. He also documented a widening north-south health gap, with the largest decreases in life expectancy in the most deprived ten per cent of neighbourhoods in the north-east, and the largest increases in the least deprived ten per cent of neighbourhoods in London.[26] And then, of course, Covid struck.

Government is very much better at commissioning reports about prevention than actively undertaking it, which is why I think the Treasury needs to get a grip.

• • •

When it comes to the Treasury's 'wiring', some progress has been made.

Rachel Reeves as Chancellor stopped the raiding of capital budgets for day-to-day spending, restoring its ring fence, and also changed the fiscal rules to encourage more investment in capital projects, a major step forward. But asset sales which deplete social infrastructure and reduce prevention are continuing despite a change of government. English local authorities reported plans at the end of 2025 to sell off more social clubs and sports centres, for example, with 60 per cent of key city councils planning to sell assets to meet the growing costs of adult and children's social care.[27]

The 2020 Spending Review introduced planning around longer-term outcomes, including some cross-cutting ones. The 2025 Spending Review set plans for only three years for day-to-day spending but did set four-year plans for capital expenditure. More significantly, since 2018, the NHS has had a ten-year plan. Seven mayoral strategic authorities in England are to have budgets which pool previously fragmented funding streams, opening up the possibility of greater innovation and more prevention (provided long-term budgets aren't plundered to meet short-term needs).

The government's public service reform agenda, as set out in the 2025 Spending Review, aims to focus on prevention rather than crisis management, as well as to devolve power to local areas to design services with people in mind and organise services around people's lives. The Scottish government had, however, promised a 'decisive switch toward prevention' in its public services in 2011, but years later little progress had been made, and a survey of local authorities showed that this was partly because they had not defined or measured prevention, and incentives including performance targets pulled in the other direction.[28] If you look at the NHS in England, a similar picture emerges. Prevention, reducing health inequalities and achieving a shift from 'hospital to community' have been NHS goals for some time, but achieving these changes has been difficult. Funding crises and other priorities keep on getting in the way.

In an extremely welcome attempt to bring together the NHS, local authorities (which run social care) and the voluntary sector (which creates health within communities), Integrated Care Boards in each local authority were established in 2022. Their focus, according to the NHS website, is on 'prevention, better outcomes and reducing health inequalities' and the idea is to join things up, which makes that a lot easier. However, Starmer's government halved their budget and reorganised them, so that more resources can go to the front line of the NHS.

So what *would* work to ensure that the Department of Health and Social Care and the NHS are not just about ill health but also about prevention and communities?

• • •

It's 16 September 2025 and I am joining an online event, run by the Institute for Government, on the incentives for the NHS to deliver the objectives set out in Starmer's new 10 Year Plan, particularly regarding prevention and moving health to the community, but also the shift from analogue to digital. The key question the expert panel of speakers is considering is whether the sanctions and incentives set out in the plan will deliver these goals. In other words, the wiring.

So, what are these incentives? Financial penalties for hospital trusts that get bad feedback from their patients, preferential funding and more autonomy for those that do well, performance pay for NHS managers and league tables against targets. Targets feature heavily, though the number has been reduced.

Will these measures work? I listen to the experts, and the answer seems to be no.

The first panellist to speak, Hardev Virdee, who is Group Chief Finance Officer at Barts Health NHS Trust, captures the challenge in a nutshell. He says he's just come from a meeting where they had been talking about how to balance the books, adding that they'd squeezed in just a little bit of time at the end to talk about what the future holds, showing with his fingers just how tiny this allotted time was. 'That's what the temperature feels [like] at the front end', he adds. He welcomes the NHS plan, but admits it's not clear to him that (as the plan suggests) moving care to communities will be cheaper. Later, another panellist, Sally Gainsbury, senior policy analyst at the Nuffield Trust, agrees.

It is great to see Anita Charlesworth, whom I knew in the Treasury. Back then, she was an economist working with Norman Glass on Sure Start, and now she's the Senior Economic Adviser at the King's Fund and the acting chair of an Integrated Care Board, and so she is an expert on both the theory and the practice. She says that she regrets that there is no ring-fencing of the relevant budgets; ring-fencing had been explicitly ruled out, even though experience suggests that significant change will remain mere rhetoric unless there are concerted efforts to force it. She doesn't spell it out but I know immediately what she is saying, as do others in the audience, I'm sure. Non-essential budgets with longer-term benefits will be raided to meet immediate pressures, especially as the 10 Year Plan states that deficits (which are common in Trusts) will not be tolerated and must be eradicated. And that's before the regular service crisis the NHS faces every winter soaks up scarce resources.

Sally describes the package of incentives in the plan as 'radically optimistic', which is think tank-speak for useless. A lot of them had been tried before, she says, and the three shifts in the 10 Year Plan are not new – they have been promised under successive governments and haven't happened. Why hadn't the shift to communities taken place, she asks herself? Because the 'resource headroom', i.e. money, hasn't been there – nor has it been ring-fenced for that matter. I'm reminded of that saying: the definition of madness is doing the same thing, again and again, even when it didn't work the first time.

Charlesworth explains that the NHS is very driven by command-and-control targets, and these prioritise the short-term health of the organisation. The performance metrics don't incentivise longer-term thinking and, in an echo of what Virdee said earlier, the immediate priorities are financial management.

Towards the end, I ask the panel a question: if these incentives won't work, what will?

The answer is surprisingly human. Virdee says that during Covid there were remarkable instances of innovation and thinking creatively and these happened because people were allowed to take risks and really lead to make change happen. People were laser-focused on purpose, stopped seeing the institutional boundaries and worked across them; for example, the NHS with pharmacies and social care. Reflecting on things post-Covid, he says that at local, neighbourhood or borough level, there is much more momentum to make changes and listen to communities, but as you 'build the layers up it becomes too fragmented and frankly too difficult to make all of those changes'.

Trust is the critical ingredient, Charlesworth says, and operations during Covid ran on trust and mutual respect, but since then people have retreated into their silos. In normal times outside of Covid, getting changes made is incredibly difficult, everything moves at 'snail's pace' and the NHS plan is extremely optimistic about what can be achieved, she adds.[29]

It seems that financial incentive levers pulled from afar, with targets set from above, just won't cut it. What is really needed is a common purpose across institutional boundaries, freeing up the people who work on the front line to work with others to do what really needs to be done in a spirit of trust rather than compliance, with enough ring-fenced resources to make real change happen.

Is that so hard to achieve?

• • •

It's 22 September 2022, and I am chairing a meeting of the leadership network, A Better Way, which brings leaders together from the public and voluntary sectors who are trying to innovate to create services that meet real needs and get things right first time.[30]

I'm listening to Mark Smith, the Director of Public Service Reform at Gateshead Council, talking about their Council Tax Recovery Team – and what he says is dynamite. This is the department that would normally send in the bailiffs when people don't pay their tax, and it's not a place that most people would think of when it comes to being at the forefront of transforming public services. But, in this case, it is.

It all started, he told us, with one of their staff asking a council tax defaulter why she couldn't pay. It turned out there was a housing problem that she couldn't resolve, and this was making it hard for her as a single parent to get her mother to do the childcare she needed to work enough hours to pay her rent, and she was getting into debt. She needed to move, and when Mark Smith was asked to take it up with the council's housing department, a move was arranged, and she was eventually able to pay her council tax.

Mark dug deeper into the reasons why other people weren't paying their tax and discovered that the vast majority just didn't have the money to do so, and when he spent some time talking to people in this situation he found that very often they had an underlying problem which, with a bit of help rather than a visit from the bailiffs, could be sorted. But it was just too much for them to fix alone, given that often multiple and often distant agencies were involved, and none of them had time to listen.

To help with this, Mark set up a small team from Citizens Advice, the Department of Work and Pensions and the Council Tax Recovery Unit and gave them a flexible budget and a lot of autonomy to work with forty people who would otherwise be about to get that bailiff visit. They could do anything they liked, so long as they did not break these two rules – 'do no harm' and 'don't break the law'. And they were given not a manual or a form to fill, but a set of guiding principles. One of those principles was to sort it out amongst yourselves or, if others need to be involved, bring the institution to the person they're working with, rather than the other way round. That way, issues that might take months to fix, if at all, could be resolved quickly. Benefits claims could be settled in an hour, not the typical six weeks. Another guiding principle was to measure only to learn and improve, not to keep scores or to make a point.

Critically, there were no targets. Free from targets, set processes and unit costs, the team had time to talk to people in depth, Mark explained, and had purchasing cards which enabled them, for example, to take a client for a coffee to talk in a more relaxed way and get to the bottom of what the problem was and how to solve it. That's a lot of trust, and it worked. Of the first forty people helped, thirty-two of them ended up living a better life, having spent years in difficulty; seven had profound mental health challenges and had a longer journey; and one didn't engage, he told us.

Does this mean you don't need managers, someone asked? No, is the answer. But managers are there to enable and problem-solve, not control. They must create an environment in which staff have license to get it wrong; they must show staff that they've got their back and that they recognise that not everything works, and support those who feel exposed if things don't work or who struggle to work without clear processes and guardrails. This is a big cultural change, Mark said. It involves 'unlearning' the old way of doing things and liberating the creativity and sense of purpose that everyone has.

I know from the Better Way network that many of these innovations are happening across the country, but many more don't happen because the system gets in the way, and those that do often fizzle out when the person championing the change moves on. It's hard to reverse a vicious cycle of poor performance that is failing the public and the taxpayer. Too often, people with problems end up in a 'revolving door' of different services without their underlying issues being solved, and they end up feeling crushed, defeated or stuck, unable to be the best they can be. Meanwhile, society and the economy also suffer. As they get pushed from pillar to post, their challenges often spiral and become more complex, and the costs of those services rise in what some experts call 'failure demand' (i.e.

not getting it right first time). The Treasury response is to cut the services back, rather than seeking to change the services that don't work. These cuts either ration services by reducing eligibility or having ever-longer waiting lists, or reduce the time spent with each person that is needed to understand and resolve their problems, all in the name of 'efficiency'. Things get even worse. Problems present later and are harder to solve. Staff get even more burnt out. Failure demand increases. The Treasury bears down with more top-down targets and more cuts, and so the vicious cycle continues…

And when something goes wrong, as it is more likely to do in these circumstances – let's say a child dies at the hand of a parent who could have been saved by social services or a dangerous prisoner is released in error – the media, the opposition and ministers come down like a ton of bricks on the public servants who are directly involved. Heads roll, and it's not usually the minister's nowadays. So why take any risks? Keep your head down and carry on – or leave, as many public servants do.

Some people still do dare to do things differently: people like Mark Smith, or the NHS during Covid, but they and others like them don't have the power to change this bigger picture, even if they shine a light on what is possible. The Treasury, however, do have such power.

• • •

At the root of the problem is the fact that the state sees itself as a controller not an enabler, and public services are focused more on meeting targets set from above than they are on working better for the people they serve. So how can this be changed and the Treasury be rewired?

A starting point is for the Treasury to see its role as not just about controlling public expenditure but also promoting prevention, as Gordon Brown did in relation to child poverty. That would save money in the medium term and boost growth, making it easier to meet the Chancellor's fiscal targets in the end. It would also make it much more likely that the government could achieve its stated vision in the NHS plan, and could ensure public service reform to deliver more prevention, integrate services around people's lives and devolve power to local areas in partnership with communities and civil society. To achieve this, the Treasury must rewire the incentives in its public expenditure planning system which promote short-termism, silo working and the underfunding of prevention.

Applying a consistent definition throughout government of early action, creating a ring-fenced budget, like the capital budget, for preventative spending and actively seeking to shift more resources to prevention over time would be a great start. Allocating dedicated resources to achieve this shift, where upfront investment is required to save money later on, and pooling existing budgets, particularly where this will encourage working across institutional boundaries, would be good steps. Introducing a much longer perspective for planning public expenditure so that longer-term costs and benefits are considered, together with a rigorously enforced system for assessing these, would reduce short-termism.

Wellbeing, not just growth as measured by Gross Domestic Product, would also be a much more preventative and person-centred overarching goal. As Robert F. Kennedy once said, GDP 'measures everything ... except what makes life worthwhile'. GDP is important, of course: it creates employment and brings in taxes. But wellbeing as a goal is longer-term and more all-encompassing. Prisons boost GDP, for example, but a decision not to lock up minor offenders and instead get them to carry out community sentences might result in them ultimately leading more productive and socially responsible lives, as well as saving money. Deforestation boosts GDP too, but is that the right goal for the wellbeing of society and the planet? Having children, caring and volunteering also create value, but this is not measured in GDP at all. Building a house contributes to GDP, but such a metric is indifferent to whether our population can afford the house.

Wellbeing Budgeting has been introduced in New Zealand and creates something of a model for the UK. It measures value in terms of social outcomes, such as healthy life expectancy and the quality and affordability of housing. Its wellbeing 'dashboard' measures the long-term impact on human and environmental capital, not just the physical and financial capital that appears on our government's balance sheet. Cutting back on prevention and selling off assets that generate wellbeing would show up negatively in that wellbeing balance sheet, whereas now they are invisible. In Wales, the Well-being of Future Generations Act (2015) also places a duty on all public bodies to think long-term, and the independent Office for Future Generations monitors progress. Something similar could also be established across the UK to help shift the culture and keep government on its toes.

This shift from controlling to enabling, and to public services centred on people, not institutions, also requires a different management model, another piece of the government wiring that currently gets in the way of delivery and good results. The operating model forged by Margaret Thatcher and refined by Tony Blair bears down on the front line of services via command and control, top-down targets and form-filling, rather than liberating them to do a much better job within a framework of agreed outcomes and principles.

Just as prevention is better than cure and collaboration is better than competition, getting it right first time by working with other services is better than shuffling off the problem to another agency or another visit. Success can then be judged on whether they are doing the right job well, rather than on whether they are doing the wrong thing ever more cheaply.

There are risks, of course, but that is nothing compared to the risk of simply maintaining the status quo. If public services start with what works for the person they serve, rather than for the institution, that could save a lot of money in the end. It could also increase trust in government, which is currently being eroded not just because the electorate feel government doesn't work for them, but also by politicians pursuing culture wars. We'll explore these in the next chapter.

Chapter 6

CULTURE WARS

'It's a hard world down there in Alabama. I made this little song about down there … I advise everybody, be a little careful when they go along through there – best stay woke, keep their eyes open.'[1]

Likely the first use of the word 'woke' in its modern sense, spoken by the Black singer Lead Belly in 1938, referring to his song about a group of Black men in Alabama falsely accused of raping two white women.

Bad government: *scapegoating and sowing division and hate, rather than dealing with real issues.*

Good government: *bringing people together, upholding rights and resolving conflicts, so that everyone can thrive.*

During my lifetime, our culture has fundamentally changed. Only a quarter of married women were working around the time I was born, abortion was illegal, homosexuality was banned and racism was widespread.[2] In parts of the US, racial segregation was in place. All of our institutions were dominated by white, able-bodied, (publicly) straight males, and nobody thought anything of it. Now three-quarters of mothers are working, gay couples can marry and adopt children and the public face of Britain – its politicians, its journalists and the senior levels of its institutions – is starting to reflect the population and be more diverse, though there is still a long way to go.

I welcome these changes and have played a small part over my career in some of the advances for women, as described in this chapter. This is the Britain in which I and most Britons want to live. In 1987, around half of people agreed that a man's job was to earn the money and a woman's was to take care of the home and the family. Only a fifth of the population thought that in 2022.[3] The proportion of people who said that same-sex relationships were 'always wrong' fell from half in 1983 to 10 per cent by 2024.[4] In 2021, the majority of people in the same survey agreed with so-called 'woke' positions on race equality, immigration and sexual identity.[5]

These changes were hard won by people at the sharp end of discrimination, intolerance and hate, and there are battles that still need to be fought and ingrained institutional cultures in the police and elsewhere that need to be changed. Before they were able to turn the tide of opinion in their favour, it was politicians who stood in the way of their rights, but then governments took steps to protect them through new laws and the policies and practices to make those laws stick.

Now some politicians and influential figures want to turn the clock back, as the forces of social conservatism have tried unsuccessfully in the past, before the days of algorithms, social influencers with millions of followers and nativist populists. Reform UK, it is being reported, is now planning not just to withdraw from international human rights treaties but also to repeal domestic human rights and equalities laws if they get into government.[6] It's not a war against injustices they're waging, but against other people's rights, and they have might and a motive on their side. As we see in Trump's America, sowing dissent, rather than resolving conflict, is one way to win elections and for powerful people to advance their own interests. It's playing political football with people's lives, setting 'us' against 'them', spreading fear and, ultimately, eroding the trust that holds our society together. It's bad government, but it makes good headlines.

And because a minority is always against other people's rights, there will always be a base on which to build, unless governments can demonstrate that injustices are real and that we all benefit from a society where everyone can thrive. That's what we tried to do at the Equal Opportunities Commission on women's rights when I was there under the Blair government. It worked, but can it now, given the forces massing on the other side?

One thing's for sure: those of us who celebrate the social advances I've seen over my lifetime and hate the injustices that still remain need to stand up for these rights, because there are people out there gunning for them. And the first casualty in war is truth.

• • •

'You either fight back or you die.'

This is what Elon Musk is telling an estimated crowd of 120,000 to 150,000 people at a 'Unite the Kingdom' protest in central London on Saturday 15 September 2025, his image beamed in from the US on large screens to this huge crowd.

> My appeal is to British common sense, which is to look carefully around you and say, if this continues, what world will you be living in? This is a message to a reasonable centre. The people who ordinarily wouldn't get involved in politics who just want to

> live their lives … they're quiet. They just go about their business. My message is to them: if this continues, that violence is going to come to you. You will have no choice. You're in a fundamental situation here where whether you choose violence or not, violence is coming to you.

He spells out the threat as he sees it: 'Other people are going to come and maraud them. There's genuine risk of rape and murder and the destruction of the country and dissolution of the entire way of life.'

On the other side of the screen is the far-right activist and convicted criminal known as Tommy Robinson, who interviewed Musk. Real name Stephen Yaxley-Lennon, he's been behind bars for fraud, assault and contempt of court. Behind him is a sea of Union Jacks and one placard saying, 'Sadiq Khan is a sleeper agent.' Khan, the three-time elected Mayor of London, is a prime target for anti-Muslim and anti-London far-right sympathisers.

Some in the crowd are carrying Christian symbols such as wooden crosses and placards featuring Bible verses (Tommy Robinson himself is said to have converted to Christianity while in jail). Some are dressed as crusader soldiers, a reference to the 'great replacement' theory, in which far-right conspiracists believe that Muslims are infiltrating Christian countries to displace the 'indigenous' populations and replace Christianity. Tommy Robinson, Elon Musk and those who follow them think they are fighting back, and they want Middle Britain to join them.

Musk shares with the crowd what he tells his UK friends who don't live in London:

> Well, if you want to know what's going to happen to your town or village, just visit London and you'll see that it's filled with crime. It

> often doesn't feel like Britain at all. And it's only a matter of time before that is what happens to your town or village. It starts in London, but it will spread to every town and village in the country, and no one will have any peace.

In fact, in 2025, murders in London were at a five-year low, and the rate is much lower than in other international cities such as New York, Paris, Brussels, Berlin and Madrid, though lower-level crimes like phone-snatching remained quite high. Musk, never one to let a fact get in the way of his argument, says things can't go on like this and calls for a 'revolutionary government change' before the next election, with 'a dissolution of Parliament and a new vote held'.

Why is Elon Musk, the richest man in the world, a South African immigrant to the US and now a US citizen, addressing this crowd in the UK and interfering in another country's politics? Tommy Robinson asks him this, only more politely.

'Well, I am of primarily British heritage, British ancestry,' Musk explains. 'I want Britain to be greater than it ever has been. I want Britain to remain Britain. I think there's something beautiful about being British.'

In other words, he's white, and so is Britain, or at least that's what he wants it to be, as he goes on to explain.

> And what I see happening is a destruction of Britain. Initially a slow erosion, but a rapidly increasing erosion of Britain with massive uncontrolled migration. A failure by the government to protect innocent people, including children who are getting gang raped. It's unreal.

Robinson tells Elon Musk that 'a lot of people don't understand why we're allowing mass uncontrollable immigration into all western nations', and asks Musk why. He says,

> There's a massive incentive on the left to import voters and if they are allowed to succeed, if this is allowed to continue, they will succeed in importing voters, swaying the elections and taking your vote away from you. That is 100 per cent what is happening.

Robinson asks about what Musk has called 'the woke mind virus'. Musk says, 'A lot of the woke stuff is – it's actually super racist, it's super sexist and it's often anti-religion, but only anti-Christian.'

Musk tells the crowd that he is wearing a George Orwell T-shirt – black, with an eye on it – and he says this is fitting because the author would 'want freedom of speech. He would want the people to know what's real. He would want the people to fight against government oppression and fight for the truth and fight for the future of Britain.'[7]

The eye is a reference to *1984*, which depicts a totalitarian regime led by Big Brother, who maintains control through constant surveillance and the Thought Police. The hero, who is inwardly rebellious, works at the Ministry of Truth, which manipulates reality and rewrites history to fit the narrative of the state, so that all meaning and truth is lost. He is eventually discovered, arrested and tortured, and then brainwashed.

This accusation against the British state comes from the man who owns X, which skews its algorithms to promote his and similar views and suppress dissent. This is a man who has explicitly trained his AI tool, Grok, to be 'anti-woke' and right-leaning. Grok has even been caught praising Hitler and telling users that Musk is smarter and fitter than anyone in the world in posts that were subsequently deleted out of sheer embarrassment.[8] Meanwhile the new head of MI6 has warned that algorithms are becoming more powerful than *countries*; AI and critical technologies are increasingly beyond the control of the state and in the hands of corporations and individuals.[9]

Musk credits himself with helping to get Trump elected as the President of the United States for a second term, despite the fact that Trump continued to deny the result of the previous election, and still does, with no evidence. As an ardent climate change denier, one of Trump's first acts in his second presidency was to remove all references to global warming from government websites. Trump has ordered the Attorney General to bring criminal charges against people who have said or done things that challenge him and said that servicemen and women should be hung because they had urged fellow service personnel (whose oath of allegiance is to the constitution, not to the President) to disobey any illegal orders. He has set up Immigration and Customs Enforcement (ICE) squads, who wear masks and arrest people in the streets for deportation, sometimes with little or no evidence of illegal residency, even killing people who stand in their way, in the case of Renee Good and Alex Pretti in Cincinnati. Under his watch, the US has revoked visas for the CEOs of the Center for Countering Digital Hate and the Global Disinformation Index and the former EU Commissioner, Thierry Breton, who was behind the EU's Digital Services Act, accusing them of 'egregious acts of extraterritorial censorship'.[10] Tourists entering the US must now reveal their social media activity for the last five years, and any telephone numbers and email addresses used in the last decade, as well as details of family members including children.[11]

So, who is Big Brother then?

It's not just Musk but also Trump's administration that is blaming the UK and the EU for allowing migration to destroy their culture and accusing their governments of crushing dissent. US Vice President J. D. Vance shocked Europeans at the Munich Security Conference in February 2025 when he said the greatest threat facing the continent was not from Russia and China, but 'from within' – through censorship, suppression of dissent and migration. He singled out the UK for creating anti-abortion protest exclusion zones. But that was just the beginning. Trump was even blunter when he said to the United Nations later that year,

> Europe is in serious trouble. They have been invaded by a force of illegal aliens like nobody has ever seen before … You want to be politically correct and you are destroying your heritage.[12]

The US's National Security Strategy, published in late 2025, made it official, warning that Europe was facing 'the real and more stark prospect of civilizational erasure' as a result of migration, as well as 'censorship of free speech and suppression of political opposition, cratering birthrates, and loss of national identities and self-confidence'. This sounds bad enough, but it also makes it clear that the US sides with 'patriotic European parties' – the far right to you and me – and says 'America encourages its political allies in Europe to promote this revival of spirit'. Like Elon Musk, the Trump administration has fostered links with the far-right Alternative for Germany (AfD) party, which has been classified as 'extreme right' by German intelligence.[13]

How did we get to the point where powerful Americans are waging culture wars in which they are portraying European allies as the enemy, while a real European war is in prospect with Russia, and they're supposed to be on our side? And it looks like they are winning. The Overton window (the range of subjects and arguments that are politically acceptable to the mainstream population at a given time) is shifting in Musk's and Trump's direction. They have allies in Europe, not just on the far right but in mainstream politics, with many promoting similar culture war talking points, policies and tactics. Nigel Farage, for example, testified to Congress about what he saw as the repression of free speech in the UK and likened the UK to North Korea.[14] At the same time, centrist politicians, because they are experiencing a loss of popularity, are modifying their policies to try to adapt to a political climate increasingly set by others.

And so we have a Labour Prime Minister who delivers a speech about migration in which he mimics words – 'an island of strangers' – from Enoch Powell's famous 'Rivers of Blood' speech,[15] and a Muslim Home Secretary who says that in order to stop people like her being called a 'Fucking P**i' – as she put it in the House of Commons – she has to say that illegal migration is 'tearing the country apart' and that 'people can see huge pressure in their communities and they can also see a system that is broken, and where people are able to flout the rules, abuse the system and get away with it'. And she introduced a draconian anti-migrant package that will prevent many migrants from ever settling permanently in this country and integrating. Will this make things better for migrants, and keep 'the other lot' out? I very much doubt it.

Welcome to the world of culture wars, in which those who shout loudest are winning and appeasement is thought to be the best policy by those who might otherwise be expected to take a principled stand.

• • •

In September 2019, I was walking around the Ulster Museum in Belfast with my husband, looking at an exhibition about the Troubles in Northern Ireland which had ended twenty years earlier. As we walked in, we were greeted by the words: 'While we have a shared past, we do not have a shared memory.'[16]

It resonated with me immediately because of a conversation I'd had with a Catholic woman some forty years earlier. She was living in the farmhouse in the Republic of Ireland which my Protestant grandparents had once owned and where my father had been born and lived until he was seven. He still proudly held an Irish passport. As my father told the story, at the time of the Irish uprising in 1922, which catalysed the Irish Civil War, his family were suddenly forced to leave for England because the IRA had come to their farm and shot one of their workers. They feared for their lives. The farmhouse and land were auctioned off from England but they believed they had not got a fair price because of the circumstances. This, and the belief that they'd been driven out of a country they considered home and could never return to, left family scars which lived on in my father.

When I was in my twenties, I tried to find their old farm while I was on holiday in Ireland with a friend. We stopped in a layby beside one farm we thought might be it, and a farmer came out with a gun and told us to move on. Despite the hostility, we continued looking and eventually found Rathkurby House, the name my father had given me to search for, which was named after the nearby village. When we got to the front door, we knocked and there was no response. We decided to have a look around the farmyard, having come so far and, when we reached the cowsheds, we found the farmer and his men, hiding. He thought we were tax inspectors, he explained.

Some minutes later, his wife, who was in her early forties and had been in the house all along, gave us tea. We sat in what looked like a rarely used parlour, where pictures of the Pope and the Virgin Mary were prominently displayed. I told her, in the manner of someone telling a rather quaint story, about how my grandparents had come to leave the house and the farm. She flatly contradicted me, saying it was not like that at all, and explained how her family had bought the farm in entirely straightforward circumstances, with no violence of any kind, talking about this as if it had happened only yesterday and she had seen it all with her own eyes. Her story was compelling and detailed; we both believed her until after we left and realised that she hadn't even been born then, as these events were sixty years ago.

A shared past but not a shared memory, indeed.

This conversation took place in 1981, when the Troubles in Northern Ireland were still raging and sectarian differences between Catholics and Protestants there were raw. The Irish constitution at that time laid claim to Northern Ireland, while Protestant allegiances lay firmly with the British mainland, so it wasn't just differences of religion but also nationality that fuelled the fire. Bombs were still exploding in Northern Ireland at that point, sectarian violence was rife and lives were being lost. In the UK, the IRA's Brighton bomb nearly killed the Prime Minister, Margaret Thatcher, three years after this visit.

On Bloody Sunday, which happened in 1972, a decade before my visit to Rathkurby House, thirteen people were shot dead and at least fifteen others were injured when members of the British army opened fire on civil rights demonstrators in the Bogside, a predominantly Catholic part of Londonderry. The facts were hotly disputed, and it was not until 2010 that a twelve-year independent inquiry finally concluded that British soldiers had shot unarmed civilians without warning and that the soldiers' initial accounts were false. A previous inquiry conducted in 1972 by Lord Widgery was heavily criticised in their report as a 'whitewash'. The Prime Minister of the UK, David Cameron, issued an apology, at long last.

A shared understanding of the truth mattered, which is why committing to the Bloody Sunday inquiry was a key part of the peace negotiations that led to the Good Friday Agreement; the inquiry was announced a few months before the agreement was signed in April 1998. It was also crucial to gaining the confidence of the nationalist community, because a common understanding of the truth matters, along with the justice that goes with it, if warring people are to lay down their arms and live together peacefully.

The Good Friday Agreement is probably the most outstanding example of good government over my lifetime, and credit is due to both John Major and Tony Blair, as well as to the United States, which played a critical leadership role in healing political and religious divisions in Northern Ireland. It was a sensitive, long and hard process, which brought political parties together. Securing peace in Northern Ireland made history, but it was not the sort of triumph that would swing British general elections, and it involved a great deal of time, patience and grief. It would have been easy to have walked away.

That's what these politicians felt they were there for, then: to resolve conflicts between communities, not inflame them. The very opposite is happening now, as hitherto shared truths are contested and people are driven apart by politicians. Climate change is one example, which until recently was a settled fact, based on overwhelming scientific evidence, and opposing parties were united in the need for action. In the UK, the value of the European Convention on Human Rights (ECHR), which the UK took a leadership role in establishing after the Second World War, had been widely accepted and was written into the Good Friday Agreement. Now, those who want to prevent asylum claims altogether and deport more migrants are calling for the UK to leave the Convention, joining unlikely bedfellows Russia and Belarus as non-signatories. This commitment to the ECHR is so important to peace in Northern Ireland because it provides an internationally agreed set of human rights standards, under the supervision of an international court, the European Court of Human Rights, which is separate from the British state. A lasting commitment to it is essential to building trust in public institutions in Northern Ireland, especially the police and security services, whom many Catholics had felt were skewed against them.

How brittle that peace in Northern Ireland remains was brought home to me when, during the same trip in which we visited the Ulster Museum, we took a taxi through Belfast and saw the unionist flags flying in areas where, the taxi driver explained, no Catholic still dared go. This was over twenty years after the Good Friday Agreement.

When I started to see St George and Union Jack flags flying in certain communities in England around the time of the Unite the Kingdom march, and heard first-hand how frightened this made people from minoritised communities feel, I was reminded of this and felt sick at heart. When Musk was calling on Middle Britain to fight, he was effectively calling on us to fight each other and tear this country apart. It would potentially be Northern Ireland all over again, but with America fomenting hate this time.

When I was taking that taxi through Belfast in 2019 I was travelling to a book festival at Mount Stewart, where I was speaking. After the event, while my husband and I were walking round its beautiful gardens, a couple in the audience stopped us to talk about Brexit. At that time, politicians were struggling to find a Brexit solution that would be compatible with the Good Friday Agreement. This was despite the assurances given by the Leave campaign during the referendum, including from the then Secretary of State for Northern Ireland, Theresa Villiers, that there would be no problems for peace in Ireland, a view that contradicted that of the experts. The answer, this couple said, was to put a border in the sea between Britain and Ireland and to allow the island of Ireland to stay in the EU. This idea was hated by the unionists, who saw it as the first step to uniting with Ireland, but the couple, who were Protestants, thought it was the only way forward and that eventually Ireland would become a single country. That will never happen, I replied, because the Tories are staunch unionists. Boris Johnson agreed to it in the end, however, as it was seen as the only way to 'get Brexit done'. That agreement was slightly moderated by Rishi Sunak's later Windsor Framework, which allowed goods intended only for Northern Ireland to abide by British custom rules in a 'green lane', while others going to Ireland were treated under EU rules – but the border in the sea effectively remains.

To rub salt in the wound, the Leader of the Opposition, Kemi Badenoch, when asked about her government's decision to put a border in the sea by a BBC Northern Ireland journalist, said 'the last time I checked, Northern Ireland did vote to leave', whereas in fact it voted heavily against.[17] Two days later, she formally announced that the Tories would leave the ECHR, following Reform's lead, denying this would undermine the longstanding peace agreement, despite an expert consensus that it would be a fatal blow.

'People in this country have had enough of experts,' said the then Justice Secretary Michael Gove, refusing to name any economists who supported Brexit and capturing a widespread sentiment among Brexiteers. Belief, not facts, are what mattered, and when you go down that route it becomes increasingly hard to find common ground or resolve disputes.[18]

The one thing that right-wing British politicians have learned from Brexit is that divide and rule, blaming something else for all your problems and asserting strong beliefs as you undermine actual evidence and basic facts works with the electorate, at least in the short term. This is probably why Nigel Farage, who spent much of his career arguing for Brexit, also wants to leave the ECHR and, like Donald Trump, is promoting the war against 'Diversity, Equity and Inclusion' (DEI) policies (or more often known in this country as Equality/Equity, Diversity and Inclusion or EDI), is threatening mass deportations of migrants and is dismissing credible media sources as 'fake news'. Reform are even threatening to remove public funding from the BBC, the most trusted media news source, while Farage continues to be a presenter on GB News, the UK equivalent of Fox News and primary BBC rival. Opinion polls at the time of writing suggest he could be our next Prime Minister.

• • •

We may be in an era of 'Truth Decay', as Barak Obama dubbed it, after a book of the same name by Jennifer Kavanagh and Michael D. Rich, but sometimes the facts speak for themselves, showing that the culture of many organisations is in need of significant improvement. This is at the very same time as some politicians are attacking the very initiatives that are designed to change those cultures for the better.

Take sexual harassment in the armed forces. Twenty years ago, the Equal Opportunities Commission (EOC), when I was its CEO, launched a formal investigation into the armed services because there were so many reports of sexual harassment against women. These statutory powers were designed to be used only where there was evidence of a systemic problem and as a last resort. It was the first time we had deployed them. Yet these problems still remain. In 2021, Gunner Jaysley Beck killed herself at the age of nineteen in an army barracks after being sexually harassed by her line manager, a superior officer twenty years her senior. He had sent her more than 4,000 messages and voicemails over two months.

Beck had not reported this incident herself because, on a previous occasion involving a different officer, sufficient action had not been taken in response to her complaint. That officer, Michael Webber, had pinned her down and kissed her, but he was given only a minor sanction in the army justice system, and he was later promoted. It took her suicide to take his case out of the jurisdiction of the armed services and into the civil courts, and in 2025 he received a prison sentence of six months for this conduct. Her mother said in court,

> She trusted people to protect her and after what he did, the trust was gone. She was very upset and scared of Michael Webber. I saw the change before my own eyes. She felt powerless and betrayed. That assault shattered her faith in the set-up that was supposed to look after her.[19]

The coroner who investigated her suicide said about this earlier harassment that 'there was a failure on behalf of the state to deal appropriately or effectively with the complaint by Jaysley'. He added that 'the failure was systemic in that every senior officer involved in the decision-based process ... failed to follow correct procedures, and in so doing breached established policies'. There was, he said, an arguable case that the state breached her ECHR Article 2 right to life for its failure to put in place a framework of laws, precautions, procedures and means of enforcement which would, to the greatest extent reasonably practicable, have protected her life.[20] Since then, two other officers in the chain of command are facing a court martial.

The coroner heard that inappropriate behaviour by male soldiers was 'commonplace amongst a significant minority' with women routinely receiving 'vile and degrading comments' while socialising. Around 700 women and men had come forward during the two-week inquest to report abuse.[21] A large-scale survey published in November 2025 found that two-thirds of women serving full-time in the UK's armed forces reported experiencing sexualised behaviour over the past year and 93 per cent of those said they believed the behaviour amounted to sexual harassment.[22]

This survey suggests things may even have got worse since the EOC took action against the Ministry of Defence twenty years earlier. What brought matters to a head then was the increasing number of servicewomen contacting us about sexual harassment because they did not trust their line managers or the complaints system to sort things out. Surveys at the time suggested that one in five women in the Royal Navy experienced sexual harassment in the preceding twelve months, one in eight in the army and one in ten in the Royal Air Force.

When we visited the Ministry of Defence to give them advance notice of our formal investigation, I couldn't help but notice that the eyes of the most senior man in the room were fixed on the legs of Julie Mellor, the EOC's chair, despite the news we were giving. Such was the culture at the time.

However, the MOD promised a three-year action plan to urgently and systemically address the problems and, as a result, an agreement was signed with the EOC that led to the formal investigation being suspended. This agreement noted that 'there is a worrying discrepancy between the proportion of people who say they have experienced sexual harassment and the actual number of formal complaints made. Furthermore, many complaints were taking too long to resolve'. The MOD committed to research into sexual harassment and for each service to establish a dedicated investigation team for formal complaints.[23] It introduced comprehensive sexual harassment policies across all three services, including helplines and trained equal opportunities officers, and the army conducted regular surveys to assess the level of harassment.

Yet the armed services still have a major issue of harassment, as well as problems with the services' internal justice system, and this applies not just to sexual harassment but racial discrimination and abuse too.[24] It is also worth remembering that the banning of homosexuality in the armed services in the UK was only lifted in 2000 after the Court of Justice of the European Union, which enforces the ECHR, ruled that it was unlawful, and the independent Etherton Review, published in 2023, uncovered the shocking scale of abuse which is still causing pain and anguish to this day.

• • •

Culture runs deep, and there is a similar pattern within the Metropolitan Police. Despite a succession of reports over many years and many promises of reform, it seems difficult to achieve the shift that is so often promised but not delivered. Louise Casey's review following Sarah Everard's murder in 2021 found the Met to be institutionally racist, misogynistic and homophobic, twenty years after the 1999 Macpherson report, following the racist murder of Stephen Lawrence, found the Metropolitan Police, and indeed the police more generally, to be institutionally racist. Two years on from Casey's review, the chair of the National Black Police Association said, 'Things have not changed', and a second, follow-up inquiry was announced in November 2025.[25]

Sarah Everard was raped and killed by a serving police office on 3 March 2021, during the Covid pandemic. My two daughters, who were in their twenties, were living with us then, and I thought it could easily have been them, as Everard was abducted close to our house. We know from doorbell cameras that she, having visited someone a few streets away from us, passed a few feet away as she walked home before reaching the point on the South Circular Road, less than a mile away, where off-duty Met Police constable Wayne Couzens presented her with his warrant card, then handcuffed and arrested her. We drive past that spot regularly and I often think of her as we do. He bundled her into his car and later raped and then used his police belt to strangle her. Her body was eventually found in Kent.

Thousands of flowers were laid at Clapham Common in her memory and a candle-lit vigil was held for her. Despite the proximity, we did not go for fear of being fined under Covid restrictions, but hundreds of women did. The police pinned several to the ground, arrested and then charged them, citing Covid rules and anti-protest legislation, and the next day, when my daughters visited the site, they saw that many of the flowers carefully laid in her memory had also been crushed by the police, such was the insensitivity of the arrests. It was the fact that we still have human rights laws that saved those women who were arrested, as the High Court ruled that this was not lawful. The police eventually accepted liability and paid compensation.[26]

An independent investigation revealed that Couzens had been reported to the police eight times for indecent exposure before Everard's murder, and said there had been 'a lamentable and repeated failure to deal, in a reasonable and professional manner, with the several allegations reported to different police forces by a number of people'.[27] A follow-up report in 2025 found that a quarter of police forces in England and Wales are yet to implement 'basic policies for investigating sexual offences', with women still being failed despite promises of change after the murder of Sarah Everard four years before.[28]

Bleak insights into the prevailing culture of the Met, at least in some places, are all too frequently revealed. Like the two police officers who took photos in 2020 of the bodies of two sisters, Nicole Smallman and Bibaa Henry, who had been stabbed to death, and shared them in two WhatsApp groups, calling the victims 'dead birds'. One group, called 'the A team', contained forty-one police officers and the other contained friends of one of the officers and was entitled 'Covid cunts'. Nicole and Bibaa's mother, Mina Smallman, the Church of England's first Black female archdeacon, believed that racism also led to a delay in finding their bodies.[29] Or the undercover filming at Charing Cross police station that revealed officers calling for immigrants to be shot, revelling in the use of force and being dismissive of rape claims. One officer told the undercover reporter in a pub that a detainee who had overstayed his visa should have 'a bullet through his head' and those who 'shag' or 'rape women' should be sexually mutilated and left to die.[30]

Violence against women and girls is at epidemic levels, with over one in four estimated to be victims over their lifetime and one in twelve each year in the UK, and a high proportion of perpetrators are known to their victim.[31] In late 2025, the government launched its strategy to tackle this epidemic, but its success will partly depend on the culture of the police that enforces it.

The leadership shown by Jess Phillips and others on this is an example of good government, and it is an issue that might normally command cross-party support. The Leader of the Opposition Kemi Badenoch, however, chose what we might call a 'culture wars' response, focusing in on migrant sexual abusers as the problem, when it is well documented that such abuse spans cultures and religions and most perpetrators are white and British. She wrote on X that 'we need to get people who have come from cultures that don't respect women out of our country! Not all cultures are equally valid'. She also took issue with the plan to teach children in schools about misogyny, saying it is 'not 11-year-old boys who are committing violence against women and girls'.[32]

When it comes to violence against women and girls, there is a need for societal cultural change and, as in institutions like the police and armed services, it needs dedicated commitment from the top to put the right policies and processes in place, to call out bad behaviour, raise awareness and win over hearts and minds, and to try and ensure that these institutions reflect the diversity of those they serve. That's what we should expect from our politicians and government.

This takes us back to the question of DEI and EDI. In the UK, the previous government banned EDI posts in the civil service under the aegis of Kemi Badenoch as the Women and Equalities Minister,[33] and Donald Trump has threatened the withdrawal of federal funding for schools and universities that pursue DEI policies.[34] The Black chairman of the Joint Chiefs of Staff in the US was fired after the Defence Secretary said he should be sacked because of his 'woke' focus on diversity, equity and inclusion programmes in the military.[35] Elon Musk partly blamed the devastating Los Angeles forest fires of early 2025 not on global warming, but on DEI policies and hires, declaring, 'DEI is DIE.'[36]

The people who believe that DEI programmes are a waste of money often also believe that they are expressions of the Thought Police, that they threaten free speech or are a result of 'cultural Marxism' that has been infiltrating our institutions, driven by graduates who have been indoctrinated at university. They believe that these institutions, including universities, have become intolerant of opposing views and are operating a so-called 'cancel culture'. In other words, they see DEI as political, partisan and poisonous and are seeking to undermine what had been something of a societal consensus around it.

Where will this end? In Russia, with whom Trump seems to be allying himself culturally against Europe, there is a 'gay propaganda' law under which public expression 'promoting' non-heterosexual relationships or gender transition is punishable by administrative fines or detention of up to fifteen days, with repeat offenders potentially facing up to four years in prison. Same-sex marriage and gender transition are banned.[37] Moving in that direction, Hungary, when it was until recently under populist control, banned Gay Pride demonstrations.[38]

We currently have laws and international conventions that stand up for the rights of minority groups in this country, but the Conservatives and Reform are already intent on repealing the ECHR, which underpins so many rights, as well as our domestic Human Rights Act, if either of them form a government. Reform are committed to unravelling our equality legislation that outlaws direct and indirect discrimination, harassment and victimisation on grounds of age, disability, gender reassignment, marriage and civil partnership, pregnancy and maternity, race, religion or belief, sex and sexual orientation.[39] It also requires public bodies not just to obey the law but also to promote and enforce equality in their functions. People undergoing or who have undergone gender reassignment are also protected from discrimination under the Equality Act 2010, and the Gender Recognition Act 2004 gives them the right to a new birth certificate and to be legally recognised in their chosen gender in marriage, pensions and inheritance.

Would those who attack EDI initiatives feel the same way if it were their daughter who killed herself because of harassment in the armed services, like Jaysley Beck, or was murdered by a serving police officer, like Sarah Everard, or discovered that police officers had taken pictures of their daughters' murdered bodies to share for the amusement of their friends, as happened to Nicole Smallman and Bibaa Henry?

• • •

Most people don't like injustice or unfairness when they see it first-hand, but it takes protesters and campaigners to raise their awareness of it when it happens to people they don't know or those they distrust. Genuine culture change often starts when people at the sharp end of these injustices force others to feel their pain through disruptive action. It's a form of culture war, if you like, but it is based on lived experience, not ideology. It takes years and often decades to achieve, so people end up devoting their life to it, and sometimes losing it for the cause they espouse.

So it was with suffragettes like Emily Wilding Davison who threw herself in front of the King's horse at the Epsom Derby and died, or Emily Pankhurst who sent letter bombs and led an arson attack against Lloyd George's empty home while he was Chancellor of the Exchequer, causing considerable damage, as well as bombing other buildings. She and many others ended up in prison and went on hunger strike for their beliefs. The parallel women's rights movement, the suffragists led by Millicent Fawcett, also campaigned tirelessly, but in their case peacefully, on behalf of women's rights. The First World War also played a role, as women became a more important part of the workforce, but it was the combination of these forces that eventually led to women getting the vote in the UK.

In the US, Martin Luther King and his non-violent protests had enormous influence in ending segregation and advancing Black people's rights. The civil rights movement was inspired by individual acts of courage, like Rosa Parks's arrest for her decision to sit in a bus seat reserved for whites, which led to the thirteen-month long Montgomery Bus Boycott and a Supreme Court decision that segregation on public buses was unconstitutional. The protests King led might have been non-violent but that did not stop an assassin from gunning him down at the age of thirty-nine.

In South Africa, Nelson Mandela and the ANC took up arms to end apartheid and he faced years in prison before his goal was eventually secured. Disabled people in the UK secured new rights through the 1995 Disability Act by chaining themselves to buses and trains and blocking roads, and similar actions were undertaken in the States.

Dedicated campaigns by charities and others, often over decades, have also won public support and have been critical in giving politicians the permission and courage to change the law, for example the campaigns for gay marriage and for the right to assisted dying. As laws are passed, new norms are created, and these are slowly established to the point where people look back at the past and see a different country.

Nigel Farage, facing allegations that he had racially abused fellow pupils at his school in the seventies – including allegedly taunting one Jewish pupil by saying that 'Hitler was right' and 'gas them', before making a hissing noise – denied the accusations, despite the fact that they've been backed up, at the time of writing, by thirty-four of his former schoolmates. Farage launched a blistering attack on the BBC in response, accusing them of double standards and demanding an apology for shows like *The Black and White Minstrel Show*, in which artists blacked up, and *It Ain't Half Hot Mum*. He also lambasted ITV for airing Bernard Manning's racist jokes.[40] Farage makes a valid point that times have changed – although I cannot recall anyone on television in the 1970s joking that Hitler was right and talking positively about the gas chambers. I think there are very few people, except perhaps the defenders of free speech who object to any form of censorship, who want to return to a country in which racist, homophobic and misogynistic slurs are common.

Nigel Farage has not denied that he admired Enoch Powell back in the seventies, who called for the 'urgent encouragement of existing immigrants to return to their home countries' through a policy of voluntary 're-emigration' and was sacked as a shadow minister for saying so. Although cultural norms have changed, political norms have shifted to the point where Nigel Farage has gone even further than Enoch Powell by threatening thousands of migrants currently living legally in the UK with deportation, refusing indefinite leave to remain to 800,000 people who might have become eligible and taking it away from those who already have that status.[41] The *Financial Times* has calculated that up to two million people might be at risk of deportation under a Reform government.[42] There are legitimate concerns about uncontrolled and excessive migration that politicians must rightly respond to, but there is a difference between that and whipping up excessive fear of migrants to achieve other political ends or pursuing policies with no regard for human rights.

The official Vote Leave campaign used migration as a key reason to vote for Brexit, claiming that Turkey and four other countries could join the EU as soon as 2020, which could lead to 5.2 million people moving to the UK by 2030 under free movement laws. Vote Leave campaigner Michael Gove warned of the threat of terrorism and 'open visa-free travel to 77 million Turkish citizens', and of the creation of 'a border-free zone from Iraq, Iran and Syria to the English Channel', though later admitted this was wrong.[43]

The irony was that, once Brexit was secured, Boris Johnson oversaw an estimated 2.6 million increase in net migration over the four years that followed. This happened without much comment, while political rhetoric about people coming in boats was escalated to the point that it was called an 'invasion' by the then Home Secretary, Suella Braverman.[44] After leaving office, Braverman wrote in *The Telegraph* in February 2024, 'The truth is that the Islamists, the extremists and the anti-Semites are in charge now. They have bullied the Labour Party, they have bullied our institutions, and now they have bullied our country into submission.'[45]

Unsurprisingly, given this escalation of rhetoric around migration in recent years, it is now a red-hot political topic. And it is generating fear and division, not bringing people together.

• • •

Politicians can play a vital leadership role, for good or bad, in creating positive social change. One of the best examples during my lifetime is the way in which in 2013 David Cameron, the Conservative Prime Minister of the coalition government, introduced laws to enable gay marriage, despite opposition from some in his Cabinet and many conservative supporters. He recognised that there was a consensus in the country that this was the right thing to do. People who loved each other were being denied the legal rights the rest of us had. Credit is also due to some of his Lib Dem coalition partners, most notably Lynne Featherstone, Nick Clegg and Jo Swinson.

The worst example of political leadership in this area during my lifetime occurred twenty-five years before that, in 1988, when another Conservative Prime Minister, Margaret Thatcher, banned the promotion of homosexuality in schools through a law known as Section 28. This included the provision that schools could not teach 'the acceptability of homosexuality as a pretended family relationship'. The teaching ban followed a *Daily Mail* campaign sparked by outrage at a children's book stocked by a school library in inner London, *Jenny Lives with Eric and Martin.* In the 1987 general election, the Tories launched a poster with the slogan: 'Labour Camp. Do you want to live in it?' with a drawing of protesters holding placards saying 'Gay Lib', 'Gay Sports Day' and 'Militant Rules'.

This was bad government, trying to turn back the clock, and it did not last.

Incidentally, there was a chasm between this ideological stance and Thatcher's personal behaviour towards gay men, illustrating the point that people faced with real life examples often behave differently to their preconceived views. She was very fond of Peter Morrison, for example, whom she appointed as her Parliamentary Private Secretary in 1990, although she knew he was gay. One of her police protection officers, Barry Strevens, told me that some time before that appointment he warned Thatcher that he had been informed by a very senior police officer that Morrison was going to parties with underage boys and might be at risk of inadvertently getting caught up in illegal activity. At the time, the age of legal consent for gay sex was twenty-one. She was considering appointing him as deputy chair of the Conservative Party at the time, which she duly did. Her political speechwriter, Ronnie Millar, was also gay and according to Howell James, a political adviser who moved in these circles, she knew that to be the case. Millar gave her the text of the Saint Francis of Assisi prayer to read out on the steps of No. 10 when she first became Prime Minister, and wrote the famous words in a conference speech, 'The lady's not for turning.'

When I was working for her, I also accompanied her to the Mildmay Hospital to visit two dying AIDS patients, in a private visit, and she sat and talked with each of them separately, just the three of us, and I can testify that she spoke with them with kindness and empathy. One of them died later that day, entirely alone, and we learnt later that he had not felt able to tell his mother he was gay and dying of AIDS. She spoke to him, human to human, and my diary remarks on her tenderness and the fact that she was 'so sweet' towards the two young men. She had an open heart if not an open mind.

Thatcher was a social conservative, a believer in Victorian family values, stigmatising not only gay people but also single parents whom she felt were living the wrong sort of life. She even toyed with the idea of making divorce more difficult, just at the time when the most prominent marriage in the land, that of Diana and Charles, was secretly falling apart. A few years later, her own son's marriage also ended in divorce.

In her case, the tide of social change was just too strong. Is it different now?

There is a good deal more force behind social conservatism today.

It's an international movement, spearheaded by the most powerful man in the world and his acolytes and allies in other countries; fuelled by think tanks with US dark money which have infiltrated political parties in this country; pursued by influencers with enormous numbers of followers who cross international boundaries and make money out of it; and aided by social media algorithms which promote anger, dissent and hate. One of the most powerful of the social platforms for political thinking, X, is owned by the richest man in the world, who also holds these views.

Financial interests may be key drivers, at least in some cases. The so-called Tufton Street think tanks – the TaxPayers' Alliance, the Institute of Economic Affairs, Policy Exchange, the Adam Smith Institute and the Prosperity Institute (formerly the Legatum Institute) – have collectively raised $9 million from American donors since 2012, Open Democracy calculated in 2022, including from oil money and climate deniers.[46] Elon Musk, in his speech at Tommy Robinson's 2025 march, was clear about his wish to see much greater deregulation and his dislike of the EU and the British government in this regard. Many speculate that the surprise support of the so-called 'tech bros' for Trump in his second term was largely motivated by the desire for deregulation.

Pushing hot buttons like migration wins votes for politicians who are then potentially free to pursue commercial objectives, like more investment in fossil fuels and deregulating AI and Bitcoin.

Another of those issues is transgender rights. There are echoes between Thatcher making homosexuality a political issue and today's transgender debate, which the last Conservative government tried to make a political dividing line, despite views cutting across political parties. During his second election campaign, Trump explicitly used anti-trans sentiment to pursue his political ambitions, in another echo of the Tories' 'Labour Camp' 1987 political campaign in relation to homosexuality. There were advertisements that declared: 'Kamala is for they/them. President Trump is for you', and $215 million was spent on network TV commercials alone specifically targeting trans and non-binary people, particularly trans women.[47] On gaining power, Trump swiftly moved to ban trans girls and women from women's sports and transgender people from the military as well as decreeing that there were only two genders and directing law enforcement to prosecute educators who 'unlawfully facilitate' a minor's social transition, such as by using their preferred name or pronouns.

Following suit, Reform promised similar policies at the 2024 general election, where the party gained a record five seats.

Transgender people make up only around 0.5 per cent of the UK population. Most people's direct experience of the issues is limited and, although there are some vocal transgender activists and defenders, it is hard for such a tiny minority to defend themselves. What's more, many may not wish to publicly identify themselves, given the high number of attacks transgender people receive, which have been increasing. People who wish to restrict or deny their rights are in a much stronger position to make their case and have increasingly had powerful politicians, influencers and newspapers on their side. Most people, myself included, tend to avoid getting involved because they observe that people who do are hounded or even cancelled by activists on either side.

As in the case of race, faith and migration, the Overton window for what can acceptably be said has shifted massively and public opinion has moved at the same time, probably in response, with an increased scepticism about transgender rights, particularly the legal right to change identity. This has accelerated over the two years between early 2022 and the end of 2024, according to one survey, a period in which politicians had brought the issue to the fore. That said, 49 per cent of the public still tend to say someone should be able to socially identify as a different gender, compared to 35 per cent who say they should not. This support is down six points from 2022, however, while the latter stance is up ten points.[48]

• • •

As well as having power and money, the culture warriors who are trying to turn the clock back on social change also have God, or at least one version of he/she/them, on their side. White Christian nationalists in the US believe Trump is their God's chosen one, and this movement enjoys a huge following in America, where a majority are religious, unlike in the UK, which is a largely secular.[49] White Christian nationalists believe the US is already and should continue to be a white Christian nation, and they are now extending this idea to Europe in the shape of anti-migrant, anti-Muslim and anti-transgender views.

Initially, abortion was their galvanising issue in the US, which has far more purchase there than in the UK. But they are also alarmed by immigration, especially by Muslims, and by the increased acceptance of different gender identities and sexual orientations which they believe are unbiblical. Many of these views have now been politically mainstreamed by Donald Trump, leading to the overturning of the Roe v. Wade decision in 2024 on abortion, among other things. He enabled this by appointing pro-life judges to the court in his first term. Many individual states have now severely restricted or banned abortion rights. Trump has, however, shown no inclination to reverse legal protections for gay people, at least to date.

Some have argued that trans rights are being used by white Christian nationalists as a deliberate 'wedge issue', where, because of lack of familiarity with trans people, it is easy to play on the general population's fears and insecurities of either rape or of the indoctrination of their children. These fears are then used to pursue other socially conservative policies, such as a ban on gay marriage or an end to abortion rights.[50]

White Christian nationalists have unlikely bedfellows, not just in Trump or Tommy Robinson, but also in the influencer Andrew Tate, a close associate of Robinson and other far-right activists. Tate believes women are the property of men, that a woman's primary role should be within a 'traditional family' and that they should obey their husbands. This is summed up by the phrases 'toxic masculinity' and 'trad wives', i.e. traditional wives. He says that feminism is a 'psyop' or psychological operation designed to divide society. Tate is a former kickboxer who boasts more than 10 million followers on X (a platform from which he had been banned when it was Twitter, only for him to be reinstated when Musk took over). He is a supporter of Donald Trump. He and his brother Tristan are facing charges of rape, human trafficking and forming an organised criminal group in Romania. At the time of writing, that case has not yet gone to trial, and further investigations are being undertaken but, in August 2024, Romanian authorities launched a second criminal investigation against the brothers, which includes new allegations of human trafficking, the trafficking of minors, sexual intercourse with a minor and money laundering. Britain has issued an arrest warrant for the Tates related to allegations of sexual assault and human trafficking in the UK dating back to between 2012 and 2015, but they cannot be extradited to the UK until after the legal proceedings in Romania have concluded.[51]

The culture wars pursued by Tate, who makes a huge amount of money out of the controversy he generates over social media and related activities, has now seeped so deeply into our culture that I heard from a colleague that her six-year-old grandson was repeating a well-known nursery rhyme which now features Tate's name in it, even though he has no idea who he is:

> One, two, buckle my shoe
> Three, four, knock at the door
> Five, six, pick up sticks
> Seven, eight, Andrew Tate.

He's gaining traction, that's for sure, at least among boys and young men. One in five men aged sixteen to twenty-nine who have heard of Andrew Tate say they have a favourable view of him.[52]

Just as Andrew Tate has turned feminism into a term of abuse, so the wider attack on liberalism has turned the term 'woke' – initially a positive word first used by the Black singer Lead Belly to capture the need to be alert to the threat of racism – into a negative term. Similarly, the Home Secretary Priti Patel under the previous Conservative government attacked the gesture of taking the knee, for example, as 'gesture politics', when the English football team adopted it. It had first been used by Martin Luther King as an act of prayer and then was later widely adopted, after the murder of George Floyd by police, by Black Lives Matter protesters in the US and Europe.[53]

Truth is being turned on its head at the same time as media outlets who pride themselves on their fact-checking are routinely attacked by Trump and Farage as peddling 'fake news'. In this *Alice in Wonderland* world, how do you keep your bearings? By holding on to your lived experience, making sure that everything you believe about the world is grounded in fact and standing up for the truth.

• • •

What does a 'trad wife' look like? Immaculately dressed and made up to appeal to her husband, she also wears an apron while baking and maintaining a perfect home and looking after the children, while her husband goes out to work. She doesn't look like me, my mother or my daughters. My grandmother might have a superficial resemblance, in that she was a homesteader in Canada, had five children, baked everything and grew her own vegetables. But she also raised turkeys and chickens to earn money for the farm and killed and plucked them by hand. She had strong arms and a formidable personality. Her youngest son was burnt to death in an accident when my grandfather was burning off stubble in a field on the farm, and my aunt lost an arm in a threshing machine as a child. My grandmother's role in the family was traditional but certainly not glamorous, and it's true that she held the view until her death that women's place was in the home.

My mother also had five children but became a lone parent when she separated from my father when I, her youngest child, was seven. She worked full-time all her adult life, largely out of economic necessity. Life for her was extremely hard and her health suffered in her later years. I had the advantage of a university education; doors were opened for me that were closed for my mother and grandmother and I started to break through what some people call 'the glass ceiling'.

The barriers to advancement were subtle and sometimes hidden. Far more men than women were successful in getting into the fast-stream civil service when I applied, and men heavily dominated the higher echelons of the civil service. When I asked the man heading up the panel that selected me what they were looking for, he said 'people like us' – the name of my first book – which he would never feel free to admit today because of much greater awareness of the value of diversity. But he was at least honest and, despite this, he let me through. A few years later, I was told by my Permanent Secretary that there was a ban on putting women forward for the role of Private Secretary to the Prime Minister because it was said that Margaret Thatcher would not accept women – but despite this he was going to nominate me. I only found out many years later that the new Principal Private Secretary, Andrew Turnbull, was unaware of the edict his predecessor had presumably put out, and having interviewed the field he chose me to put forward to the Prime Minister as the top candidate. She had turned down preferred candidates before but she decided to accept me, despite genuinely preferring the company of men in senior professional roles, I later concluded.

Margaret Thatcher may have been a social conservative who believed in the traditional family and wore pearls, but she was no 'trad wife'. She was our first female Prime Minister, and I was the first female Private Secretary at No. 10. It was a man's world, but we were in it, and it was tough. Like my grandmother, she was formidable and, although she didn't kill turkeys by hand, she didn't let men (or very much else) get in her way.

I ended up devoting an important part of my life to trying to get women a better deal in the workplace, which was not the direction I had originally intended. I wanted to change the world in general but found that the working world for women was part of what needed changing.

I was given no choice when I was posted to Head of Personnel in the Treasury (or what today we would call Head of Human Resources) after the birth of my first child. I was told by my boss, a man, that it was suitable for someone who needed to step back in order to look after their baby. I was angry about this, as I was interested in government policy, not HR, and felt the move might damage my career, where I was aiming for the very top of the civil service. Looking back, I am grateful I had that experience because it allowed me to do something about how HR policies affected women's careers, especially when they became mothers. It was part of a sequence of events that eventually led to me becoming CEO of the Equal Opportunities Commission, which of all of the things I did in public service was the role that I most loved.

I finally left the Treasury after the birth of my second child, departing from my job in General Expenditure Policy because I didn't quite fit and, as I found out when I was in HR, I was not alone. A group of senior women came to me and told me that they could not thrive or feel comfortable in the Treasury. Its culture of long hours was one aspect, which worked for men with wives at home but made it hard for women to combine a family and a career. Women felt that skills they thought important, like management and team building, were not valued in the Treasury. Bullying was one issue which, as I have said earlier, staff surveys confirmed after I left. A small thing, but to relax people at the beginning of meetings the talk was often about football, which at the time before women's football became a thing was very much male-dominated. Jobs were not advertised and people either had a tap on the shoulder or were posted, which given the feeling of a 'boy's club', made women feel excluded. Women also had to leave a job when they went on maternity leave and start a new one on their return, meaning that they sometimes had insufficient time in one job to prove themselves and get the track record of good performance required for promotion before starting another. And rather than returning to a familiar role they faced a steep learning curve in a new job when they might not be sleeping normally, as maternity leave then was only three months. Part-time and flexible working was rarely available, and certainly not for the best jobs most likely to secure you promotion.

While I was in charge of HR, I was able to make some changes to help other women – I ended the requirement to move jobs when going on maternity leave, extended flexitime to higher grades and made it a requirement to advertise all jobs and to offer part-time and flexible options. When I took up my new job after giving birth a second time I opted to work four days a week, but I soon discovered that this was a hollow victory, as the job description and culture remained the same. I found myself working six days a week and being paid for four instead of five. And I used to set my alarm in the middle of the night so that I could fit in an extra hour or two of work then. Once, on my day off, Friday, when I was looking after my baby daughter but still working on a deadline that had to be met that day, I had put her in front of a video but, when she started to cry, I sat her on my lap while I was typing. She slammed her hand down on the hard drive at the front of the laptop and it stopped working. Rather than giving up, I drove us to the Treasury and carried on working there instead, with her on my lap and me unpaid.

I remember going to a Cabinet Office lunch for senior women and hearing from many mothers who were there that they were becoming ill from the strain of it all. Later, when my daughter Victoria was a little older, my new boss Suma Chakrabarti, who was an enlightened man and a great manager, suggested something novel to me: work for five days a week but work from home on Fridays, fitting your hours around family responsibilities. It was a pattern that

I adopted for the rest of my career. It made it possible for me to take my children to school and pick them up on one day a week, and it allowed me to get to know their friends when they came round to play after school.

Now that Covid has changed cultural attitudes to working from home, this way of working has become more widespread and has made it much easier to combine parenthood with work. It has also brought wider benefits including making work more accessible for disabled people. However, homeworking is also experiencing a major backlash and was even made something of a culture war issue under the last government, with Jacob Rees-Mogg leaving notes on civil servants' desks saying, 'sorry you were out when I visited. I look forward to seeing you in the office very soon', signed off 'with every good wish'. At the same time, heavy-handed edicts were set by ministers to force their return.[54] Many studies suggest hybrid working is good for employees and improves retention and productivity, though some others show a drop in productivity.[55] I know of many private and voluntary sector employers who no longer have premises, saving greatly on overheads, and operate almost entirely remotely very effectively, while some City firms now require employees to attend full-time. Many workplaces now have hybrid working.

In my own work, operating remotely has been transformative, removing geographical barriers that had virtually excluded people not working in London and the south-east from attending most meetings, and making it possible to have far more meetings in the day, because travel time is no longer needed. Communication and connectivity have increased and improved greatly, and many find it is easier to focus on work without office distractions and noisy environments, though face-to-face meetings when they occur do add a huge amount of value, too. In recent years, I have been a regular commentator in the media, and most interviews are now undertaken remotely, as this saves hours of travel time and means they can be carried out wherever you are in the country. However, when I was invited by GB News to be interviewed by Jacob Rees-Mogg about the civil service, I was told this could only be done if I was prepared to travel to his home in Somerset, as he had installed his GB News studio there. A whole day of my time but a few minutes of his. I declined.

Another cultural revolution that has taken place over my lifetime is the growth of affordable, quality childcare, though there is still a long way to go. I am pleased to have also played a part in expanding the amount of childcare available, increasing the government subsidy and raising the quality through new childcare standards when I was at the Department for Education and Employment, and pushing for better childcare, including childcare wrapped around schools, while I was at the EOC.

Part of the revolution that has made it easier for mothers to work is fathers taking a more active role in childcare, though women still do far more than men, according to surveys. When our children reached secondary school, my husband retired early to write his novels, but it also allowed him to be there when they came home and share childcare at a different point in their lives, which they appreciated. And it also helped me. Back then, he was the only father among thirty-five mothers at a parents' coffee morning get-together, and our daughters told him that other girls were envious of them having a father at home.

Working women at that time often had to carry an extra psychological load. The pressure to be better than any man makes you work even harder – too hard, perhaps. It can also leave you isolated, as you eat your sandwich at your desk while you work and rush home at the end of the day to look after the children, while the men meet colleagues for lunch or for drinks after work and relax. They instinctively know that relationships and networks matter because they can help you get on and protect you if things go wrong. No wonder Nigel Lawson said of Margaret Thatcher that she was not 'clubbable', with no sense of shame given that men's clubs did not admit women at the time. No wonder, either, that she fell out with her two most senior ministers, Nigel Lawson and Geoffrey Howe, which led to their resignations and precipitated her fall.

There's a price to be paid by women like Thatcher – feelings of guilt, resentment and a 'why do I have to do it all' type of anger, which in her case would sometimes damage her relationships with her peers. 'Your paper is twaddle, complete and utter twaddle, and I don't know how you have the nerve to submit it', she once said to Geoffrey Howe, her Deputy Prime Minister. In response, he had a habit while she was exploding of opening his ministerial box and signing letters.[56] Much later, he wrote, 'She was an intellectual void that others had to fill.'[57]

Working harder than any man can get results, even if it is bad for work-life balance and sometimes for career prospects. It worked well for Thatcher for much of her career even if, at the end, it led to her tunnel vision. Hard work was not something that Boris Johnson as Prime Minister ever felt he needed, but he found his nemesis in Baroness Hale, who styled herself as a 'girly swot', a reference to a phrase used by Johnson about David Cameron because he reintroduced the September session of Parliament 'to show the public that MPs were earning their crust'.[58] This was the session during which Johnson decided to prorogue to drive Brexit through, action which the Supreme Court, led by Baroness Hale, decided was unlawful, forcing him to reverse his plans.

Baroness Hale, who became the first female Law Lord in 2003 and the first woman to head the Supreme Court in October 2017, knew a thing or two about getting on in a man's world. She told a girls' school association event in 2019, 'Let's hear it for the girly swots!', and added that her main advice to young women is: 'Don't let the bastards get you down.'[59]

These days, women in the workplace are a norm, not just in popular fiction but in reality. It's no longer a question of choice for most people but an economic necessity, as mortgages and rent cannot be paid without it. At the same time, a lot of the pressure seems to have been removed from the shoulders of women – to prove themselves, to demonstrate they can make it, to pretend that they are invulnerable – and there's less drive to reach the top. I've seen examples of a number of young women who have entered coveted professions and decided in the light of experience that that is not what they want from their lives. Work–life balance matters more to them than conventional success.

My own daughters are definitely not 'trad wives' – they are themselves, with their own careers. It's true that Victoria likes to bake in a traditional way – and she's good at it – but her partner Ayush does most of the cooking. Lizzie and Ryan tackle domestic challenges, and parenthood, together as a team. Advances such as these have been hard won, and they could be lost again if we become too complacent. There will always be a minority who disagree with such progress, and we should never take consensus for granted.

• • •

On Sunday 6 July 2003, I was digging in a ton of manure that had recently been delivered by a local farmer so that we could improve the sandy soil in our new garden in Suffolk. We were creating huge new flower beds, which over the following twenty years or so would lead to great joy and appreciation. It was very hard work and it seemed like it would take forever.

However, it suited my mood, because the organisation I was leading as a relatively new CEO, the Equal Opportunities Commission, had got itself into some deep shit, and it was my job to get us out of it. The EOC's sponsoring department were on my back, asking how the hell this had happened, and I was wondering if I was going to have to resign. It was a culture war, and I was in the middle of it.

'Official: inequality is natural.' This was the headline I had woken up to on the previous Sunday, about an EOC publication I had no idea was being released. It was a piece by Yvonne Roberts in *The Observer*, which said that our report, which was partly based on focus group research, showed that 'despite countless personal experiences of discrimination, women do not see it as a major issue. In comparison with their mothers, they believe they are doing well. They regard discrimination as a private problem with which they "put up and shut up".' Roberts claimed our report suggested 'the equality lobby often speaks an alien language. People find phrases such as "gender pay gap", "work/life balance" and "glass ceiling", too "woolly" and "abstract", and the concern of only a small minority of high-flying females.' She also repeated some Andrew Tate-like views which were expressed by some people in the focus groups. As one man from Glasgow put it, 'women discriminate against men now. Women fought for equal opportunities. They got them. But if you take your wife out at the weekend, she still won't buy a round of drinks.'[60]

On the following Tuesday, Zoe Williams had weighed in with her column in *The Guardian*, 'What Women Want'. She said that 'only last week, the Office for National Statistics found that six out of seven mothers would rather be at home, looking after the kids, than working'. She concluded that 'if the workplace is a disappointment, that's not a failure of feminism, it's a failure of capitalism'.[61]

Before we knew it, the story was everywhere, taking hold like a wildfire, with the broadcast media running light-hearted stories along the lines that feminism is dead and equality is done, according to the EOC.

Two days before these headlines, the celebrated if controversial feminist Germaine Greer had written an article entitled 'Equality is dead: Long live feminism' in *The Times*. 'What the EOC has chosen to put its name to is no more nor less than a suicide note, and probably not before time,' she wrote (referencing a political decision to set up a new body, the Equality and Human Rights Commission, or EHCR, incorporating the EOC and the other existing equality bodies on race and disability, along with some brand new responsibilities, which came into being four years later in 2007). Her main conclusion was that equality is the wrong goal and that 'women's liberation was as radical as equality feminism was conservative'. 'Equality feminism,' she explains, is in her view 'essentially conservative in that it seeks merely to induct women into existing masculinist structures, where success depends upon conformity', whereas woman's liberation sought 'a new world where women could blossom into full self-realisation, and exert new kinds of potency in protecting life against the forces of death'.[62]

Not too many ordinary women were reading this kind of stuff, of course, or would agree with it, but nobody in the EOC enjoyed this attack on what it was trying to achieve, and I certainly didn't. That morning, before I started shovelling the manure, I had read Joan Smith's piece in the *Independent on Sunday* entitled 'I'm a feminist so I must be dead', who weighed in with a slightly more grounded piece, which I had been speaking to our chair about before going out into the garden to clear my mind:

> Talk about being late with the news: feminism is finished, *The Guardian* announced last week, devoting a whole page to a new study which apparently shows that the fight for equality is an 'outmoded' concept. 'The term has been equated with hatred of men,' the paper revealed, shocking readers who live in caves in the Outer Hebrides and were unaware that feminism has not enjoyed a universally positive press.[63]

This was the whole point of the research: to find out what a range of people felt about equality so that we could connect to and address their concerns. Good idea, I thought, but these headlines were not making this at all clear.

The document in question, *Talking Equality*, was based on research which we had commissioned, but which had in fact been conducted by the Future Foundation, involving discussions with thirty-five people. To rub salt in the wound it was published on the seventy-fifth anniversary of women winning the vote. The reality shown by the research was that some people, including some women, had felt either that the battle for equality had gone too far or that it was not working for them. But a large-scale survey also confirmed a 'high level' of concern about sexism and discrimination in the workplace. Traditional divisions of roles were accepted as 'natural' in the home, but not at work. But that wasn't making the headlines or even being reported in the think pieces.

The phrase from the focus groups that was sticking in my mind, as I piled manure into my wheelbarrow and emptied it into trenches dug by my husband, was from a young woman who is quoted as saying 'every time I think of feminism, I just get this really awful feeling'. She feels sick. When you want to move forward, you need to start from an honest assessment of where things are, and the EOC's job was to promote equality between women and men, not feminism as such. The truth, which I knew very well from my work with Margaret Thatcher, was that there were still many, women included, who disliked the ideology of feminism because they felt it did not reflect their worldview. The numbers might be smaller now, but Andrew Tate is out there, fuelling the flames.

For social conservatives at the time of *Talking Equality*, feminism was often seen as man-hating, bra-burning and telling people how to live their lives. Thatcher never liked the idea of the Equal Opportunities Commission, nor the legislation it was set up to enforce: the Equal Pay Act 1970 and the Sex Discrimination Act 1975, which were put in place by a Labour government by that equally powerful woman, Barbara Castle. Thatcher's intense dislike of Elspeth Howe, Geoffrey Howe's wife, started when she agreed to become the deputy chair of the EOC, according to Charles Moore.[64] However, she left the EOC and the legislation in place when she became Prime Minister a few years later.

She believed that breaking through gender barriers was down to individual talent, determination and choice, and she wanted to be seen 'as a person, not as a woman leader'.[65] Nevertheless, I wrote a speech with her for the 300 Group, whose objective was to get more women into public life, in which she spoke from the heart about how few women there still were in Parliament, and her wish to see 'lots more'. She said she didn't want women to be 'granted special favours' but wanted 'to see more women in public life because this country will be better served if it draws fully on the rich talents of women as much as men.'[66] That last point – more women in work being good for the country – was the common ground which united ideological divides, and it was something on which we could build.

The key lesson we took from *Talking Equality* was that we needed to do more to break through the complacency and make the case for further action to achieve gender equality, bringing the public and business with us by demonstrating with evidence that discrimination negatively affected people's lives. I saw it as my job to reorientate the organisation towards doing just that, as I worked with the EOC and staff to create a new vision and plan for our work going forward.

Were we wrong to publish *Talking Equality*? Back in the office and away from my literal pile of shit in Suffolk, I undertook a review which concluded we should have thought more about what we were walking into and framed the publication accordingly, because the message that came over, despite our best intentions and the substance of the report, was: 'job done.' And in future, all publications were to be signed off by the CEO, i.e. by me, with a risk management strategy for communications. The government accepted this and we moved on with even greater energy and a new sense of direction for all the controversy we had generated. Plus, we knew what we were dealing with.

The EOC was blessed with brilliant, creative and knowledgeable policy, communications and legal teams, led by the extremely talented Amanda Ariss, Sarah Wootton and Alice Leonard respectively, and we had fantastic commissioners, chaired by the deeply committed Julie Mellor and later Jenny Watson, who were bent on modernising the EOC, like me. Up to that point, the different parts of the EOC had not worked particularly effectively together and there had been some tensions, but once we had a strong shared vision of what we were about, they did just that, working in groundbreaking ways as one team. Alongside the formal investigations we launched into the armed services and the Post Office, the Commission agreed that we could use our statutory general investigative powers to better understand the barriers that were contributing to the gender pay gap, raise awareness and make recommendations for addressing them. Some of these were largely hidden from sight, but remarkably prevalent.

We launched an investigation into discrimination against pregnant women and new mothers at work later that year. It turned out that the large number of legal cases we knew about were just the tip of the iceberg and we were stunned by the vast number of women revealed by our surveys who were being dismissed, demoted, denied training or promotion or bullied into quitting, just because of their pregnancy. Around 45 per cent of pregnant women reported experiencing some form of 'tangible discrimination' and we estimated that more than 30,000 women a year were being forced out of their jobs and left without work, and income, perhaps even access to benefits. Only a tiny proportion were seeking any advice or redress.

Awareness of the problem up until that point had been low, something we quickly rectified as we published our interim and final reports, which both attracted massive media interest. People were listening because we were chiming with their everyday experience. We also discovered that there was a consensus that pregnancy discrimination was wrong. 87 per cent of people in a poll of 1,000 adults carried out in January 2005 agreed that Britain needed to look after pregnant women at work because the economy needed them, but there was still a minority who did not agree…[67]

• • •

On the day we published our final report on pregnancy discrimination, I was sitting in the *Channel 4 News* studio being interviewed about the results. It was the end of a long day which had involved breakfast television, around fifty radio interviews, national and local, made from a specially hired recording studio, and now this – another tremendous opportunity to raise awareness of the problem and put forward our solutions.

I had been expecting a one-to-one interview, but as well as the interviewer I faced Sylvia Tidy-Harris, a larger-than-life figure – quite literally, as she was beamed up on a huge TV screen in front of me. Tidy-Harris was the founder and owner of The Speakers Agency, a small business employing three people in Leicestershire which acts on behalf of people seeking a platform. I already knew about her because she had gone on record saying that she would never employ a woman of child-bearing age.

'If someone who worked for me found she was pregnant and needed to have six months off, it would absolutely kill my business,' she said, before continuing,

> I would have to keep her job open and if I hired someone to cover the job, while she was on maternity leave, it would be impossible to find somebody else to be as enthusiastic and as committed because that person would know that at the end of the maternity leave period they were going to be booted out. It would be incredibly debilitating for my business.

I pointed out that it is unlawful to discriminate against women in this way, making the business case for employing and supporting pregnant women and new mothers because you won't get the best talent unless you do. I talked about our particular recommendations for better financial support for employers with fewer than ten people. The bottom line, I said, is that we all benefit from women having children and as a society we need to share the cost in a fair way. But Tidy-Harris was not a woman to change her mind lightly and I knew she wasn't going to budge an inch.

I felt pretty confident because we'd taken great care to ensure that employers were on our side, and in this – and indeed all our other formal investigations into the causes of the pay gap – we had brought in employers of all shapes and sizes to advise on the design and development of our research and conclusions, through an external advisory board. The advisory board in this case was chaired by Fiona Cannon, one of the EOC commissioners, who was then the Head of Equality and Diversity at Lloyds TSB, and it included a representative of the Federation of Small Businesses.

Sylvia Tidy-Harris's views about not employing women of child-bearing age were also publicly shared by Godfrey Bloom, a UKIP Member of the European Parliament, who gained even further notoriety when he said that a woman's role was to clean behind the fridge.[68] Back in 2013, Nigel Farage actually suspended Bloom from UKIP for similar remarks. When women at a UKIP conference event said they had never cleaned behind their fridges, Bloom responded that 'this place is full of sluts', then tried to explain this away by saying it was a joke (as if that made it any better). It was said Farage suspended him because these remarks had overshadowed his conference speech.[69]

Godfrey Bloom's comments are not so different from Andrew Tate's widely quoted and far more recent remarks that women should 'have kids, sit at home, be quiet and make coffee'. As the Overton window of what is acceptable continues to shift, we may see a resurgence of what we would now call 'trad wife' and 'toxic masculinity' views on the right, just as anti-migrant, racist and Islamophobic views are now being openly expressed by some politicians.

Back in 2005, although some dissenting voices remained, the EOC was winning the culture wars debate around women by pointing to the facts and demonstrating the social and business costs, and indeed the sheer injustice, of what was going on.

• • •

Across a range of issues, we were able to demonstrate that Britain then was stuck in a 1950s 'trad wife' model of employment, which ran against the grain of what people needed as society moved on. For example, many women were forced to take up lower-paid, low-skilled part-time jobs after having children, as shown by another of our formal investigations, 'Britain's Brain Drain', which we published a few months after the pregnancy report in 2005. At that time, opportunities for flexible working were restricted to relatively few, often senior, people, while the majority of the workforce lacked flexibility. We worked closely with employers during the investigation and demonstrated that the best of them had already found that offering flexible working not only benefitted employees but also employers, for example by leading to reduced absenteeism and increased productivity, as well as the economy as a whole.[70] Because of outdated stereotypes about 'women's' and 'men's' work, women were also often stuck in lower-paid roles and faced barriers to work in higher-paid, male-dominated areas, while employers experienced skill shortages that were damaging the economy, another of our investigations revealed. We also sought to remove the penalty of a lower pension for women who took time out for caring responsibilities by building a new coalition of interests to progress our case.

At the same time, through our annual 'Sex and Power: Who Runs Britain?' publication, we demonstrated the snail's pace of progress towards women gaining equal power in politics, the boardroom and within the judiciary.

In doing so, we laid the groundwork for subsequent changes, which include stronger protection against discrimination for pregnant women, better maternity and paternity rights and the right to ask for flexible working – all of which have been progressively strengthened under successive administrations – as well as better childcare and equal pensions. We won the intellectual battle, as our polling of opinion-formers at the time revealed.

However, abuse still exists to this day. The charity Pregnant Then Screwed, which is chaired by Sam Smethers, a key person in the EOC back then, said on its website in 2025,

> Every year, 54,000 women lose their job simply for being pregnant, while 390,000 working mothers face negative or discriminatory treatment at work. These figures have almost doubled in a decade – the situation for mothers is getting worse, not better. Yet fewer than one per cent take legal action, with limited access to justice leaving discrimination unchallenged.

And a significant pay gap still exists, though it has fallen slowly but significantly over time.[71]

We thought that the creation of the Equality and Human Rights Commission would make it possible to better reflect the lived reality of people's lives, and we championed the idea, even though it put us out of business. Women, and indeed men, have multiple identities – based on race, faith, sexual orientation, disability, age and caring status – and gender runs through all of them. People often experience multiple forms of discrimination. It made no sense to put people in just one box: human rights would provide a way of balancing competing rights where they came into conflict, we thought.

Despite this, I think there has been a loss of focus on the issues for women, and the same may be true of other groups, probably not helped by a considerable reduction in the resources available to work on these issues, despite promises at the time that this would not happen. What's more, the gender issue that seems to have absorbed the EHRC in recent years has led to a perceived conflict between women's and transgender rights, despite the law already providing for the exclusion of transgender women from safe spaces for women. The issue certainly cannot be ignored, especially given the landmark Supreme Court ruling in 2025 on the meaning of gender in equalities legislation, the implications of which are wide-ranging and, depending on how it is finally applied, potentially in conflict with the legal and human rights of transgender people. But has the EHRC, and indeed the rest of society, lost sight of the main plot? So many longstanding, widespread and deep-rooted challenges to the safety and equality of women remain to be resolved.

Achieving equality and resolving injustices is a long game, and you can never afford to take your eye off the ball.

• • •

If you listen to certain politicians and influencers, it seems we are at war over issues which often have limited impact on most people's lives, while a real war is waging in Europe. Despite the fact Russia is the aggressor, the US seems to think Putin's nation is a better cultural bedfellow than democratic countries in Europe.

Bad government is about driving wedges, playing on fears and breaking rather than mending things. It often goes with another aspect of poor government: campaigning rather than governing. Pointing the finger at others so that they don't look at your own faults, playing on people's fears of people who are different and their fear of change, so that they see you as their saviour. Spreading hate, not compassion and mutual respect.

Culture wars can catch fire relatively quickly, but good government takes time. It means listening to those affected, understanding the problem, explaining why change is necessary and bringing people with you. Good government involves solving real problems that people can see are damaging and even ruining lives, identifying and resolving any conflicts, but also laying a firm line in the sand about specific rights and putting in the hard graft to change ingrained institutional cultures that stand in the way, as we saw with peace negotiations in Northern Ireland. This kind of government seeks consensus but doesn't shy away from conflict. It brings people together and ensures that everyone has an equal opportunity to thrive.

This is government responding positively to people experiencing injustice, recognising the lived reality of their lives and facilitating lasting cultural change that the rest of society can accept. If politicians, tech bros and social influencers are embarking on these wars, beware. It's the facts that matter, not opinions, prejudice or vested interests.

Yet truth itself is now under attack, whether it's the issue of climate change or how our society as a whole is portrayed, and facts are being inverted to suggest that the rights that help us live together peacefully are a cause of injustice and conflict, not the answer to them. Our very strength – our diversity – is being presented as a threat. And 'woke', which once meant being alert to discrimination, has now become a dirty word.

Governments need to stand firm in defence of rights and root out injustices when they see them, and so do we. Complacency is our enemy, not other people.

But what if politicians aren't listening to the problems people are facing? This is explored in the next chapter.

Chapter 7

BROKEN BRITAIN?

'So with respect and humility, I invite you all to join this government of service in the mission of national renewal.'

SIR KEIR STARMER ON THE STEPS OF NO. 10

***Bad government**: talking up what's wrong while never fixing things; putting financial interests above those of the people; demonising civil society.*

***Good government**: joining forces with others to address shared challenges and listening to those who are least heard.*

Is Britain broken? Many people, especially those on the right, will tell you so. It strikes a chord, just like the Brexit slogan 'Take Back Control', because we can all see plenty of examples to fit that narrative. It may win votes but fixing what's broken is much harder to do when you get into government. So many other things seem more important.

Take David Cameron, for example, who repeatedly told us that Britain is broken when he was in opposition. Once in power, however, he decimated public services and social infrastructure through his policy of austerity, which reduced growth. Then, to try to heal divisions in his own party, he called a referendum on Brexit which tore the country and families apart and further damaged the economy and living standards. Before he became Prime Minister, Cameron had promised to fix 'Broken Britain' by giving more power to people, fundamentally changing how government works through his 'Big Society' initiative. He also committed to tackling the 'far too cosy relationship between politics, government and money' that he said eroded trust.[1] Once in power, after some half-hearted attempts, he eventually lost interest in both. But that doesn't mean they were the wrong goals.

Now Keir Starmer is also seeking to work with 'civil society' – including people and communities, charities, other not-for-profits, community groups and social enterprises – to achieve his 'decade of renewal'. This isn't surprising, as so much of what governments seek to do can only be achieved by mobilising social forces beyond their direct control. But will it work this time?

Since 2011, I've been seeking to strengthen government's connection to civil society to deliver better services, stronger communities, a fairer society and a healthier democracy, and to ensure that everyone's voice is heard. I've seen many positive examples of this across the country, but no systemic change in central government as yet. Ultimately, if governments are going to fix the things that are broken, or stop them from breaking in the first place, they have to put people, not financial interests or politics, first.

Unfortunately, I've been observing an entirely contrary trend, where governments start to see charities, campaigners and even ordinary people as blockers, getting in the way of what they want to do or slowing them down. And all the while, Cameron's 'secret corporate lobbying' persists and trust seeps away.

It's Jekyll and Hyde government. But which side will win?

• • •

On 14 June 2017, I woke up to the horror of Grenfell Tower. First, I heard it on the radio, then I turned on the TV, staring in disbelief and terror at television footage of a block of flats in Kensington engulfed in fire, a fire that continued to rage throughout the day and was only fully extinguished the next morning. I saw pictures of exhausted firefighters collapsing outside the tower, as efforts to bring people out down a single staircase continued and the death toll slowly began to rise, and heart-rending stories of those who escaped began to emerge.

Like that of the Gomes family, Marcio and Andreia and their two daughters, twelve-year-old Luana and ten-year-old Megan, who lived on the twenty-first floor. Or their neighbours, Helen Gebremeskel and her twelve-year-old daughter Lulya, who came to the Gomes flat to wake them up in the early hours of the morning and then stayed with them, huddled together in fear, following instructions from the fire brigade to stay put and wait to be fetched, while other people who had already escaped frantically called them and urged them to leave. An hour and a half went by in an increasingly smoke-filled flat, and they lay on the floor to stop themselves from breathing it in, until, at about 3.30 a.m., Marcio's and Andreia's bedroom caught fire, the empty Moses basket in the corner going up in flames, and they decided that they had no choice but to leave. Marcio tied wet tea towels on all their faces and wrapped wet sheets around them, and they opened the door.

The staircase was pitch black and filled with smoke, and they found themselves treading on others who had died or were dying as they descended. 'We were just going, just going and going, because if we don't keep going, we're going to die,' Helen later told reporters.

Helen, Andreia and Megan, who were at the front, managed to reach safety. But Marcio turned back to try and find Luana and Lulya as soon as he realised that they were no longer behind him. The girls had been overcome by smoke at about the tenth floor and, when he called out, his daughter finally responded and said she couldn't go on. Then a light held by two firefighters appeared and, because of their breathing apparatus, they were able to carry both the girls down to safety.

All three children and Andreia Gomes were put into induced comas and treated for cyanide poisoning, but they survived. Andreia was seven months pregnant and their son-to-be, Logan, was stillborn in hospital.[2]

Seventy-two people died and most of those who survived lost everything except the clothes on their backs. During the course of the day, local residents, charities and businesses quickly sprang into action to give immediate aid to those who fled. There was an angry protest at the local council for their lack of responsiveness.

Theresa May visited the site the following day but only met with firefighters – for reasons of security, it was said. The initial response to the disaster was 'not good enough', May later admitted, adding, 'I include myself in that.' She went on to say,

> What I did not do on that first visit was meet the residents and survivors who had escaped the blaze. But the residents of Grenfell Tower needed to know that those in power recognised and understood their despair. And I will always regret that by not meeting them that day, it seemed as though I didn't care.

People say harsh things about Theresa May, unsurprisingly given her role as Home Secretary during the Windrush scandal, but at least she was prepared to admit her mistakes. She had promised to tackle the 'burning injustices' of society on the steps of No. 10, and after she left office she wrote a book called *The Abuse of Power*,[3] which lists Grenfell Tower as one example of such abuse. Her heart was in it, even if in government her head generally was not.

On the day May resigned as Prime Minister, she listed initiating the Grenfell Tower inquiry as one of her achievements. The inquiry took seven years, and when its final report was published in 2024 it concluded that the disaster 'was the culmination of decades of failure by central government and other bodies in positions of responsibility in the construction industry'. Recommendations that could have stopped the fire had been made, but were shelved, it pointed out, following two earlier cladding fires in high-rise buildings in 1992 and 1999.

The needs of business were put above the lives of those people the government claimed to serve. Deregulation policy so 'dominated' thinking in government that 'even matters affecting the safety of life were ignored, delayed or disregarded', the inquiry concluded.[4] David Cameron's New Year's resolution in 2012 was to 'kill off the health and safety culture for good',[5] and two years later he promised the Federation of Small Businesses that one hundred standards and building regulations would face the bonfire.[6] Cameron denied that deregulation played a role in the disaster, but the conclusion of the final report was that the stripping back of building regulations and other documents had had a material impact on how construction firms approached fire safety.[7] The Grenfell Next of Kin group responded to Cameron's denial by saying 'There was a bonfire, Mr Cameron, and the ashes of that bonfire were returned to us...'[8]

The report found that the Building Research Establishment (BRE)'s testing process, which should have spotted the flammability of the cladding, was flawed and subject to manipulation by 'unscrupulous' manufacturers, with senior BRE staff accused of 'unprofessional behaviour' in advising their customers on the best way to pass their tests and secure compliance with regulations. The BRE had apparently been captured by financial interests after it was privatised in 1997 by John Major's government. There 'was systematic dishonesty' by the manufacturers of the highly combustible material used in Grenfell Tower construction, with information on the safety of the cladding falsified, the inquiry said. Yet none have faced prosecution to date.

At the same time, the voices of the residents of Grenfell, who had repeatedly raised well-evidenced concerns about the safety of the building, were ignored by the Tenant Management Organisation set up by Kensington and Chelsea Council to run their building, which failed in its fundamental duty to keep them safe.

The inquiry may have taken seven years, but it was recognised well before then that the cladding was dangerous, and residents in high-rise buildings with similar material were notified and advised to take remedial action, with no solution in sight for getting the situation rectified except a government loan to help them with the costs. They were left in limbo for years, unable to sell their flats, often having to employ night managers to monitor the risk of fires while they slept. Finally, in 2022, five years after the fire, Michael Gove got property developers to agree that they would meet the cost, but progress was still glacial. Angela Rayner promised to hurry things up shortly after the 2024 Grenfell report was published, and launched her 'Remediation Acceleration Plan', but it will not be until 2029 that all such flats will be safe, assuming that deadline is met. That's twelve years of living in fear for your life for many people.

There's a wider pattern here. People have not been listened to, both before and after injustices occur; recommendations from previous disasters have been ignored; there have been endless delays and much prevarication in taking remedial action; and many fingers have been pointed but few if any bodies held accountable. The charge list includes the Hillsborough disaster and the infected blood, Windrush, Post Office and NHS maternity care scandals, but there are too many to mention here. Sometimes those who suffer at the hands of others are initially blamed for the injustices or disasters that are inflicted on them, as in the case of Hillsborough and the Post Office. In many cases, the burden of seeking justice falls to the victims, not the state, and the state works against them. Achieving justice often takes decades, by which time many of those affected have died and some have committed suicide.

The victims pay a heavy price, while those who are responsible mostly go scot-free. In France, by contrast, a former Prime Minister faced a trial for involuntary manslaughter over the country's infected blood scandal, and though he was acquitted, his health minister was found guilty in 1999, and the head of the national blood service was jailed for four years. But not here. Twenty-five years after France made that conviction, the UK finally agreed a compensation scheme for victims of infected blood.

Amber Rudd did resign over the Windrush scandal even though it was her boss, Theresa May, who set it in train, but she is the exception that proves the rule.

To the great credit of Keir Starmer's government, a so-called Hillsborough Law is in the works, which places a new 'duty of candour' on public bodies and officials to tell the truth and cooperate with investigations. It's shocking that such a thing should be needed, but the police lied about the cause of the Hillsborough disaster, which saw ninety-six people crushed to death in 1989 during an FA Cup semi-final. Officials said that Liverpool fans had broken into the stadium, when in fact the doors had been opened at the command of the senior police officer in charge, David Duckenfield, to ease crowding outside. In evidence to the Hillsborough inquiry, over one hundred statements given by junior police officers were amended, before being submitted, to remove or alter comments unfavourable to South Yorkshire Police.[9] After the Manchester Arena terrorist attack, a public inquiry also found that MI5 had not given an 'accurate picture' of the key intelligence it held on the suicide bomber but it was only after concerns that individual security services personnel might be exempt, and after many months of deliberation, that the government finally signalled that the Bill was likely to be partially amended to take them into account, though whether this will satisfy campaigners is far from clear.[10]

It is also to the credit of the previous government that an independent victim advocate is now responsible for ensuring victims of large incidents know their rights, get access to support and are represented in inquiries and inquests, and the advocate will regularly report to Parliament on their findings.[11] All bereaved families will also have access to non-means-tested legal aid at all inquests where the state is involved. The imbalance of power between wronged individuals and the state will hopefully be reduced as a result.

But the question remains – why aren't ministers quicker to sort things out when disasters occur? The high cost of compensation may be one reason why ministers and institutions do not want to accept blame, which is often the starting point for setting things right. The constant change in ministers, which has worsened in recent years, may make it more difficult for them to get to the bottom of things. It is relatively easy to announce inquiries knowing that you won't be around to pick up the recommendations, and when these finally do report, hands are wrung but the news headlines quickly move on, and memories are short.

Fixing broken things is not as good for your career as announcing new things, and if you accept responsibility for government failure then your career is often over. Only those affected will notice if you drag your feet, and the numbers are tiny compared to the electorate who ultimately decide your future.

Perhaps the biggest reason is that governments are institutionally bad at listening to people at the sharp end of their policies, as opposed to the vested interests that often fund their political parties, the think tanks that are sometimes funded by dark money and the lobbyists who often use contacts to get their attention. This is what some people call a democratic deficit: listening to the people with power and influence, but not to you.

• • •

The truth is, the government knows this. That's why David Cameron shortly before becoming Prime Minister promised not just the Big Society but also to 'clean up politics' and tackle what you might loosely call corruption in government, 'secret corporate lobbying' and (this has been quoted before but bears repeating) the 'far too cosy relationship between politics, government, business and money'.[12] It's why Keir Starmer on entering No. 10 said that rebuilding trust is 'the battle that defines our political era' and also introduced reforms on taking power.[13]

'We all know how it works', Cameron said back then. 'The lunches, the hospitality, the quiet word in your ear, the ex-ministers and ex-advisers for hire, helping big business find the right way to get its way.' He added, 'I believe that secret corporate lobbying, like the expenses scandal, goes to the heart of why people are so fed up with politics. It arouses people's worst fears and suspicions about how our political system works.' Cameron vowed to introduce 'vigorous, wide-ranging reform' to increase transparency and restore public trust in political institutions.[14]

The result was the coalition government's so-called Lobbying Act of 2014,[15] which was widely criticised at the time, and indeed since, for being too narrow in scope, with one estimate by the Association of Professional Political Consultants suggesting that only one per cent of lobbying is regulated by the law. Only professional lobbyists have to register and only meetings with ministers and Permanent Secretaries have to be recorded. Most lobbying is undertaken by in-house lobbyists and individuals, however, and meetings with civil servants are excluded entirely from records.[16]

Just two years after leaving office, David Cameron himself joined a company called Greensill Capital as an 'adviser' and lobbyist and acquired stock options that could have been worth tens of millions of pounds. The founder of Greensill Capital, Lex Greensill, had worked as an unpaid adviser in No. 10 while Cameron was there, and a later Cabinet Office investigation concluded that this job enabled him to 'promote a product which did not, in fact, provide material benefits to government, although it could have been of benefit to his incipient business and was of immediate benefit to his former employer, Citibank'.[17] Greensill Capital provided loans to tide companies over while they paid debts due, whereas the public sector does not rely on creditors for its cash flow and can generally pay on time, if it wishes.

While benefitting from Greensill's business, Cameron sent sixty-two texts to his former colleagues who were still ministers, pleading with them to help the controversial bank through Covid support schemes, including nine WhatsApp messages to the then Chancellor Rishi Sunak and twelve texts to the then Permanent Secretary of the Treasury, signing his messages with a 'Love DC' or a thumbs up emoji.[18] Greensill Capital was unsuccessful in gaining direct Covid support for itself, but it did gain government accreditation to make government loans to others, the vast majority of which it made to Sanjeev Gupta's steel empire GFG Alliance. In May 2021, the Serious Fraud Office opened an investigation into GFG over suspected fraudulent trading and money laundering, including its financing arrangements with Lex Greensill's company.

It later transpired that Greensill Capital was in financial difficulties while Cameron was pestering his former ministers to help it, though he denied knowledge of this at that time. Eventually it went into administration, leaving the taxpayer potentially liable for the loans it made to GFG of up to £355 million.[19] A Treasury Select Committee report in 2021 heavily criticised David Cameron's 'significant lack of judgment' and added salt to the wound when it said that he had not broken any rules, but the rules (which Cameron had made) should have been tighter.[20]

This was bad enough but, in early 2026, a bombshell dropped that was so significant it put Keir Starmer's entire premiership in jeopardy. The Epstein files had already revealed that Lord Mandelson, whom Starmer had appointed as Ambassador to the US in 2024, remained close to the disgraced billionaire paedophile Jeffrey Epstein, even after his conviction. When this came out in the autumn of 2025, he was sacked. But, as more files were released, it emerged that Mandelson, when he was Secretary of State for Trade and Industry under Gordon Brown, had sent highly confidential and market sensitive information to Epstein just after the financial crash of 2008, after personally receiving money from him. Epstein and his close associates might well have benefitted financially, and the leaks could even have put the stability of the pound at risk, at a time of unprecedented peril for the economy of the country. Mandelson even counselled the head of J.P. Morgan, via Epstein, to threaten the Chancellor in order to reverse government policy on bank bonuses, which the banker duly did. At the time of writing, Mandelson is under a criminal investigation for misconduct in public office, at the same time as Andrew Mountbatten-Windsor, who allegedly also passed trade secrets to Epstein when he was a trade envoy.

This seemed to show how easily rich and powerful men can worm their way in and corrupt people in politics, at the same time as demonstrating how easy it apparently was to ignore the plight of the girls and women Epstein had abused. Lord Mandelson was not just any man but the person often credited for New Labour's success, who had helped bring Starmer to power and had been giving his team confidential advice once in office. Starmer was blamed for appointing him as Ambassador despite evidence showing he could not be trusted (Mandelson's nickname, the Prince of Darkness, is telling). The Prime Minister was aware that he had maintained a relationship with Epstein after his conviction, though he said that Mandelson had lied about the closeness of that friendship. Starmer also knew when he appointed Mandelson that he was forced in his past to resign twice as Secretary of State over incidents connected to rich and powerful men. How could someone committed to restoring trust in politics take this kind of risk?

Starmer managed to avoid a leadership challenge, despite considerable pressure, apologising and forcing his Chief of Staff to resign instead, as well as promising to release key documents and clean up politics. His Chief Secretary in a statement to Parliament committed to pick up or at least consider some of the suggestions made by Gordon Brown during the crisis to strengthen safeguards. These included a ban on Members of the House of Lords being paid as lobbyists, parliamentary hearings into top appointments, stronger powers for the anti-corruption commissioner and no longer allowing MPs to hold second jobs except where this is necessary to maintain professional qualifications.[21] Starmer's Ethics and Integrity Commission – which among other things could enforce penalties for the first time for politicians ignoring business appointment rules – had not gone far enough, Brown argued, and needed to have statutory powers of investigation. What emerges from this remains to be seen but the Ethics and Integrity Commission was formally asked to carry out a review of 'lobbying, disclosure and access to government' in March 2026, and to report in May.[22]

It's a pattern we've seen again and again: companies and rich individuals using former ministers, MPs and even government ministers to lobby behind the scenes for them, for example with the Michelle Mone scandal and the fast-track Covid contracts which relied on who you knew, not how good your products were. There are also powerful lobbies who prevent regulation if they can.

And now we have Donald Trump, who is allegedly benefitting financially from his political decisions, with Forbes estimating in September 2025 that in his current presidency he had already boosted his personal wealth by $3 billion.[23] The 'tech bros' are supporting the President, with reports that this is largely because of his deregulatory stance toward cryptocurrency and AI. A different but related example: by the beginning of 2026 Nigel Farage had earned £1.6 million on top of his MP's salary from fifteen 'second jobs' since being elected as an MP in July 2024, including £415,000 for being an ambassador to gold traders Direct Bullion and £180,00 from video messaging on the site Cameo, something which is entirely above board under current rules.

Donations are another area of weak regulation which have the potential to buy influence, and some of them are huge. The Tories took £20 million from Frank Hester via his company The Phoenix Partnership (TPP), including £5 million just before the 2024 election. The donation was accepted only a few weeks after it emerged that Hester had made inappropriate comments about Diane Abbott, then the shadow Home Secretary, saying she made 'you want to hate all black women' and 'she should be shot'.[24]

Hester denied any connection between his donations and the £135 million TPP had already received from the Department of Health and Social Care for supplying computer systems to the NHS. However, TPP had recently announced that it had 'a suite of AI solutions about to launch, focused on the NHS's key clinical and operations priorities'.[25] Hester boasted to *The Telegraph* that 'I've had some quite long conversations with Rishi [Sunak] about AI and it's not just that he understands it, we were talking about different algorithms'.[26] According to parliamentary records, he also gifted Prime Minster Sunak the use of a helicopter for a political visit in November 2023, valued at £15,900.[27]

Sometimes even relatively small donations have the potential to generate controversy, if not influence. Remember those suits and glasses, worth more than £16,000, provided to Keir Starmer during the 2024 general election by Lord Alli, who gained a temporary Downing Street pass when Starmer came to power despite having no formal role?[28]

Do political donations change parties' policies? It's difficult to prove, but recent examples are telling. The Tories received £50,000 in January 2025 from Neil Record, the chair of Net Zero Watch, the campaign arm of the UK's foremost climate science denial group, the Global Warming Policy Foundation. Two months later Kemi

Badenoch announced that the Conservatives would no longer be advocating for the UK to achieve net zero emissions by 2050, the goal set by Theresa May and enshrined by her in legislation, saying that we are 'bankrupting ourselves' in the pursuit of that target.[29] On a bigger scale, Reform, a strong advocate for fossil fuel investment and against net zero policies, has reportedly received as much as £24 million from oil and gas interests since it was formed, including over £20 million from Thai-based Christopher Harborne, who owns a firm, AML Global, which sells jet fuel, which is made from crude oil.[30] This figure excludes the £5 million donation given directly by Harborne to Nigel Farage before he became an MP which Farage has said was given for his personal security.[31]

Who can forget the rumoured donation to Reform UK of $100 million by Elon Musk, only for Musk to let it be known that he didn't think Farage was up to the job. The incident provoked much debate about the need to cap large donations and stop loopholes in foreign donations as well. Following calls from the Electoral Commission, the government is now committed to tightening loopholes that still make it possible for foreign donations to be made, but it has no plans to cap donations. There are also no new controls planned on donations made through cryptocurrency, which makes the source hard to trace. Reform UK is the first party to declare that it will accept such donations. The party also received a £9 million donation in 2025 from Harborne, who is also a leading cryptocurrency investor, but this donation at least was given in conventional currency.[32]

Meanwhile, the kind of deregulation we saw before the Grenfell Tower disaster is gathering pace. Keir Starmer pledged in March 2025 to cut regulatory costs for business by 25 per cent, referring to regulators as 'a cottage industry of checkers and blockers slowing down delivery for working people'.[33] The government is also embarking on another cycle of deregulation in other areas, for example in the City and with regard to planning regulations, including nuclear power. It is also committing to low regulation of AI, all in the name of growth, but to whose benefit and at what cost?

Because we don't have proper control of lobbying or full transparency, at least as yet, we're unlikely to find out about the commercial influencing, if any, that has happened behind the scenes. What we do know from the example of Peter Mandelson is that integrity cannot, under current rules, be taken for granted. It took the Epstein scandal and the unprecedented bulk release of confidential correspondence to identify his wrongdoing, which otherwise would have been hidden. If it wasn't for that drop of emails, government might never have had to justify why someone who had kept in touch with Epstein after his conviction was a suitable candidate to be our Ambassador to the US.

And, as the daily business of government grinds on, the voices of those who had been abused by Epstein, alongside all those other survivors or potential victims of disasters and scandals, seem rarely to be taken account of when the big decisions that affect them are made. But maybe all this is finally changing?

• • •

On 17 October 2024, I was standing in a crowded room in No. 10, full of leaders from civil society. In some ways the scene was very familiar to me. Back in my day in No. 10, all those years ago, one of my jobs as a Private Secretary was to stand by the side of the Prime Minister during these receptions, listening in to conversations and making sure that anything that was agreed was recorded and, where necessary, followed up. I don't ever remember a room quite so packed or the noise so loud; guests who would normally be milling throughout the reception rooms talking to each other were now congregating almost entirely in the Pillared Room where a podium had been set up. Clearly everyone was expecting Keir Starmer to speak. No one wanted to miss a word, because this was so exceptional for most of them, given how cold relations became under the last government.

When he started speaking, the Prime Minister didn't disappoint.

> To fix the foundations of our country we need a fundamental reset of the relationship between government and civil society. That is why we're building a new partnership with the sector to tackle the complex social and economic challenges we face as a country. By harnessing the dynamism, innovation and trusted reach of civil society organisations, we can boost growth and deliver better outcomes for communities right across the country.[34]

The occasion was the launch of a consultation on the principles for a new Civil Society Covenant which will underpin these commitments, including a partnership between government and civil society and respect for the latter's independence.

Lisa Nandy, the Secretary of State for Culture, Media and Sport, who was leading on the new Covenant, was equally welcoming in her remarks, and afterwards I gave her a hug. She is no stranger to working with government from within civil society. We worked together when we were both in the charity sector trying to secure more humane arrangements for asylum seekers, particularly children, through the Home Office. We also met again when she was shadow Civil Society Minister to discuss the challenges the sector was facing. She knows what she's talking about, and is determined to make this work, I'm absolutely sure.

But the question in my mind, as it probably was in others, is, 'Will it be different this time?'

Before the Big Society, Tony Blair signed a national Compact between civil society and government, which had similar goals and even stronger foundations, as it took forward the recommendations of the Independent Commission on the Future of the Voluntary Sector, led by Professor Nicholas Deakin, which reported before New Labour came into power. Successive administrations signed up to the Compact, including David Cameron's. Gordon Brown, when he became Prime Minister, also promised 'civic renewal', publishing a White Paper in 2008 entitled 'Communities in control: real people, real power'. Yet somehow the ship of state kept sailing on the same course, at best dragging civil society after it on a tow rope, rather than inviting it on board, and sometimes the rope was cut.

The stakes were even higher when David Cameron launched the Big Society early on in his coalition government, largely because it received far more fanfare and publicity than we are seeing today – the media hadn't even been invited to Starmer's event and the only coverage of his words appeared in the civil society press. But Cameron's promises were very similar – to 'turn government completely on its head' and work with charities, community groups and others, because, as he put it, 'If we want real change for the long-term, we need people to come together and work together – because we're all in this together.'[35] By 2011, he said the Big Society was all about a 'social recovery to mend the broken society' which included 'broken families' and communities breaking down, high levels of crime and gang membership, 'people stuck on welfare, unable to work' and a 'sense that some of our public services don't work for us'.[36]

• • •

In 2011, not long after Cameron first promised his Big Society (the timing wasn't entirely coincidental), I set up a think tank, Civil Exchange, a not-for-profit organisation with the aim of strengthening the connection between society and government, and it is where I work to this day.

I'd seen government from both ends – working at the very top of government in No. 10 and in the Treasury and then at the receiving end, in the years leading up to the formation of Civil Exchange, when I was the Chief Executive of the charity Refugee and Migrant Justice (RMJ), providing legal advice for immigrants and asylum seekers going through the asylum application process, which was funded by legal aid. I'd also seen it from the middle of central government, working in the Department for Education and Employment (DfEE – as it was then) and as the Chief Executive of an arms-length body, the Equal Opportunities Commission. It was clear to me that a better appreciation of how processes and policies work in practice – or don't – would make government much more efficient and effective and help it not just fix problems but stop them happening in the first place.

I knew this was possible because I had seen effective partnership with the voluntary sector first-hand when I was Joint Head of Early Years and Childcare at the DfEE. We worked closely together to design quality standards for childcare and nursery education and exponentially increase the amount offered across the country. The partnership was also local, with Early Years and Childcare Partnerships bringing local authorities and voluntary and private sector providers of childcare together to make it happen on the ground.

My decision to set up Civil Exchange was partly spurred by the events that forced the charity I had been leading, RMJ, to close. This had been caused by a change of funding by the government, which had decided to make payments for legal aid cases in arrears instead of as cases went along. We specialised in complex cases, which often took a year or more to resolve due to the slowness and inefficiency of the asylum process, and this left us with a multi-million-pound cash flow problem. We'd been given assurances from the shadow minister that he would fix the funding issue for us and others just before the general election which, as we had expected, brought the coalition into power, but he was then appointed to a different role, our hopes were dashed and we were forced into administration.

Our experience of government had not been all bad. RMJ had piloted a different way of working on asylum cases with the UK Border Agency in Solihull, which was designed to shorten the time it took to get a final decision. These cases were taking much longer than necessary because the Home Office was making too many poor initial decisions that were later overturned on appeal. The Solihull pilot suggested that if more of these could be got right first time it would be better for asylum seekers and much cheaper for government. I joined forces with other asylum charities to argue successfully for a much wider pilot of the same approach, and I was personally involved in the subsequent Early Legal Advice Project as a member of a joint national working group with the Home Office, until RMJ closed. The project did demonstrate that this way of working was beneficial for complex cases but failed to show it reduced costs in every case.[37] I was told privately after RMJ had closed that this was largely because of a lack of expert asylum lawyers to take part in the pilot after RMJ had gone. We were the largest provider by far of asylum advice, our lawyers were the acknowledged experts in this area, and we trained most of the specialist immigration lawyers across the country. The following year, the largest provider of both immigration and asylum legal advice, the Immigration Advisory Service, also collapsed. Fast forward to now, and the issue persists: nearly half of initial asylum decisions were overturned on appeal in 2024, there is now a huge appeals backlog, during which asylum seekers are unable to work and so are supported by the state at considerable cost,[38] and part of the problem, experts suggest, is an increasing lack of access to legal support.[39]

By design, I set up Civil Exchange as an unconventional think tank. I called it a 'link tank' because I thought that there was already a lot of knowledge in civil society about what worked, but a lack of connection within it and between civil society and government in all its forms, which made such knowledge difficult to convey. As well as linking up individuals and organisations, sometimes through new networks like A Better Way (of which more later), Civil Exchange also works in partnership with others, bringing in external expertise and people as needed for different projects, so that the sum can be greater than the parts. In addition to building connection, it makes recommendations to tackle the barriers that stand in the way.

Civil Exchange has worked to show that a better kind of government is possible, ideally one in which the public, voluntary sector and indeed private sectors build and share a common vision of the changes needed, and work together to achieve this, as we had done when I was at the DfEE working on childcare. My experience is that civil society is often undervalued by government and seen as the poor relation of business. But civil society has qualities and knowledge that are vital to government. It knows from working with people at the sharp end what works and what doesn't, its reach into society goes far deeper than government can achieve and it has the trust of individuals which public bodies rarely have. Civil society organisations also give voice to the needs and stories of their communities which may otherwise not be heard, and they build connection and capacity that help people to thrive and communities to come together.

Getting the attention of government can be a challenge for such bodies, partly because of the difficulty of speaking with one voice when the sector is so heterogenous, and also because of lack of time and resource. Many are run on a shoestring, struggling to survive from day-to-day. Connections between business and government, in contrast, are generally strong, partly for the reasons given earlier and also because they have more resources for lobbying, which means that, as was the case with Grenfell Tower, the voices of business and vested interests are more often heard and taken on board than the voices of people who are most directly affected when something goes wrong.

Back in 2011 when Civil Exchange was founded, the Big Society seemed like a priceless opportunity to correct this democratic deficit and strengthen the connection between civil society and government, because the will in government seemed to be there.

• • •

I suspect for David Cameron the Big Society was a largely theoretical concept, based on a conservative view that value is generated between individuals as locally as possible and that the state is too large and should get out of the way. When Margaret Thatcher told *Woman's Own* that there was 'no such thing as society' she went on to qualify this by saying that 'the quality of our lives will depend upon how much each of us is prepared to take responsibility for ourselves and each of us prepared to turn round and help by our own efforts those who are unfortunate'.[40] One thinks of wealthy wives carrying a basket of supplies to a struggling family in the village, before the welfare state was invented.

The reality of modern charity is very different, and much of it is highly organised, but almost all of it does come down to passionately caring about other people. My mother, who was a struggling lone parent of five children herself, supported charitable causes despite being extremely short of money and time for her own family, and used to collect money for charities as a volunteer. I used to cower in embarrassment behind her as a very young child as she rang doorbells in our local town to collect donations for Christian Aid, but people on the whole were polite and generous.

In her fifties my mother worked as an area organiser for the charity Help the Aged (which later merged into a new charity, Age UK), which provided support to older people at home and abroad. She and her manager, Vi Courtenay, organised Help the Aged's charity shops in Dorset and the south-west, and my mother used to collect and then sort donations of second-hand clothes in our small bungalow, often asking me to help, then driving round Dorset and delivering them to their different stores, as well as sending off suitable clothing and money to elderly people in need in other countries. My older sister Diana and I managed one of those Help the Aged shops in Lymington as volunteers over the summer holidays one year, while she was an art student and I was at school, and we also visited an old people's home in Greece while we were on a backpacking holiday. We saw with our own eyes how much these donations were appreciated by the residents there, and we took back photos to my mother and Vi of their smiling faces upon receiving the things Help the Aged had sent them. In their retirement, my mother and

Vi went to Africa once to visit projects their efforts had helped fund, and it brought them great joy.

Even after they retired, and into very old age, my mother and Vi, who ended up living together, used to crochet blankets for people in need abroad and raised money for good causes through boot sales and stalls at local events. They lived on very little but always helped others, and as they grew frail a charity that provided home care workers, which they had supported for many years themselves, helped care for them. The carers often did that little extra thing, especially for Vi after my mother had died and she was all alone, and the carers were always lovely women, worth far more than they were paid.

The state, however, was less caring. As the adopted only child of a working-class family, and a Salvation Army officer in her prime, Vi was immensely self-reliant for most of her life and extremely well-organised. She had nursed her parents in old age, as well as my mother and a mutual friend who lived with them for a time, Jess, until they both died and she was left alone. But eventually she became so frail she asked to go into a council care home and she was entitled to a free place by statute, as she did not have the means to pay for it herself. With failing sight and hearing, she needed more support but also wanted the company, as she could no longer listen to the radio or watch TV to stay connected. I used to ring her regularly from London but it got to the point where she struggled to hear me. Most of all, she told them she didn't want to die alone.

The answer from her council in Dorset was no. Due to lack of funds caused by austerity cuts, they could only accommodate people who were a danger to themselves or others. At the age of ninety-nine, shortly before her hundredth birthday, Vi was found dead on the floor of the bathroom of her tiny flat. She had fallen over in the night, had pressed the alarm on her wrist to get help, but no one had come in time to save her life or hold her hand as she died.

I once met a hedge fund manager who told me that the trouble with politics is that politicians are not paid enough, and so were of poor quality. Only a salary of a million pounds a year or more would attract people of the right calibre, he said. And yet it is my experience that people working in the charitable sector, or volunteering for it, are often of the highest quality, and are driven by passion and love, not status or money. It is also the case that surveys consistently show that poorer people give a higher proportion of their income to charity than richer people. The best people who work in politics are often those who know what they are talking about when it comes to the problems they are trying to fix, either through first-hand experience or through listening with empathy to people who have first-hand experience themselves.

The lesson I took from my mother and Vi is that helping other people through charity is immensely important, and generates great value, but so are adequately funded public services, which should treat people with the same love, care and respect that we would expect from the very best charities and from families and friends.

• • •

On 13 July 2017, a month after the Grenfell Tower fire, I was sitting around a table on a warm summer evening listening to a small group of civil society leaders talking about the tragedy and why it happened, and what needed to change. We came together through A Better Way, a leadership network I co-founded the previous year with Steve Wyler, who had been the CEO of the charity Locality, which represents local community organisations, and we were the co-convenors. Many of our founding members were round the table. We didn't yet know the full picture about the causes of the fire, but one thing was clear: the residents, who were articulate and well informed and had been raising concerns about the building for years, were not heard.

A Better Way had ultimately come out of an overnight gathering at St George's House in Windsor Castle in early 2013, where the civil society organisation Community Service Volunteers (CSV, now known as Volunteering Matters) had brought together civil society leaders and thinkers to discuss the role of civil society in a time of austerity. As one of the participants, I gave a presentation about the Big Society and why it wasn't working. A number of people attending, including me, thought it worth continuing a conversation about the potential for a new, positive narrative for the future focused on the common good. What we had in mind was an alternative to the Big Society, originating from civil society, based on its direct experience of what was possible and how to achieve it, with a hopeful narrative at a time when austerity was causing so much pessimism and destruction.

CSV's Chief Executive at the time, Lucy de Groot, chaired the discussions, and we subsequently worked together on 'A Call to Action for the Common Good'. From this foundation Steve and I decided to set up A Better Way, starting with a small group of people within civil society: Kathy Evans, then the Chief Executive of Children England which represented children's charities; Professor Mark Gamsu, from Leeds Beckett University; Danny Kruger, then leading a charity working with young offenders; James Perry, founder of the ethical business COOK, and promoter of B Corp; David Robinson, the founder of Community Links and the Relationship Project which is encouraging public and other sectors to build relationships into the heart of their services; Sue Tibballs, then Chief Executive of the Sheila McKechnie Foundation, which supports campaigners and promotes campaigning; Karin Woodley, the Chief Executive of Cambridge House, a London-based charity which tackles poverty and promotes social justice; and, joining a little later, Polly Neate, then the Chief Executive of Shelter, and Cate Newnes-Smith, the chief executive of the charity Surrey Youth Focus representing youth charities there.

Together, we drew up an initial list of founding principles, which were later refined in discussion with the growing network and then published. They run like a thread through this book: prevention is better than cure; principles are better than targets; collaboration is better than competition; mass participation is better than centralisation; building on strengths is better than focusing on weaknesses; local is better than national; and relationships are better than transactions. We also thought changing ourselves is better than demanding change from others. You learn through doing.

These reflect what they and grassroots and national leaders were telling us worked from their direct experience of trying to improve services, strengthen communities and build a fairer society, across many different challenges and in different places and contexts. In subsequent discussions over a number of years with all the different people in our network, which by then straddled both the public and voluntary sectors as well as some businesspeople, we identified four behaviours that people who were successful in bringing about this change found were essential to success: putting relationships first as a society and in services and organisations, because people cannot thrive without good relationships; sharing and building power, because power is held in too few hands and we have more power than we think to change things for the better; listening to each other, particularly those least heard, because that's how to find out what works and what doesn't; and joining forces with others, because most problems are too complex to solve alone.

As we talked about Grenfell Tower on that evening in 2017, many of those principles and behaviours were evident. David Robinson told us about how a similar tragedy had been averted in the past. The charity he co-founded, Community Links, in Newham, East London, had heard from local residents about the problems they were experiencing in Ronan Point, one of nine identical tower blocks. They could smell cooking in other flats, despite the fact that they were supposed to be sealed off from each other to stop fire spreading. This was the same Ronan Point which in 1968 experienced a partial collapse that killed four people, and which had since been refurbished. Community Links wanted to help, and so joined forces and forged strong relationships between the residents of these tower blocks and a campaigning architect, Sam Webb, and his students, as well as with journalists. Together they shared and built their collective power and used this to get their concerns heard and acted upon.

Getting the council to hear them and act was a real struggle. David's wife, Frances Clarke, who was also working at Community Links at that time, had written about this in *The Guardian* directly after the Grenfell Tower disaster. 'Ranks were closed,' she wrote,

> and many suggested that one problem was the prevalence then, in the municipal and construction worlds, of freemasonry. Ronan Point itself stood on the Freemasons Estate. Whatever the motive, nothing was made easy. When the tenants' campaign organised its early meetings, council staff delivered leaflets pretending the

> meetings had been cancelled. When Newham's chair of housing authorised the emptying of Ronan Point, his recommendation was blocked by a legal challenge pursued by his own housing director, and referred to the borough's full housing committee.

However, the result of their collective efforts was that the residents were relocated and the tower blocks were demolished, very probably saving many lives.[41]

Hearing about this account from David, that evening, we concluded that the stories that are told after disasters really matter. The Ronan Point story was a positive one about how new alliances – in this case a charity working with local people and others who can amplify their voice – can make a world of difference. But wouldn't it be so much better if the public sector could be encouraged to listen much earlier? We hoped that the heart-rending stories of individuals from Grenfell Tower that were being aired in the media would help shift the dial.

Our network started small in 2016 but by 2025 had grown to 1,500 members, from across both the voluntary and private sectors and including national and grassroots leaders. Our conversations continued, sharing insights to help members in their own work and to spread to others in the network, including our principles and behaviours, and using their example to demonstrate to others that positive change is possible. Together, we've been making the collective case that fundamental change is needed if these are to become the norm.

We found much to be proud of in our society, our communities, our services and institutions and heard about brilliant work, sometimes led by forward-thinking councils like Camden, Gateshead and Newham, and sometimes spearheaded by charities like Grapevine in Coventry and Warwick, and Cambridge House in London. We've heard about new ways of engaging the public in setting priorities for their communities and deciding how resources were allocated, including through citizen's juries and participatory budgeting. We've seen how services are being transformed by basing them on good relationships, trust and genuine communication and how people coming together can create change in their own lives and bridge divisions in their communities. Collaborative leadership across sectors, listening to the people they serve, can be transformative for services and communities. In Chapter 5, I have written about one example of the work in Gateshead where the council brought different agencies together, including the local Citizens Advice Bureau, to solve problems much earlier for those unable to pay their council tax bills.

As a network we agreed our ultimate vision of how things could be better, which we call 'A Bigger We', in which 'everyone can enjoy a good life, where everyone is heard and believed in, given a fair opportunity to thrive, and the ability to influence the things that matter to them; where every community comes together, looks out for each other, respects difference, and enables everyone to belong; and society as a whole values and invests in everyone and in every community.'[42]

This is a long way from how things are now, certainly, but not a million miles from what is already happening in some organisations, communities and places across the country, at their very best.

On that evening in the summer of 2017, when we were talking about Grenfell Tower, we reflected on the many acts of kindness after the Grenfell Tower disaster by local people, rich and poor, across different faiths and backgrounds, and by charities and businesses, who spontaneously came together in solidarity to support and comfort the victims, demonstrating the power of community when there's a shared cause. An example of the 'Bigger We' in action, we would say today.

However, government, both national and local, can struggle to rise to these occasions, as happened immediately after the fire. The hidden wiring of government – what we in A Better Way call the 'operating model' – works against collaboration with others, as discussed in earlier chapters, and the Big Society experiment demonstrated this all too well.

• • •

The Big Society failed, certainly in its grand ambitions, partly because austerity resulted in more and more being offloaded from the state to civil society, sometimes by government contracts but also by the expectation that society would just pick up the pieces when the state withdrew. But it also foundered because the state didn't change the way it worked, as I painfully documented in Civil Exchange's three annual 'Big Society Audits'.[43]

Some valuable things were done, for example more devolution and community ownership of local assets, but Cameron's original promise to 'reimagine' government turned out to be hollow. Cameron said he would end top-down, over-centralised government, but that didn't stop him from announcing national initiatives at the expense of what was already there. For example, money was found for the new, flagship National Citizenship Service, which offered three- to four-week programmes once a year for some fifteen- to seventeen-year-olds, while resources were taken away from established youth clubs which offered services and connection to far more young people, right across the year. By 2018 more than 600 of them had closed.[44]

Cameron promised to open up public services to new ways of doing things through innovative contracts with civil society. But big contracts with large private sector providers were still favoured, for example in the Work Programme, and charities ended up as their subcontractors with little or no freedom to do things their own way. Increasingly charities and similar organisations were seen as just another arm of the state.

The aim had been to allow civil society the agency to create value in a way the state could not do, and for there to be a partnership with government that would give a voice to those least heard. However, the operating model of government, as mentioned earlier, is based on the belief that you generate value through markets and competition, rather than collaboration, and ensure value for money and results by setting targets in contracts, through what I have called megaphone government (see Chapter 5), rather than agreeing principles and shared outcomes. It all began to look like co-option, not partnership. And buzz words like 'co-creation' were commonly used to cover cursory consultation, rather than genuine engagement on equal terms.

The impact of this kind of lip service and co-option can even be seen with the Grenfell disaster. As my colleague on the Early Action Task Force, Professor Anne Power, pointed out to me, the very concept of Tenant Management Organisations had been subverted by the council. These organisations had originally been established by local residents to self-manage their own blocks of flats, giving power to those people, but only the title and not the reality was being practised here, with this TMO being wholly owned by the council and used to ignore residents, rather than give them control.[45]

• • •

Fast forward to July 2025. I was at a summit at the National History Museum, where the new Civil Society Covenant was being launched by Keir Starmer, Lisa Nandy and an impressive collection of other Cabinet ministers. I was pretty invested in this occasion as I was a signatory to this Covenant, as a member of the Civil Society Advisory Group which, as the government put it, co-created it with them. That was hard work on both sides, but the words on the pages which finally emerged are all the better for it.

The Prime Minister promised a fresh start from a past over which Cameron and others had presided. 'We're not going to shut charities out and then expect you to pick up the pieces,' he said, 'nor am I interested in slogans that sound good but end up being gimmicks for governments to simply hide behind. I'm interested in solutions.' And it certainly sounded like a fundamental shift away from the control-freakery of government in the past. 'Not the hierarchical, top-down approach of the state working on its own,' said Starmer. 'Not the transactional approach of the markets left to their own devices. But a way forward in partnership – together – by giving civil society a home at the heart of government.'[46] This was all backed up by warm words from Lisa Nandy, Wes Streeting, Bridget Phillipson and Darren Jones, among others, many sharing platforms with people from the sector who were already partners in some of the work they were doing. And underpinning all this was the Covenant, with its strong commitments to respecting and upholding the sector's independence and to partnership working. It was impressive.

There's very good reason for the government to want this change. They know that voluntary and social enterprise organisations reach places they can't, and a partnership has the potential to unlock much greater social good than they can achieve alone. Government can build and run hospitals, albeit sometimes with the help of the private sector, but to deliver good health it needs everyone in society to do their part, not just medical professionals. And that's the same across most of society's challenges. Some local authorities and devolved administrations and authorities are already starting to work in this way, and Integrated Care Partnerships, as mentioned in Chapter 5, are a definite step in this direction (notwithstanding the fact that their budgets have recently been halved by the government).

Somewhere in the mix, I suspect, is a very real wish to rebuild that sense of trust and connection that politicians have increasingly lost.

This was certainly what I'd thought about the Big Society. When I was writing about it back in 2012, around two in ten people trusted governments to put the country above their party, compared to around four in ten under Thatcher in 1986.[47] Bad enough, but by 2024 only around one person in ten trusted governments to put the country's interests first 'just about always' or 'most of the time'; and nearly 80 per cent of people in the same survey said the system of governing Britain could be improved 'quite a lot' or 'a great deal'.[48] Party before country.

Politicians have lost some of that deep connection with communities which they had when there was mass party membership. Over 2 million people were members of the three main political parties in the 1970s, but there were only half a million in 2012.[49] In contrast, membership of the three main nature charities stood at 5 million at that time. Despite some ups and downs, this is not much better now. Labour had 370,450 members at the time of the 2024 general election and the Lib Dems 86,599. The Conservatives have stopped publishing the figures, presumably because they are so low.[50] Reform UK, on 16 January 2026, had just over 270,000, according to its website, but is still building its local party structure, and membership of the Greens is beginning to grow.

With that loss of connection, it's easier to step on political landmines, like the cuts to Winter Fuel Payments and to disability benefits put forward by Keir Starmer's government in its early days, which had to be reversed after a revolt from its MPs. If they had built up the trusted relationships that would have allowed them to discuss these proposals in confidence with the charities and campaign groups that knew a lot more about the consequences in the real world, they might have announced workable reforms that could have stuck, even if they would not reflect everything that those groups would have wished.

At the launch of the Civil Society Covenant, I was hoping that government would open hitherto closed doors, surrender some of its power and start to define problems and create policies together with civil society, building trust and mutual learning and genuinely unlocking the potential of the Covenant. In the process, I hoped they would reset the relationship that went so badly wrong under the previous government, despite the positive commitments that government had made to civil society.

The Starmer government has since set up a new Civil Society Council to help them deliver the Covenant, which it says will be driving the transformation in government we hope to see. I will be watching closely to see if that vision will actually be achieved. It's going to be an enormous challenge to change the way government works, and a challenge for civil society too, especially when it comes to finding sufficient resources to engage and being prepared to have an 'insider' role without losing independence.

And I can't get out of my mind how previous governments ended up treating the social sector like a contractor, or even an enemy, after solemnly declaring it to be a partner. The memory of what happened then is still vivid in my mind, and I see some seeds of it now.

• • •

Let's go back in time to see what this Jekyll and Hyde approach to charities and other civil society organisations looks like.

In June 2014, we were listening to Chris Mould, the Chair of the Trussell Trust, the charity that operates foodbanks, telling us about how the Trust had been criticised by ministers and even threatened for raising legitimate policy issues in relation to food poverty. He was giving evidence to the Panel on the Independence of the Voluntary Sector, which had been set up by charitable trust the Baring Foundation, to advise on growing threats to the sector from the government that once championed the Big Society.

To be fair, the decline in the relationship was part of a longer-term trend. As successive governments contracted out parts of the welfare state to the social sector, they started to see it as a contractual arm of the state, interchangeable with the private sector. To be seen but not heard.

Things had definitely got much worse. Earlier in 2014, Chris Grayling, then the Justice Secretary, had told an audience of charity leaders that he strongly disagreed with the campaigning role of charities.[51] They could alleviate poverty but not seek to end it, it appeared. The message seemed to be 'shut up', some might say.

Chris Mould was telling us about the more-than-frosty reception his charity had received from Iain Duncan Smith, the Secretary of State for Work and Pensions, who in 2004 had set up the think tank the Centre for Social Justice in order to find solutions to deep-rooted poverty and social breakdown by working with civil society. You'd expect him to have wanted to talk to the Trussell Trust about what they were seeing when they handed out food parcels. But once Duncan Smith was in government, he no longer wanted any advice.

Mould had requested a meeting with him to discuss evidence they were picking up that welfare reforms were contributing to people being unable to feed themselves. Universal credit, Duncan Smith's flagship reform, which replaced a number of individual benefits, was then being rolled out and there was a minimum six-week delay in the first payment, leading to financial hardship along with a host of other problems.

Duncan Smith responded to him in a letter leaked to the press, dismissing his claims and attacking the charity for publicity-seeking. He criticised the 'political messaging of your organisation', which 'despite claiming to be nonpartisan' had 'repeatedly sought to link the growth in your network to welfare reform'. He asked the Trust to 'stop scaremongering in this way', adding, 'I understand that a feature of your business model must require you to continuously achieve publicity, but I'm concerned that you are now seeking to do this by making your political opposition to welfare reform overtly clear.'

And there was more hostility aimed at the charity, we heard, including angry conversations with ministerial aides accompanied by threats. The members of the Independence Panel were listening, and they were well qualified to understand the gravity of the situation. Sir Roger Singleton, its Chair, was a former Chief Executive of Barnardo's, and was now chairing two bodies in the children's sector. At his right hand was Professor Nicholas Deakin, the man behind the Compact, as mentioned earlier, which the government was still signed up to. He knew this sort of thing should not be happening. Beside him was Sir Bert Massie, the man who had policed the Compact as the former Commissioner on the Compact Commission, until it was abolished. Andrew Hind, a former regulator of the sector as Chief Executive of the Charity Commission, was listening intently. Julia Unwin, then Chief Executive of the Joseph Rowntree Foundation, was there too, along with Louise Whitfield, an expert in public law and judicial review, Joanna Holmes from Locality and the Barton Hill Settlement in Bristol; and Nick Wilkie from Save the Children. Supporting the panel was David Cutler, the Director of the Baring Foundation, a great expert on the relationship between government and the sector, who had also been on the Compact Commission, serving with Bert Massie. (And then there was me, furiously scribbling down everything that was said. I was the head of the panel's secretariat, the main person advising on the challenges and writing the reports.)

These were big hitters in civil society – they knew their stuff, and they were shocked.

Later that day, we also heard from Women's Aid, which brings together charities working with women who experience domestic abuse and sexual violence. They were telling us about how they were being prevented from speaking out about any problems women were experiencing in the services they were delivering because of 'gagging clauses' in the contracts they had with government. It was resulting in self-censorship stemming from a fear of withdrawal of vital funding and active threats by some local authorities to do just that. We knew from other testimony and research that 'gagging clauses' were being used more widely and that self-censorship had been happening across the sector, not just in women's services.

We also heard about the negative impact of the Lobbying Act 2014, which, as I mentioned earlier, had proved ineffective in tackling what Cameron had called 'secret corporate lobbying', but seemed instead to be having a much greater impact on the ability of the charitable sector to continue to campaign for policy changes in the run-up to elections. This was something which a later report by the Tory peer Lord Hodgson said should be regarded simply as their normal business – not party political lobbying at all – and should be left to charity law alone to regulate.[52] The Lobbying Act imposed new restrictions and bureaucratic burdens on charities and other not-for-profits, requiring them to register twelve months before a general election if they might potentially exceed a low limit of spending on 'political lobbying' during that time (and this is a rule applied retrospectively to whenever elections might eventually be called). Fearful of additional bureaucracy and fines, we heard that the law had a chilling effect on them advocating for changes in policy or law in the run-up to elections. Fast forward to the present day and, despite some subsequent softening of its provisions in statutory guidance, this has persisted, surveys suggest.[53]

The panel also knew that many government consultations were breaking the minimum period requirements of the Compact, while the ability to challenge the government through judicial reviews was also being curtailed. We observed then a trend that continued to worsen over subsequent years. I was involved in producing five annual reviews of the independence of the sector for the panel, starting in 2012 and, after the panel had been disbanded, my think tank Civil Exchange produced a final report in 2017,[54] with the support of both the Baring and the Lankelly Chase Foundations.

By 2016, under Cameron's second administration, the promise of working together through the Big Society had been long forgotten and a contrary argument, driven by the right-wing think tank the Institute of Economic Affairs (IEA), had taken hold that government was simply funding charities to lobby for more government intervention and so should not be funded to work with government at all. The then Cabinet minister, Matt Hancock, introduced new 'anti-advocacy' restrictions on the use of government grants to civil society organisations, which were later softened, but nonetheless the principle being put forward by the IEA seemed to stick in people's minds: civil society and government should not be working together.

As part of my professional work, I have continued to watch this space very closely and to seek to repair the damage, with ongoing support from the Baring Foundation in recent years. Increasingly I observed under the last government that our 'civic space' – in which individuals and civil society organisations help shape the policies, services, laws, and cultural norms that affect everyone's lives – has become increasingly constrained and hostile, most notably through a series of restrictions to the rights to peaceful protest, as documented by a report published by the Sheila McKechnie Foundation and Civil Exchange in 2023.[55]

That report also found that opportunities were decreasing for civil society to engage positively with government to ensure good laws and policies, with a failure to publish and consult on draft bills and the abuse of regulation-making powers (sometimes called Henry VIII clauses) to make and amend legislation with almost no parliamentary scrutiny. Indeed, the previous government tried to use these regulation-making powers to curtail peaceful protest rights by redefining 'serious disruption' in the Public Order Act 2023 as 'more than minor', even though a successful House of Lords amendment had ruled out 'more than minor' as the Bill went through Parliament. However, the High Court, and later the Appeal Court (in a case continued by the incoming Labour government), ruled that the use of regulations in this case was unlawful.[56]

Another problem the report listed was the increasing politicisation of public appointments. The potentially compromising nature of this became clear when the then chair of the BBC, Richard Sharp, was forced to resign in 2023 because, while his application for the job was being considered, it emerged that he was trying to facilitate financial support for the then Prime Minister Boris Johnson via Johnson's distant cousin.[57] He was also a Conservative Party donor. The good news is that after concerns had been aired about the role of Sir Robbie Gibb as a BBC board member, the Labour government announced that it was considering making all BBC board appointments independent of government.[58]

Even the integrity of elections had come into question. The Elections Act 2022 gave the Secretary of State the right to direct the Electoral Commission, until then an entirely independent body, a clear conflict of interest given that it has an enforcement role against political parties. Again, the Labour government has signalled it will overturn this. The introduction of Voter ID for elections by the Tories was also described by the former Tory minister Jacob Rees-Mogg as 'gerrymandering', which he added had not worked.[59]

Culture war attacks on institutions that are central to our democracy have also continued to grow, with some politicians, including ministers under the last government, portraying judges, lawyers, charities, campaigners and parts of the media as a block to democracy rather than key components of it, and there have been sustained attacks on the National Trust, the RSPCA and, more recently, the RNLI and migrant charities. Since we wrote that report in 2023, culture wars have been waging even more fiercely, as the last chapter discussed, and some refugee charities are having to close doors or create safe rooms for fear of attack.[60] Who would have thought when the Big Society was launched that it would end like this. Jekyll and Hyde, indeed.

There are a few signs emerging of a similar negativity toward the sector from the Labour government now, despite the Covenant's promise of partnership and respect for civil society's independence. The government sometimes portrays campaigners as one of the blockers: the people who advocate for bats thereby increasing the costs of infrastructure projects; the protesters whose rights need to be restricted so that national infrastructure can be protected and people can go about their daily lives unrestricted; and the people who slow government down and generally get in the way.

In this worldview, these are people who, as Starmer's former Director of Political Strategy Paul Ovenden wrote in January 2026, contribute to the 'Stakeholder State': a 'complex coalition of campaign groups, regulators, litigators, trade bodies and well-networked organisations' who are holding government back from delivering its goals and bogging it down. 'Consultations and reviews are the sacred texts of the Stakeholder State,' Ovenden wrote.[61] It's beginning to sound a bit like the resurgence of Liz Truss's tirades against the 'Blob', the 'anti-growth coalition' and the 'deep state'.

Flip the coin over and you see the people in Grenfell Tower whose warnings were ignored and who were seen as troublemakers getting in the way of what the council wanted to do. Or the victims of the Windrush scandal, whom no one thought to consult before they pressed on with an unworkable policy that would end up ruining their lives, or the victims of the infected blood scandal who were pushed aside year after year while the business of government ground on.

And as Trump's second term has shown, this has the potential to get even worse. We already saw signs of it in Johnson's administration, with his attempts to sidetrack Parliament and his cavalier attitude towards parliamentary scrutiny. In mature democracies there are insufficient protections against those who refuse to play by the rules. Project 2025, which was drawn up by Trump's supporters before his election as a plan for seizing more power and derailing checks and balances, is now being emulated by Reform UK who, according to press reports, are planning their own Project 2029 to dismantle protections in the state. These reports suggest such efforts include directly appointing judges and sidestepping Parliament through Orders in Council, wherever possible, and repealing human rights and equalities legislation and international treaties.[62]

And here the Jekyll and Hyde story of politicians' attitude toward civil society can be seen clearly in one man: Danny Kruger. Kruger is now in charge of Reform UK's Project 2029, but was formerly one of the men behind Cameron's Big Society when he was in opposition, before he became a founding member of A Better Way when he was leading a charity. When he later became a Conservative MP, he worked for Boris Johnson in No. 10 as his Political Secretary, when he told me that he was an admirer of Dominic Cummings's approach. Kruger went on to found the Social Covenant Unit with Miriam Cates MP, in which he argued that the real 'enemy' of Brexit was not the EU but 'the British Establishment' and that 'the great threat to liberty is elite estrangement, the supercilious disdain for patriotism by leading public servants, academics, and the lobbyists who gain airtime in our public debates'. And so, he concludes, 'if we are to defend liberty, we need to be more robust in insisting on the implicit deal that is the basis of their privileges', saying that the government, as 'the principal funder of civil society', would be 'right to nudge elite culture in a more popular and patriotic direction'.[63] So much for the independence of civil servants, academics and so-called 'lobbyists' (meaning charities and campaigners). Kruger remains positive about the power of community within neighbourhoods but it looks like he has become increasingly wary of civil society otherwise.

A similar story can be seen with Steve Hilton, David Cameron's one-time adviser, who is often regarded as the architect of the Big Society. Hilton has become increasingly authoritarian in his views. He moved to the US, presents on Fox News and is a supporter of Donald Trump, standing as a MAGA Republican candidate for governor of California.

• • •

So is Britain broken? There are plenty of things not working well in this country. As the Better Way network puts it,

> We live in an 'us and them' society, where other people are seen as the problem. Deep-seated inequalities and injustices continue but are swept under the carpet. Too many people and places are ignored and left behind … When people need help in their lives, services and systems too often let them down. From food poverty to climate change, we address things only when they're in crisis.[64]

You, like me, will have your own long list of examples. I think of my dear friend Vi, who cared for so many others over her long life but ended up dying alone at the age of ninety-nine for want of a free place in a care home to which she was entitled by law. Or the many children in care who have been placed in illegal and unregistered accommodation, often far from the people and places they know, half of them under fifteen, many with complex needs and a third of them subject to deprivation of liberty court orders which means they are locked up.[65] And the much-loved streams and rivers of my childhood, many of which I discovered on a recent holiday in Dorset are now polluted and devoid of life. Beside them, most of the wildflowers I remember have gone. And when there are institutional failures – like Hillsborough or the Post Office – it's a scandal that institutions often seek to protect themselves rather than sorting them out. The needs, and sometimes safety, of individuals too often come last, as we saw with Grenfell.

However, there are also public services that are working well or have been fixed, like the Passport Office, which for a period experienced long delays in issuing passports but now is doing so very quickly again. We often take for granted our confidence in the independence of institutions like the judiciary, a confidence that derives from the relative lack of corruption in our country, as well as the separation of powers, especially compared to some other democracies. And then there are the many charities and community groups that people treasure and support, and the neighbours who look out for each other in good times and in bad, like the Gomes and Gebremeskel families on the twenty-first floor of Grenfell Tower, who saved each other's lives. Despite all the hate that politicians and far-right activists are spreading, many people in this country are tolerant, compassionate and kind.

It's not Britain that is broken but how our government, led by politicians, works. There are so many resources in society, in government and across the wider public sector that could be deployed to tackle the challenges that face us, if there is a will to do so. That means bringing people together to understand the problems and listening to people at the sharp end to find out what will work and what won't, which is what the Starmer government promised to do. It also means putting in the hard work over years to put all this into action, rather than moving on to the next initiative.

It also means accepting and strengthening accountability and correcting the imbalance of power that leaves families facing disaster with an impossibly uphill struggle to get justice. The Hillsborough Law and new Victims Advocate are a step in the right direction, but what about politicians? What we're seeing from politicians from previous administrations is a failure to take responsibility and be accountable, or to sort these things out. Take Robert Jenrick, a former housing and immigration minister, who when he defected from the Tories in 2026 said that Britain was broken and that the Tories had broken it, pointing the finger at everyone to avoid having the finger pointed at himself. In this kind of politics, everyone is the enemy, except yourself and the people you are asking to vote for you.

And there is still the suspicion, as David Cameron admitted and then later demonstrated after he left government and Peter Mandelson's behaviour in office showed, that the people who have the ear of government are lobbyists with financial interests, rather than those like charities who try to represent the needs of those with little or no power and influence. More needs to be done to sort this out, too, with much tighter controls on that kind of lobbying – along the lines of that proposed by Gordon Brown in response to the Mandelson scandal – and caps on the amount of political donations, along with fewer restrictions on charities, in the Lobbying Act and elsewhere, to campaign and advocate.

We seem to be on a negative spiral, as trust in government falls ever lower. Governments that are high on rhetoric but low on delivery lose more of it. As trust goes through the floor, politicians ratchet up that rhetoric in ever more dramatic terms to get the voter's attention, because many of those voters have switched off as they feel that they have no influence. The harsher the rhetoric about 'broken Britain', the easier it is for them to justify authoritarianism. We've increasingly seen the demonisation of the forces in society that actually hold government to account and constrain its power, from lawyers and judges, NGOs and campaigners, to the BBC and even the civil service. If those politicians who are ratcheting up things even further get into government, expect them to take more power and ramp up action against those they deem to be 'enemies of the people'.

Right-wing populist politicians increasingly portray themselves as the superheroes of their own dramas – Trump being the prime example – pretending that they have all the answers when they certainly don't, always announcing initiatives while never fixing things, and saying that smashing things down, particularly checks on their own power, is the way to make space for new things to grow.

It's through creativity and solidarity, not fear and division, that Britain's resourcefulness and energy will be unlocked and government will be transformed to work better for its people.

Chapter 8

HOW GOVERNMENT ENDS

'I wasn't the best version of myself as PM.'

RISHI SUNAK, 2025

It's 22 May 2024 and Prime Minister Rishi Sunak is stood at a podium outside No. 10, where he's announcing a surprise general election. As he speaks, it begins to rain heavily, at first drenching his shoulders and then running down his suit. The song 'Things Can Only Get Better' can be heard from beyond the gates, played by the anti-Brexit protester Steve Bray, a song that was also playing when Tony Blair first entered Downing Street as Prime Minister. Sunak ignores what is going on and reads out his prepared script like an actor. I find it hard to focus on what he is saying as I wait for him to at least acknowledge the rain. Some quip would make him seem more human and self-aware. But he has a plan, and he isn't deviating from it.

Funnily enough, that's what he is saying in his speech, too, referring to his plan of action for Britain:

> I hope that my work, since I became Prime Minister, shows that

> we have a plan and are prepared to take bold action necessary for our country to flourish. Now, I've stuck with that plan and always been honest with you about what is needed, even when that's been difficult, because I'm guided by doing what is right for our country, not what is easy.

No one inside No. 10 has the good sense to come out with an umbrella to shield him. I guess that's because they are paralysed with panic about how it might look, or maybe they are simply hoping the rain will pass. When he turns into No. 10, we can all see that the rain has run right down the back of his very expensive suit. He holds his head high. Job done.

Rishi Sunak was twenty points behind Labour in the polls at that time and, after he had spoken, commentators lined up to say that the reason he was calling this surprise election, months before he needed to, was because things would only get worse in the autumn. That day's fall in inflation to 2.3 per cent, and the news that the UK had just crept out of recession, was probably as good as it was going to get.

Not long after, Keir Starmer, safely undercover and flanked by two Union Jacks, told the electorate that Labour had a 'long-term plan to rebuild Britain, a plan that is ready to go and is fully costed and fully funded', with an unfortunate echo of Boris Johnson's phantom 'oven-ready' Brexit plan. Fast forward a few months, and No. 10 staff were blaming Starmer's first Chief of Staff at No. 10, Sue Gray, for the lack of one. It was her job to develop a plan, apparently, while everyone else focused on winning the election.

'Things can only get wetter' was the headline in *The Telegraph* the next day.

• • •

'All political lives, unless they are cut off in midstream at a happy juncture, end in failure, because that is the nature of politics and of human affairs,' wrote Enoch Powell in 1977, whose own political career effectively ended a decade earlier when he was sacked from the shadow Cabinet for his inflammatory speech against migration and the proposed Race Relations Bill.

Most Prime Ministers lose their job, as Rishi Sunak did, at the hands of the electorate, but over my career that pattern has changed, first with the defenestration of Margaret Thatcher, which broke the great taboo that Prime Ministers in office should not be brought down by their colleagues, then Tony Blair handing over in a back office coup to Gordon Brown, and now with ever-increasing speed the premature departures of David Cameron, Theresa May, Boris Johnson and Liz Truss. Changing Prime Ministers in midstream has become something of a norm as a means of restoring waning fortunes and winning elections, though the strategy doesn't always work, as Sunak found out.

We've become used to seeing Prime Ministers at that podium outside No. 10, announcing their resignations in their own inimitable styles: David Cameron whimsically humming as he turns his back on us after delivering his bombshell. Theresa May's voice breaking as she expresses her 'enormous and enduring gratitude to have had the opportunity to serve the country I love'. 'Them's the breaks,' from Johnson, shortly after letting it be known that he would barricade himself in No. 10 rather than leave voluntarily. Liz Truss's terse and factual hostage-like statement, as she stands in front of the twisted plinth of her prime ministerial podium, which had been specially crafted for her premiership of just forty-nine days. Who knew each PM has a different podium?

As soon as it is done, it is done. There's no turning back, unless there's a comeback sometime in the future, which Boris Johnson hinted at when he finally left No. 10, comparing himself to Cincinnatus, a Roman leader who returned to rule Rome once more. Before that moment, Prime Ministers fight hard to stay in power, as Sunak's decision in the weeks before the election to ignore ever more urgent calls to release prisoners from overflowing prisons to stop the collapse of the criminal justice system goes to show. Politics before country.

It's a mystery why politicians say the right things in order to get elected, do the opposite while in power and then are surprised when the public lose faith in them as a result. Promising more power to the people only to centralise government and even reduce their accountability, if they can. Promising to fix broken public services but then indulging in distracting public sector reorganisations instead. Promising to rebuild Britain's future but then fighting short-term political battles from one day to the next. Promising to bring people together to solve common problems but then sowing dissent instead of bringing harmony. Promising to right injustices and then ignoring them. Promising to clean up politics and restore trust but getting mired in scandals. They start by wanting to be their best selves in government, then turn away from the path.

It first began to dawn on me that Starmer's premiership might end abruptly, despite his resounding majority, when I read the quote in the book *Get In* that claimed Starmer had only been put in place by others to become Prime Minister and was like the driver of a Docklands Light Railway train, which is operated by others remotely. If a Prime Minister is just a figurehead, they can easily be replaced, especially when even insiders start saying they don't have the skills for the job. It's mighty hard to focus on running the country as Prime Minister when you're constantly protecting your back from the people who are supposed to be by your side, on the same team, and while all that is happening, No. 10 is viciously briefing out about your colleagues, apparently in your defence. Rats in a sack, the electorate might be entitled to think.

But that was the spectacle we have been watching for quite a long time now…

• • •

On 11 November 2025, I was getting ready for bed when I caught a comment by the BBC's political editor on *The World Tonight* on Radio 4. He said that Starmer wasn't going anywhere, which made me tune in to *Newsnight* straightaway. I'd been hoping for an early night but now I was wide awake. Victoria Derbyshire was introducing the programme by saying that allies of the PM were making it clear he would fight any leadership challenge. What challenge, I'm thinking? And then she turned to Nick Watt, *Newsnight*'s political editor, to explain what was going on.

'Well, Vic,' he said,

> what we know is that right now there is a rift between the two people who we thought were closest in this government and were essential to the stability of his Cabinet and that is Keir Starmer and his Health Secretary, Wes Streeting. There are people in Downing Street who believe Wes Streeting is on manoeuvres, hence those remarks that we've heard that the PM would fight a challenge, and it would be irresponsible, they say, for a challenge to be launched. That has produced quite a response in parts of this government. One person has said to me, these briefings out of No. 10 are not accidental; they don't believe that people are speaking out of turn. It is a pattern of behaviour that has followed

> Keir Starmer from Opposition to No. 10, which is people around him briefing against people. Who is briefed against? Lisa Nandy. Bridget Phillipson was briefed against … Ed Milliband's been briefed against. Angela Rayner's been briefed against, and now they're saying it is Wes Streeting's turn. Perhaps it would be a good idea, I've been told, that the PM and the Chancellor might want to focus on the Budget.

He then read out another briefing from No. 10 claiming this story had been overwritten and another from Wes Streeting, who categorically denied the allegations and said he was focusing solely on cutting NHS waiting lists.

Lord Glasman, of Blue Labour, who Victoria Derbyshire claims is believed to be influential in No. 10, rested his elbows on the back of the *Newsnight* sofa, jutted out his paunch and said it's not going to happen, dismissing Wes Streeting as a 'Blairite apparatchik out of the Student Union'. Barry Gardiner, the left-wing Labour MP and former shadow minister, arrived in the studio mid-programme (such was the haste with which all of this had been put together). Derbyshire waved him in and moved across from her seat on the sofa to make room. 'The question is why has No. 10 started circling the wagons?' he said. 'You circle the wagons and you end up in a circular firing squad – that's what they're doing. And people want a government that is going to say "this is what we're about", but they don't know, that's why our poll ratings are so low…'

It was all very dizzying.

The next day, on Radio 4's *Today* programme, Wes Streeting called for the No. 10 staff who briefed out in this way to be sacked and said they did not align with Starmer's model or style of leadership. Starmer later let it be known that he had apologised to Wes

Streeting and that he would sack the person who had done this, but after his staff assured him none of them did, he let the matter go.

It's one thing for this sort of thing to happen behind the scenes, which is bad enough, but another to have it in public in such dramatic terms, with a senior Cabinet minister accused of mutiny, then openly putting the knife into Starmer's No. 10 in response. And effectively calling for Morgan McSweeney's resignation, the kingmaker and man behind the throne, who some months later, in response to the Mandelson scandal, finally did go.

A few days later, I saw Streeting in a restaurant talking to a political journalist – which some people would say is what you do when you are 'on manoeuvres'.

And so it went on, with constant talk of challenges, usually denied, not just by Streeting but also by Andy Burnham, the Mayor of Greater Manchester; Angela Rayner, the former Deputy Prime Minister; and others. And as the speculation grew and the next crisis came, we started to see reporters and photographers once again gathering in Downing Street, only for that crisis to subside, and for another to arise not long after...

So it was with the second Mandelson crisis for Keir Starmer, this time in February 2026, when Anas Sarwar, the leader of Labour in Scotland, called on him to resign but, despite talk of a wider rebellion, all of Starmer's Cabinet then issued statements backing him. Speculation about challenges persisted, however, and only increased when Starmer's sacking of Olly Robbins in April pushed Mandelson back into the headlines. A few weeks later, after truly disastrous May election results for Labour in Scotland, Wales and some local councils, things came to a new, even more chaotic climax, ending in Wes Streeting resigning and Andy Burnham finally being allowed to stand as a Member of Parliament so that he could, if successful, take part in a leadership challenge. By Burnham's own account, as Mayor of Greater Manchester he has managed to create the conditions for people to pull together and to govern in a different way, as mentioned in Chapter 2, and this has made him popular.

As this book goes to print, it is unclear exactly how this story will end, but Starmer's position looks precarious.

Change is what Labour had promised at the general election, but people expected change in the country, not change of this sort. When Starmer and his colleagues arrived in government, people wanted competent, trustworthy politicians delivering Starmer's promised 'decade of national renewal' and, as he puts it, a government that puts 'country, not politics, first'. He said he would restore trust and bring the country together, but those May election results showed the country had little faith in this administration and was instead fracturing in all directions. As Streeting's resignation letter said of Starmer's government, 'Where we need vision, we have a vacuum, where we need direction, we have drift.' We hoped for good government when Keir Starmer became Prime Minister but sadly got quite a lot of bad government instead.

Will the next instalment be any better?

• • •

Whatever the merits of each individual departure, as more and more Prime Ministers leave prematurely the entire office of Prime Minister is potentially diminished. It's like that moment in *The Wizard of Oz* when the curtain is drawn back and everyone sees that the seemingly all-powerful wizard is just an ordinary man amplifying his voice through machinery and smoke and mirrors. It begins to look like no one is up to the job and government is just an illusion. Or that it's time to look outside the mainstream political box and vote for someone like Trump who would govern in a very different way.

Meanwhile, many people are noticing that government isn't working so well for them, with lower living standards, a lack of affordable housing and increasingly poor public services. Some also feel that government's ability to protect them from destructive wider headwinds is diminishing as the UK's influence declines, from trade wars to real wars and global warming and the potentially negative impact of AI. They're worrying not just about their own future but their children's and grandchildren's.

Some feel there is no credible plan to address the things they care about and only one consistent plan across the political spectrum: to stay in power. No wonder trust in government is at rock bottom and many people have just tuned out, with 40 per cent of the voting population choosing not to vote at the last general election.

There's a feeling we might be on an inevitable slide toward a government like Donald Trump's in the US, that wants to sweep away the checks and balances that prevent it from taking more power and start to dismantle parts of what we think of as the state.[1]

• • •

What could our Prime Ministers do differently to deliver for the people they serve and save us from this? Rishi Sunak was asked a similar question in an interview in *The Times* after he left office: with hindsight, how would he have conducted his brief premiership differently? His answer was one of a salesman who had failed to get his message across, not someone who thought he might have been doing the wrong things, in the wrong way:

> I did not communicate enough and in the right way. You get into this habit – you do an announcement for the evening news, post some things on social media and video, and your team briefs the press. Repeat. That wasn't sufficient. I took it for granted that people would know why I was doing things. I assumed people thought I had the right motives. I spent too much time talking about the what and how and not enough about the why. I wasn't the best version of myself as PM. But I am absolutely determined to make the best possible job of being a former PM.

And then he added, 'Clearly, I miss the levers of power. I'm proud I brought in the smoking ban for the young. I miss playing cricket in the garden with the England cricket team and the staff. But not much else.'[2] It's a tough job, being Prime Minister, and when it rains you get wet.

At least he, like Theresa May, has kept some dignity after leaving office, and stayed in Parliament. Liz Truss lost her seat, to be fair, but then wrote a book, *Ten Years to Save the West*, in which she accepted no blame for her failure in office and, as she said to a far-right summit in the US, she'd faced 'a huge establishment backlash and a lot of it actually came from the state itself'.[3] Within five months of leaving office and Parliament, Boris Johnson had declared income of almost £4.8 million and, as later exposés alleged, 'in his international dash for cash, Johnson appears to have repeatedly broken ethics rules as he tried to trade on relationships made in Downing Street'.[4] Don't get me started on David Cameron and Greensill Capital: enough has already been said in Chapter 7.

Others have grown in stature after office. I admired John Major's principled stance on Brexit and on standards in public life during Johnson's premiership, a stance which doubtless lost him many friends in his own party. Gordon Brown's unrelenting focus on his lifetime mission of ending child poverty has been inspiring, if initially unpopular with No. 10 (until the recent U-turn on the two-child benefit cap). Out of office, these men have demonstrated the vision and integrity that we need to see more of in Prime Ministers, while they are in power.

• • •

As future Prime Ministers walk up the Downing Street stairs, what will they remember about the faces they pass by, so serene now, despite those often painful departures from office in their last days? Each leaves a legacy, good and bad, and here's what I might choose to list for each.

Margaret Thatcher? The end of the Cold War and decades of peace; the restructuring of our economy that left a persistent north-south divide and an overdependence on financial services; the City deregulation that eventually led to the financial crash and the austerity that followed; privatisations with decidedly mixed results; and a new operating model for government, sometimes called New Public Management, that remains firmly in place.

John Major? The Nolan principles of good governance and the foundations he laid for the Good Friday Agreement.

Tony Blair? Finally achieving peace in Northern Ireland; investing in public services; introducing Sure Start; and, not so good, introducing the whole idea of megaphone government.

Gordon Brown? Saving our financial system from collapse after the 2008 crash.

David Cameron? Introducing gay marriage but also unleashing Brexit and austerity.

Theresa May? On the plus side, her anti-slavery laws, making coercive control an offence in domestic abuse legislation, and legislating for a target to reduce global warming. And she *tried* with Brexit.

Boris Johnson? The Covid vaccine in double-quick time but a botched Brexit, Partygate, corruption, poor Covid planning and chaotic government.

Liz Truss? A nil return.

Rishi Sunak? New smoking restrictions (which were eventually passed by Labour) but also weaponising global warming and other culture wars for his own political ends and choosing to carry on with Johnson's ill-conceived Rwanda scheme for relocating asylum seekers.

And Keir Starmer? The dust will need to settle, but he initiated some closer ties to the EU, helped create a stronger defensive coalition in Europe and introduced greater worker and tenant rights, the Hillsborough Law (if passed), the Ethics and Integrity Commission and the Civil Society Covenant.

Which politician wouldn't want a chance to be Prime Minister and make a difference, for good or bad?

• • •

At the turn of the year in January 2026, Laura Kuenssberg started her interview with Keir Starmer by asking him to recall his first steps into No. 10 as Prime Minister. As she talked with him, they were walking together back out of the No. 10 door and down the street, a journey we normally only see when Prime Ministers leave the building for the last time. This thought must surely must have occurred to the show's production team, but Starmer happily played along.

It was, he said,

> an amazing feeling, it was only the second time I'd been in the

> building and I walked straight through and all the staff were here [at this point, Kuenssberg and the Prime Minister were in the corridor walking away from the Cabinet Room] clapping into the Cabinet Room, where I met Vic and the kids and Vic's Dad and had about ten minutes with them. And then I was taken down the stairs to be given the security briefings.

As they left No. 10 and entered Downing Street, he said, 'I knew this would be tough – there's nothing easy about this – and so it has been, but the question now as we turn 2025 into 2026 is we're turning a corner.' Is that a question, I wondered?

He added that he felt 'ready, confident, optimistic and looking forward to it, so I am glad that we've got to this stage'. But the thing which touched me most is when he said of No. 10: 'It's an amazing place to work, it's incredible.'[5] I suspect most Prime Ministers would agree about that. That's how I felt about it, too.

• • •

I wonder what ex-Prime Ministers would say to each other about how to do government well if they were gathered together privately, under Chatham House rules of confidentiality.

I'm guessing, but I suspect something along the lines of: don't worry too much about being unpopular. Try instead to do the right thing. Stop thinking about dominating the daily news cycle and be clear about what you want to achieve in the medium- to long-term and focus on that. Be true to yourself and act with integrity. Put country before party. People will thank you for it in the end…

In the final chapter, I list the advice I would give, based on my own humble experience.

Chapter 9

HOW TO MAKE IT BETTER

Public patience with government is running out, and far-right populism, with its unrealistic promises and hostility toward the state, is on the rise in this country and elsewhere. The fashion is to say that government is broken, but how about trying to fix it rather than smashing it up?

Here are my seven priorities for creating a better government and restoring public trust:

1. No. 10 should be strategic, setting and maintaining direction, values and purpose, rather than taking on more and more responsibility.
2. Government should create a shared vision with the country as a whole, so that everyone pulls together.
3. It should decentralise, setting clear roles and accountability, and strengthen the civil service rather than attacking it.
4. The Treasury should be rewired to incentivise prevention and long-term value, rather than short-termism, with services that focus on people, not institutions.
5. Replace the tired command-and-control management operating model with principles not targets, collaboration not competition.

6. Respect and uphold rights and the truth, and address social tensions without inflaming them.
7. Protect democracy and civic space, upholding high standards and strengthening checks and balances, not diminishing them.

A STRATEGIC NO. 10, SETTING AND MAINTAINING DIRECTION, VALUES AND PURPOSE

When Prime Ministers first enter No. 10, they often know what they need to do to restore trust but then they fail to deliver. Politics, personality, events, the daily news cycle and many other things too often get in the way. It all goes so fast, and before too long governments can find themselves hoarding power rather than thinking of how to make the best use of it, managing a media grid of daily announcements and waging wars on those with whom they should work to be effective. They blame everyone else but themselves.

What the public want is governing, not performing: governments doing what they say, dealing with today's problems and fixing things, but also thinking ahead and looking to the long-term, with a clear sense of purpose, values and vision that they can understand and share.

At the very top, government should be strategic, focusing on the bigger picture, because no other part of government can do this. They should engage with the public so that they can see and buy into the direction of travel too. A Prime Minister should set out a clear sense of purpose, direction and values for their government and make sure that it stays on course, rather than taking more and more decisions themselves, and away from others, with the result that No. 10 gets larger and larger, and is sucked in to ever more micromanagement. Of course, a Prime Minister also has a vital political role and needs to be able to command the confidence of the country, but the population is better served by them explaining what they are trying to do and how they are going about it, rather than acting as a salesperson for a myriad of micro-initiatives orchestrated by No. 10.

If you are not clear about what you are trying to achieve, you leave your civil servants in a fog and they cannot help you plan how to get there, and you alienate the public who want to feel the country is in safe hands. For all of her faults, Thatcher had this clarity, and it enabled her to take charge of the civil service and the wider public sector and transform government and the country, however one feels about the result. With her strong beliefs, vision and values she was also able to react swiftly when things went awry, as she did when the Falklands War erupted unexpectedly, and put things back on course.

But at what cost, you might ask? And it's a fair point: the way in which Thatcher steam-rollered change through against all opposition caused social division and left lasting scars, including the north-south divide. Eventually her inability to listen and bring people with her led to the riots and the party rebellion which eventually brought her down. Which is why I suggest…

CREATING A SHARED VISION WITH THE COUNTRY AS A WHOLE

It's far better in the long run if governments bring people with them, rather than trying to impose change from above, and in today's world of social media, where people can coalesce around a view very quickly, and where there is less deference to traditional sources of power like governments and the mainstream media, you can far more quickly find yourself unable to proceed than in Thatcher's day. That is, unless you build a consensus first. Starmer's many U-turns illustrate this well.

There are so many problems that government cannot solve alone – the apparent epidemic of poor mental health in young people is one example – and employers and charities, communities and families all have a part to play. Government's role should be to create a shared vision and strong relationships built on trust, so the country can pull together with a common sense of purpose. Listening all the while, not dictating.

For issues where continuity is essential to give people confidence in the future, like social care policy, governments need to get far better at building coalitions of support across political parties, rather than parking the issues in the 'too difficult' box or farming them out to yet another inquiry. It may be that proportional representation is the only way to shift the damaging culture of our Punch and Judy politics, so it's worth thinking about that, too.

DECENTRALISING, AND STRENGTHENING THE CIVIL SERVICE

The UK remains one of the most highly centralised governments of any advanced democracy, and more needs to be delegated, particularly to the places where people live and work. As we say in *A Better Way*, local is better than national. We also note that

> some things do need to be organised at national level, and stewardship is a shared task … governments and other national agencies should stick to what they do well and stop trying to organise services and community life from the centre, set out aspirations not blueprints, recognise the value of locally based organisations, and only get involved in things which local people can't or won't do by themselves.

The good news is that successive administrations have been pressing ahead with more mayor-led combined authorities in England and are increasingly delegating more authority to them. But this only creates another middle layer of centralisation if they do not delegate more to local areas within their authorities, and to local people, where they can do things better.

More delegation is needed within the wider public sector as well, but here things seem to be moving in the other direction, with the abolition of NHS England and ministers taking its delegated powers to themselves. There are also promises to abolish even more quangos, as we have seen happening over many years. A prerequisite of good delegation is being clear about the job to be done and the respective roles of ministers and agencies, avoiding the overlap and confusion about who does what, which only slows government down and reduces its effectiveness. It also means ensuring people are held accountable for what they deliver.

Civil servants are the means through which ministers deliver change, and in recent years that trust between ministers and civil servants has been damaged, with the latter appearing to be a scapegoat for non-delivery. Lack of trust has led to more and more decisions ending up in ministers' red boxes, which has also slowed the machine. Empowering civil servants to take more decisions without reference to ministers, establishing task forces to cut across institutional boundaries to deliver wider goals, using technology to increase productivity and implementing tougher measures to address poor performance – all of which were promised in 2026 by the current Chief Secretary to the Prime Minister, Darren Jones – are all important modernisations.[1] So is bringing in external expertise. Greater clarity from ministers about their priorities, combined with honest conversations between ministers and officials about what needs to be cut back, would also strengthen the civil service and improve delivery, instead of using blanket instruments to cut the civil service, like headcount cuts, recruitment and pay freezes. Such measures have been counterproductive, leading to ever more frequent moves from job to job and overpromotion in order to increase pay, random gaps in key areas and a general loss of vital expertise, capacity and accountability, all of which also clogs up the works.

Ministers and civil servants also need to work on the civil service's culture, which still tends to reward senior civil servants for how they manage ministers day to day, rather than for how they collaborate with others inside and outside government or ensure that government is delivered.

REWIRING THE TREASURY TO INCENTIVISE PREVENTION AND SERVICES CENTRED ON PEOPLE

The Treasury should take on the role of promoting prevention, rather than just controlling total expenditure regardless of the impact, longer term. As several departments and agencies often contribute to outcomes, and costs and savings often fall across multiple budgets and departments unevenly, only the Treasury has the incentive and overview to do this. It took on this responsibility in relation to Sure Start and should do so across the piece again. It should rewire itself to incentivise prevention, including public services that get it right first time, rather than frequently recycling problems, as some do. This will reduce costs over time and put government in a better position to meet its fiscal rules.

Bean-counting tends to favour small, incremental changes which do little to shift the dial, rather than taking a risk to do things differently. The Treasury is good at seeing the risks of trying something new, but not the risk of staying as we are, in terms of higher costs not just to society but to the Exchequer, and less growth and so less funding for services in the future. It is easier to lock people up in prison expensively now rather than invest in tackling the causes of crime to reduce prison numbers in future, for example.

Wellbeing should be the Treasury's top goal, as it is longer-term and more encompassing than mere growth, as measured by Gross Domestic Product. GDP is boosted by locking people up, for example, but excludes having children, caring and volunteering, on which our society depends. As set out in Chapter 5, the Treasury could adopt New Zealand's Wellbeing Budget approach, which aims to support social outcomes such as healthy life expectancy and the quality and affordability of housing, and measures the long-term impact of decisions on human and environmental capital. To help shift the culture, the Well-Being of Future Generations Act, developed and implemented in Wales, which places a duty on all public bodies to think long-term, might also be introduced.

If the Treasury is charged with pursuing prevention, it will itself want to rewire the incentives in its spending rules that deter others from investing in it. A ring-fenced budget for preventative spending, like the capital budget, would protect it from being raided to finance short-term pressures and make it easier to actively shift more resources to prevention over time. The Treasury should also introduce a longer time frame for planning public expenditure and assess the relative long-term costs and benefits of acute and preventative interventions, which tend to be forgotten when only the next few years are formally considered. Longer-term planning also helps the rest of government to focus on the delivery of outcomes which cannot be delivered in just a few years.

One aim should be for services to put the people they serve first, rather than the needs of individual institutions. False economies often lead to a reduction in unit costs, frequently crowding out time spent listening and building trusted relationships. Frontline staff should be given the autonomy, time and space to resolve issues first time round, rather than people being passed from pillar to post at ever greater expense to them and the Treasury, leading to even sharper pressure on unit costs in an effort to retain control of the overall budget. This often requires professionals to work across different agencies, while targets and budgets push them in the opposite direction. To create financial incentives for agencies to work together, more pooled budgets should be created.

The Treasury has begun to move in this direction, but a much bigger push is needed.

REPLACING THE EXISTING COMMAND-AND-CONTROL OPERATING MODEL

To support this shift, the outdated operating model of government, which Margaret Thatcher introduced and Tony Blair refined, should be replaced with an enabling, not a controlling, one, moving away from their command-and-control management model, which some call New Public Management. This only inhibits collaboration, stifles innovation and gums up the works through a culture of compliance, often generating bureaucracy, not results. As one businessman told me at a recent Better Way event, if the private sector's operating model was making it so difficult for its front line to meet the needs of its customers, it would go out of business.

Agreeing broad outcomes and clear principles for how things should be delivered – 'prevention is better than cure', for example

– is more likely to be effective at gaining results than targets (which are frequently gamed). These would encourage public servants to work together rather than focus on their own territory and give them the flexibility to adjust what they do to match the needs of different individuals. Success can then be judged on whether they are doing the right job well, rather than on whether they are doing the wrong thing ever more cheaply.

RESPECTING AND UPHOLDING RIGHTS AND THE TRUTH, AND ADDRESSING, NOT INFLAMING, SOCIAL TENSIONS

Good government is about helping people lead good lives, not pitting them against each other. Rather than pursuing culture wars for their own political ends, government should be upholding people's rights, not suppressing them, and tackling continuing injustices, including the hostile cultures in some organisations that discriminate against individuals and stop organisations from serving us all. There is a particular responsibility for governments to sort out their home patch, including the police and the armed forces.

And where there is conflict between different communities, as in Northern Ireland, it is the job of government to find a way through, as it did with the Good Friday Agreement, creating a solution that works for everybody, rather than fanning the flames.

Governments have a particular duty to stand up for the rights of communities and individuals who are being attacked and stand firm against a growing tendency to invert the truth and portray human and equalities rights as our enemy, rather than our friend.

They should ensure that arguments are based on facts, not falsehoods, so that we all stand on solid ground.

STRENGTHENING DEMOCRACY AND CIVIC SPACE, AND UPHOLDING HIGH STANDARDS

The bedrock of good government is good character and a respect for democratic institutions, but as Boris Johnson's premiership showed, one cannot depend upon it. The Nolan principles of selflessness, integrity, objectivity, accountability, openness, honesty and leadership are a good start, but what happens when a Prime Minister doesn't apply them and yet remains the last port of call for enforcing them?

Despite the creation by Keir Starmer's government of the Ethics and Integrity Commission, the strengthening of the Ministerial Code and the new power given to the Prime Minister's independent ethics adviser to initiate investigations, tougher, independent enforcement of standards in public life is still needed. These steps should include 'the comprehensive and immediate action to clean up our politics' proposed by Gordon Brown in the light of the Mandelson scandal, including those set out set out in Chapter 7, to address weaknesses in the current system, of which there is a long list. The Ethics and Integrity Commission, for example, may have a duty to advise Prime Ministers on gaps in the system and the changes it thinks are necessary, but Prime Ministers can still ignore its recommendations. They have certainly ignored such recommendations in the past from its predecessor body, the Independent Committee on Standards in Public Life. Prime Ministers themselves still decide whether a breach of the Ministerial Code has taken place, not their adviser, and that adviser is appointed by him or her anyway, not independently, and has no independent powers of investigation. The Ministerial Code, unlike the Civil Service Code, is not enshrined in statute. There is no ban on parliamentarians taking on second jobs, the anti-corruption commissioner needs stronger powers and there should be parliamentary scrutiny of major appointments.

So many factors of good government rely on the 'good chaps' assumption that Prime Ministers mean well and will abide by unwritten constitutional rules. If you look across the pond to Donald Trump, the potential dangers are clear (even when the constitution is written down).

To guard against future authoritarianism, guardrails need to be strengthened. The independence of the Electoral Commission should be restored, as already planned by the current government, and judicial appointments, as well as some other appointments to public bodies where political control could be used to increase the executive's power, should be made entirely independent from government. Political appointments to the BBC board should be stopped, as the government has now said they will. As recommended by a recent report, a supermajority vote for any change to laws that enshrine fundamental rights and constitutional protections should be considered, so that these cannot be changed simply at the whim of the political party currently in power. The Scotland Act of 2016 already requires a two-thirds majority to change core election rules to the Scottish Parliament, and many other countries have supermajorities in place for constitutional laws. And there is a case for giving the Supreme Court a more proactive power to maintain the constitution.[2]

The public interest defence should be restored to the Official Secrets Act, so that civil servants who are asked to assist ministers in breaking both the Ministerial Code and Civil Service Code have a defence for whistleblowing, as they do in many other countries. The proposed new Hillsborough Law and Victims Advocate are definitely positive moves in the right direction in correcting the imbalance of power between the citizen and the state when things go wrong. But accountability at both ministerial and official level should be strengthened so that there are more resignations and successful prosecutions in future, particularly in egregious cases.

We would have better policies, laws and services if people had more of a say, including through citizens' juries and other measures to increase deliberative democracy, as well as government working at all levels in partnership with civil society and people with lived experience, as promised by the government's new Civil Society Covenant.

Civil society has a key role in ensuring a healthy democracy, not just by using its expertise to inform public debate and policy and telling authentic stories about the negative impact of existing services and laws, but also through holding government to account, alongside the media, when things go wrong, laws are broken or people's lives become intolerable.

It's especially important that positive steps are taken to roll back the legal and administrative rules against campaigning, advocacy and protest, the rights to which have been built up over time and which are now threatened, including through the increasingly draconian laws that have been progressively introduced over the years.

Last but far from least, stronger measures are needed to stop undue influence from the rich and powerful. The rules for funding political parties, including those that are designed to prevent foreign influence, should be tightened and donations capped. More effective political lobbying laws should be put in place that don't restrict charities from doing their job and do put limits on lobbying by big money.

• • •

In short, a new model of government is needed – much more inspiring and enabling, and less controlling, because governments cannot solve most problems alone and need to work with society, not manage it. Rights must be respected and enforced by government, tackling continuing injustices, including negative cultures in places like the police and armed forces, that undermine those rights, and the truth must be upheld. Democratic safeguards must also be strengthened so that governments uphold our constitution, and everyone has a say on the things that affect them, not just those with influence and power.

ACKNOWLEDGEMENTS

I'd like to thank the many people who have helped shape this book, starting with everyone I've worked with over the years, many of whom are named in the text, including some, sadly, who are no longer with us. I spent a wonderful evening with former colleagues from the Equal Opportunities Commission while I was working on *Bad Government*, reminiscing, reflecting on the world now and talking about the themes of this book. All of them are continuing to do amazing things to create a fairer and kinder world and I am in awe of their energy and brilliance. I have learned so much from them and others over my career, including from those ministers across the political spectrum who were determined to make change happen and had the vision and the skills to do it, as well as from the civil servants who worked with them. In more recent years, I have gained both hope and inspiration from taking part in discussions between the public, social and private sectors – particularly in the Early Action Task Force and the Better Way network – on how to solve the great challenges of our day, and I would like to thank them for their collective wisdom, which is reflected in this book.

I'd also like to thank warmly all those with whom I have spoken in the civil service, and the people who have kindly read draft chapters and commented on them, including my former EOC colleagues Sam Smethers, Kristine Ziwica and Sarah Wootton, my Better Way co-founder, Steve Wyler, Gus O'Donnell, and David Cutler from the Baring Foundation. I am indebted to my husband, John Nightingale, for putting up with me writing every weekend, during holidays and even in bed, and for giving me encouraging feedback on each chapter as it emerged. Our daughter, Victoria, was also kind enough to cast her copywriter's eye over drafts and give a young person's perspective. Our dog Flossie also has my thanks for taking me on walks to clear my mind, and I forgive her for constantly trying to climb over my laptop as I wrote.

I would also like to thank my editor at Biteback Publishing, Alex Pathe, for his expertise and input, and all those who read the book in advance and endorsed it. I should also add with gratitude that this book would not have happened without the initial encouragement of James Stephens, who has now moved on from Biteback, and Olivia Beattie, who is currently on maternity leave.

Early on in the gestation of this book, I was surprised and delighted to learn that Olivia was expecting a baby on the same day as my daughter, Lizzie, and both babies safely arrived in March just a few weeks after I submitted the manuscript. As I watch my first grandchild grow, I hope to see governments do more to shape a better future for him and all the other children growing up here and across the world, but fear that things may instead take a turn for the worse. We must all do what we can to make things better and, as colleagues in A Better Way would say, we have more power than we think.

NOTES

PREFACE

1 'Trust and confidence in Britain's system of government at record low', National Centre for Social Research, Press Release, 2024
2 'UK trust in government among the lowest globally', John Smith Centre, 2024

CHAPTER 1

1 Danielle de Wolfe, 'Boris Johnson likens Downing Street decor to "a crack den" as he defends lavish £200k refurb amid Starmer gift row', LBC, 2024
2 'Downing Street refurbishment: What is the row about?', BBC News, 2022
3 'Boris Johnson mocked by John Lewis over "nightmare" furniture Downing Street debate', Virgin Radio, 2021
4 Rhiannon Du Cann, 'Jeremy Hunt humiliates Boris Johnson after revealing No10 gold wallpaper "peeling off"', *The Express*, 2022

CHAPTER 2

1 Tom McTague, 'Is Trump a blessing for Starmer? Labour will be forced to show its hand', 14 November 2025, *Unherd*, 2025
2 'Findings of the Second Permanent Secretary's Investigation into alleged gatherings on government premises during Covid restrictions', Cabinet Office, 2022
3 Ibid.
4 Patrick McAlary, 'Labour's special advisers: a growing cohort is learning on the job', Institute for Government, 2025
5 'Power with Purpose: final report of the Commission on the Centre of Government', Institute for Government, 2024
6 Sean Seddon, 'Number 10 staff "made puppy gate to stop Boris Johnson leaving Covid isolation"', *Metro*, 2022
7 Richard Stone, 'Thatcher Finds a Home at No. 10', *Mail on Sunday*, 2009
8 'PM explains decision to move Thatcher portrait', BBC News, 2024
9 Sam Francis, 'Keir Starmer defends praising Thatcher in pitch for Tories', BBC News, 2023
10 'Tony Blair: "My job was to build on some Thatcher policies"', BBC News, 2013
11 Gus O'Donnell, 'The insider's guide to preparing for power', *New Statesman*, 2024
12 James Heale, 'Boris Johnson pens touching reply to seven-year-old girl who wrote to tell him she had cancelled her birthday party twice due to coronavirus', *Mail on Sunday*, 2020

13 Charles Moore, *Margaret Thatcher: The Authorized Biography, Volume One*, London, Allen Lane, 2013
14 Charles Moore, *Margaret Thatcher: The Authorized Biography, Volume Two*, London, Allen Lane, 2015
15 Caroline Slocock, *People Like Us: Margaret Thatcher and Me*, London, Biteback Publishing, 2018
16 Bernard Ingham, *Kill the Messenger*, London, HarperCollins, 1991
17 Milmo, Cahal, 'Margaret Thatcher aides "buried' plan to make her condemn apartheid', *The Independent*, 2016
18 Claire Ellicott, 'Queen was "so enraged" by Margaret Thatcher's refusal to back sanctions on apartheid that she wanted to scrap their weekly meetings', *Daily Mail*, 2017
19 Patrick R. H. Wright, *Behind Diplomatic Lines: Relations with Ministers*, London, Biteback Publishing, 2018
20 George Younger, 'Thatcher: The Inside Story', *Scotland on Sunday*, 1993
21 Geoffrey Howe, *Conflict of Loyalty*, London, MacMillan, 1994
22 Speaking at a question and answer session at the Institute for Government event, 'The Nolan Principles at 30: What does the future hold for standards in public life?', 2025
23 Andrew Rawnsley, *The End of the Party*, London, Penguin, 2010
24 '"Absence of humanity": Helen MacNamara's evidence to Covid inquiry', *The Guardian*, 1 November 2023
25 Rowena Mason, 'The advisers behind the birth of Mayism: dream team or terrible twosome?', *The Guardian*, 2017
26 George Parker, 'Theresa May's tight rein at No 10 fuels cabinet tensions', *Financial Times*, 2016
27 Simon Murphy, '"A couple of black eyes": Johnson and the plot to attack a reporter', *The Guardian*, 14 July 2019
28 'UK civil servant said Boris Johnson changed "direction every day", Covid inquiry hears', *Financial Times*, 2023
29 'Boris Johnson admits it's ludicrous he's PM, says Cummings', BBC News, 2021
30 '"Absence of humanity": Helen MacNamara's evidence to Covid inquiry', *The Guardian*, 2023
31 'Boris Johnson's f-word WhatsApp message about "hopeless" Hancock revealed by Dominic Cummings', ITV News, 2021
32 'NHS test and trace "failed its main objective", says spending watchdog', *The Guardian*, 2021
33 Dan Hodges, 'Sue Gray is told Carrie Johnson's friends "held a Downing St Winner Takes It All Abba party" on the day Dominic Cummings quit and left with his belongings in a box – so will it be in redacted report to be published this week?', *Daily Mail*, 2022
34 'Sunak ignored police chiefs' warning to act on prisons crisis before election', *Civil Service World*, 2024
35 Jesse Norman, 'My letter of No Confidence in Boris Johnson', 2022
36 Andy Burnham, 'Place First: A Unifying Path for a United Kingdom', Institute for Government lecture, 2025
37 Tom McTague, 'Keir Starmer interview: What he can't say', *New Statesman*, 2025
38 Patrick Maguire, Gabriel Pogrund, *Get In*, London, Bodley Head, 2025
39 Tom Baldwin, 'The private trials of Keir Starmer', *The Observer*, 2025

CHAPTER 3

1 For a transcript of the speech, see https://www.gov.uk/government/speeches/a-message-from-prime-minister-keir-starmer-to-the-civil-service
2 Jim Dunton, 'Ministerial code update stresses need for "partnership working" with civil servants', *Civil Service World*, 2024
3 'Dominic Raab hits out at "activist civil servants" after resignation', BBC News, 2023
4 Adam Tolley KC, 'Investigation Report to the Prime Minister on formal complaints about the conduct of the Rt Hon Dominic Raab MP, Deputy Prime Minister, Lord Chancellor and Secretary of State for Justice', 2023

5 Dominic Raab, 'The people of Britain will pay the price for this Kafkaesque saga', *The Telegraph*, 2023
6 'Philip Rutnam resignation: his full statement', *The Guardian*, 2020
7 'Priti Patel: Summary of official report into bullying claims', BBC News, 2020
8 'Boris Johnson "asked for Patel report to be palatable", source claims', BBC News, 2020
9 Catherine Haddon, 'The manner of Mark Sedwill's exit shows how easy it is to undermine civil service impartiality', Institute for Government, 2020
10 Rowena Mason, 'No 10 regrets choice of "insipid" new cabinet secretary, sources say', *The Guardian*, 2025
11 Antony Jay, 'Informed Sources', *London Review of Books*, 1980
12 For a full transcript of the speech, see https://www.margaretthatcher.org/document/105519
13 Michael Kandiah, Rodney Lowe *The Civil Service Reforms of the 1980s*, CCBH Oral History Programme, Centre for Contemporary British History, 2007
14 Alan Travers, 'How Margaret Thatcher asked for cuts – and ministers asked for more', *The Guardian*, 2009
15 Bernard Ingham, *Kill the Messenger*, London, HarperCollins, 1991, p.396
16 Source: author's interview with Charles Powell, cited in Slocock, *People Like Us*
17 'Then and now: Sue Cameron looks back on Margaret Thatcher's relationship with the civil service', *Civil Service World*, 2015
18 David Leigh, 'Clive Ponting obituary', *The Guardian*, 2020
19 'Spy law reforms will redefine 'enemy' and refresh "outdated" Official Secrets Act', *The Telegraph*, 2020
20 Beckie Smith, 'Closing argument: ex-legal chief Jonathan Jones on Brexit, Covid and leaving government, *Civil Service World*, 2021
21 See https://x.com/Dominic2306/status/1467907520840744961
22 Nathan Sparkes, 'Johnson evidence confirms *The Times* was briefed on ex-PM's Birthday party, later found to be illegal', *Byline Times*, 2023
23 'Chris Pincher: No 10 not telling the truth, says ex-senior civil servant', BBC News, 2022
24 'Updates on Standards in Public Life: Oral statement in the House of Commons from the Chief Secretary to the Prime Minister on standards in public life', 2026
25 Jim Dunton, 'Wormald departure: Gus O'Donnell criticises "shabby" briefings from No. 10', *Civil Service World*, 2026
26 Dave Penman's comments on the departure of Chris Wormald as Cabinet Secretary, 2026
27 'Where does Wormald sacking leave Sir Keir Starmer?', BBC News, 2026
28 'Keir Starmer "pressured Foreign Office into Mandelson appointment"', *The Times*, 2026
29 Gus O'Donnell, 'Keir Starmer's clash with the civil service exposes three ironies', *Sunday Times*, 2026
30 'Mandelson crisis exposes no. 10's civil service rift', *The Rundown Podcast*, Politics Home, 2026
31 For a transcript of the speech, see https://www.gov.uk/government/speeches/a-message-from-prime-minister-keir-starmer-to-the-civil-service, 2024
32 'Starmer tells civil servants to speak "truth to power" after vetting row', BBC News, 2026

CHAPTER 4

1 Helen MacNamara's written statement to the Covid-19 Inquiry. Although this is Cummings's account, she did not deny it in her written evidence, saying it was 'essentially accurate'.
2 Steven Greenhouse, 'As Musk steps back, experts say Doge cuts have harmed government services', *The Guardian*, 2025
3 Jessie Blaeser, 'Just how much has DOGE exaggerated its numbers? Now we have receipts', *POLITICO*, 2025
4 'Trump administration rehires hundreds of federal employees laid off by DOGE', CNN Politics, 2025
5 'Argentina's President Milei divided his nation but won over Trump' BBC News, 2025

6 Rowena Mason, 'Farage said Andrew Tate was "important voice" for men in podcast interview', *The Guardian*, 2025
7 'Tougher than Thatcher?', Institute for Fiscal Studies, 2010
8 'Summary letter from Lord Darzi to the Secretary of State for Health and Social Care', Department of Health and Social Care, 2026
9 Peter Walker, 'No. 10 distances itself from Robert Jenrick over planning row', *The Guardian*, 2020
10 Richard Bilton, 'HS2 blew billions: here's how and why', BBC *Panorama*, 2024
11 Gemma Tetlow, 'HS2: costs and controversies', Institute for Government, 2023
12 Tevye Markson, '"Stark" drop in real-terms civil service pay at all grades since 2010, analysis reveals', *Civil Service World*, 2023
13 'Summary letter from Lord Darzi to the Secretary of State for Health and Social Care', Department of Health and Social Care, 2026
14 The Right Reverend James Jones KBE, 'The patronising disposition of unaccountable power: a report to ensure the pain and suffering of the Hillsborough families is not repeated', House of Commons, 2017
15 See https://www.dailymail.co.uk/video/news/video-2517099/Video-Boris-says-build-batter-stuffing-battered-cod.html
16 'UK Covid-19 Inquiry: Core decision-making and political governance (Modules 2, 2A, 2B, 2C) Report', Cabinet Office, 2025
17 MacNamara's witness statement
18 Denis Campbell, 'Abolition of Public Health England just "passing of blame for coronavirus mistakes"', *The Guardian*, 2020
19 'Gavin Williamson's oral evidence to the Covid Inquiry: Shutting schools in 2021 put "NHS over children"', BBC News, 2025
20 Susan Acland-Hood's oral evidence to the Covid inquiry, 15 October 2025
21 Boris Johnson's oral evidence to the Covid inquiry, 21 October 2025
22 Susan Acland-Hood's oral evidence to the Covid inquiry, 15 October 2025
23 MacNamara's witness statement
24 Ibid.
25 Nehal Panchamia, Peter Thomas, 'The Next Steps Initiative', Institute for Government
26 'Howard's "triple deceit": the Widdecombe charge', *The Independent*, 1997
27 Charles Polidano, 'The Bureaucrat Who Fell Under a Bus: Ministerial responsibility, Executive Agencies and the Derek Lewis Affair in Britain', in *Governance*, 2002
28 'The Home Office's management of asylum accommodation: Fourth Report of Session 2024–26', Home Affairs Committee, 2025
29 'Academies and LA Maintained Schools: Inspection Analysis', Local Government Association, 2018
30 Nehal Panchamia and Peter Thomas, 'Public Service Agreements and the Prime Minister's Delivery Unit', Institute for Government
31 Ibid.
32 Heather Stewart and Dennis Campbell, 'Hancock says UK hit 100,000 tests amid claims tally is artificially boosted', *The Guardian*, 2020
33 Jamie Wilson, 'Psychiatric unit dismissed killer's appeal for help', *The Guardian*, 1999
34 'Wife killer sent to mental hospital', BBC News, 1999
35 Sue Quinn, 'Treasury man bludgeoned wife to death', *The Guardian*, 1999
36 'Ministers let NHS make patients wait longer to save money', *The Times*, 2025
37 Helen MacNamara's written statement to the Covid-19 Inquiry.
38 'A reset squandered: the civil service in Labour's first year', Institute for Government, 30 June 2025
39 Ibid.
40 MacNamara's witness statement

NOTES

CHAPTER 5

1 Derek Wanless, 'Securing Good Health for the Whole Population', HM Treasury, 2002
2 See https://www.gov.uk/government/organisations/hm-treasury/about
3 Norman Glass, 'David Walker obituary', *The Guardian*, 2009
4 Petr Bouchal, Emma Norris, 'Implementing Sure Start Children's Centres', Joseph Rowntree Foundation and Institute for Government, 2014
5 Richard Adams, 'Sure Start centres generated £2 of financial benefits for every £1 spent, study finds', *The Guardian*, 2025
6 Kate Ogden, David Phillips, 'How have English councils' funding and spending changed? 2010 to 2024', Institute for Fiscal Studies, 2024
7 Caroline Slocock, 'Why don't we invest in early action?', Lessons from the Early Action Task Force, Civil Exchange, 2022
8 'Giving every child the best start in life', Department for Education policy paper, 2025
9 Caroline Slocock, 'Why don't we invest in early action?', Lessons from the Early Action Task Force, Civil Exchange, 2022
10 Ibid.
11 'Unequal pandemic, fairer recovery', The Health Foundation report, 2021
12 Jatinder Hayre, 'Reinvesting in Sure Start is crucial for children's health', LSE British Politics
13 Caroline Slocock, 'Why don't we invest in early action?', Lessons from the Early Action Task Force, Civil Exchange, 2022
14 'Revenue, capital, prevention: A new public spending framework for the future', Demos, 2023
15 See https://www.cipfa.org/services/integrating-care/investing-in-prevention
16 'Early Action: landscape review', National Audit Office, 2013
17 'NAO: Public Accounts Committee – Second Report: Early Action: landscape review', National Audit Office, 2013
18 'Being in a Good Place: Investing in social infrastructure', Community Links, 2020
19 'Government commits to further £2 billion of property savings', Cabinet Office press release, 2022
20 Frank Field, 'The Foundation Years: preventing poor children becoming poor adults', The report of the Independent Review on Poverty and Life Chances, 2010
21 Graham Allen, Frank Field, 'Early Intervention: The Next Steps' and 'Early Intervention: Smart Investment, Massive Savings', Cabinet Office report, 2011
22 Andrew Dilnot, 'Fairer care funding: Reforming the funding of adult social care', 2011
23 Derek Wanless, 'Securing Good Health for the Whole Population', HM Treasury, 2002
24 Michael Marmot, 'Fair Society, Healthy Lives: The Marmot Review, Strategic Review of Health Inequalities in England post-2010', 2010
25 Caroline Slocock, 'Why don't we invest in early action?', Lessons from the Early Action Task Force, Civil Exchange, 2022
26 Michael Marmot, Jessica Allen, Tammy Boyce, Peter Goldblatt and Joana Morrison, 'The Marmot Review 10 Years On', Institute of Health Equity, 2020
27 Phillip Inman, 'English councils plan to sell off social clubs and sports centres to balance books', *The Guardian*, 2025
28 Paul Cairney, 'A "decisive shift to prevention" in Scotland: the next steps', National Records of Scotland, 2021
29 'How can changes to NHS incentives help deliver the 10 Year Health Plan?', Institute For Government live event, 2025
30 See https://www.betterway.network/past-events-feed/ putting-relationships-first-liberating-the-method?rq=Mark%20Smith

CHAPTER 6

1 Ronald E. Hall 'Back in the day, being woke meant being smart', *The Conversation*, 2024

2 Data on working mothers was not typically collected then, and married women were used as a proxy.
3 Jules Allen, Imogen Stevenson, 'BSA 40: Gender roles', National Centre for Social Research report, 2023
4 Jingyuan (Gloria) Zhang, 'Key takeaways from the British Social Attitudes Survey in 2024', Survey Monkey, 2025
5 Patrick Butler, 'Majority of UK public agree with liberal views on race and sexual identity', *The Guardian*, 2025
6 Tim Shipman, '"We will use the power of democracy to blow you away": Reform plots a path to No. 10', *The Spectator*, 2026
7 Charlotte Ambrose, 'What did Elon Musk say at the Unite the Kingdom march?', *London Evening Standard*, 2025
8 Josh Taylor, 'Elon Musk's Grok AI tells users he is fitter than LeBron James and smarter than Leonardo da Vinci', *The Guardian*, 2025
9 'New MI6 chief: Tech bosses are becoming as powerful as nations', *The Times*, 2025
10 'Trump bars boss of Starmer-linked charity from entering US', *The Telegraph*, 2025
11 Chris Michael, 'Tourists to US would have to reveal five years of social media activity under new Trump plan', *The Guardian*, 2025
12 'Trump UN speech: Seven years ago his audience laughed, this year they were silent', BBC News , 2025
13 'Trump administration says Europe faces "civilisational erasure"', BBC News, 2025
14 'Nigel Farage urges US to oppose UK on free speech laws', BBC News, 2025
15 'PM remarks at Immigration White Paper press conference', 2025
16 The full text reads: 'The Troubles and Beyond. The history of Northern Ireland from the late 1960s onwards has been dominated by the civil and political conflict commonly referred to as 'the Troubles'. The traumatic events of the years after 1968 touched almost everyone who lived here and many others from further afield. Inevitably, the interpretation of these events is contested in terms of their significance, meaning, and responsibility. While we have a shared past, we do not have a shared memory.' National Museum NI, drafted by the Director of Collections, William Blair, National Museum. Thanks to the museum for permission to reproduce it.
17 'Kemi Badenoch mistakenly says NI voted in favour of Brexit', BBC News, 2025
18 Henry Mance, 'Britain has had enough of experts, says Gove: Brexit campaigner offers to have disputed EU contribution figure audited', *Financial Times*, 2016
19 'Jaysley Beck: Ex-sergeant jailed for sexual assault on soldier', BBC News, 2025
20 Steven Morris, 'UK government may have breached young soldier's right to life, coroner concludes', *The Guardian*, 2025
21 'Mother of Gunner Jaysley Beck thought to have killed herself after sexual harassment angry at lack of support', Sky News, 2023
22 'Two-thirds of military women experienced sexual harassment, survey says', BBC News, 2025
23 'Armed forces admit sex harassment', BBC News, 2005
24 'Racism "prevalent" in the armed forces, ombudsman warns', BBC News, 2019
25 Vikram Dodd, 'Met police to face "Casey 2" inquiry amid recent scandals', *The Guardian*, 2025
26 Alexandra Topping, Vikram Dodd, 'Met police pay damages to women arrested at Sarah Everard vigil', *The Guardian*, 2023
27 Emine Sinmaz, 'Police "could and should have" stopped him: key points from Wayne Couzens report', *The Guardian*, 2024
28 Vikram Dodd, 'Quarter of police forces missing basic policies on sexual offences, says Sarah Everard report', *The Guardian*, 2025
29 Vikram Dodd, 'Two Met police officers jailed over photos of murdered sisters', *The Guardian*, 2021

30 'Secret BBC filming exposes hidden culture of racism and misogyny inside Met Police', BBC News, 2025
31 'Tackling violence against women and girls: Summary', National Audit Office, 2025
32 'Badenoch calls on people "from cultures that don't respect women" to "get out of our country"', Sky News, 2025
33 'Labour considers tearing up Tory ban on civil service diversity jobs', *The Telegraph*, 2024
34 Leonie Chao-Fong, 'Trump administration threatens to withhold funding from schools with DEI programs', *The Guardian*, 2025
35 'CQ Brown: Trump fires top US general in Pentagon shake-up', BBC News, 2025
36 Elon Musk on X, 2025
37 'Country policy and information note: sexual orientation and gender identity and expression', GOV.UK, 2025
38 'Hungary Bans LGBT Pride Events', Human Rights Watch, 2025
39 Rob Moss, 'Reform UK would "repeal Equality Act"', Personnel Today, 2026
40 Daniel Boffey, Henry Dyer, Rowena Mason, 'Farage turns on broadcasters over racism allegations as number of claims hits 28', *The Guardian*, 2025
41 Eleni Courea, Jessica Elgot 'Farage vows to scrap indefinite leave to remain, placing thousands at risk of deportation', *The Guardian*, 2023
42 Delphine Strauss, Anna Gross, 'How many people would Reform UK deport?', *Financial Times*, 2026
43 Dan Sabbagh, 'Michael Gove admits leave campaign wrong to fuel Turkey fears', *The Guardian*, 2018
44 'Illegal immigration is "out of control", claims Suella Braverman as she defends actions over Manston centre', Sky News, 2022
45 Suella Braverman, 'This is no longer the great country I knew. Islamists are bullying Britain into submission', *The Telegraph*, 2024
46 Adam Bychawski, 'Conservative-linked UK think tanks given millions by US climate deniers', openDemocracy, 2022
47 Zane McNeill, 'Republicans Spent Nearly $215M on TV Ads Attacking Trans Rights This Election', Truthout, 2024
48 'Where does the British public stand on transgender rights in 2024/25?', YouGov, 2025
49 Kristin Kobes Du Mez, 'White Christian nationalists are poised to remake America in their image during Trump's second term', CNN, 2025
50 Florence Ashley, Blu Buchanan 'The Anti-Trans Panic Is Rooted in White Supremacist Ideology', Truthout, 2023
51 'Andrew and Tristan Tate will return to UK to face charges', BBC News, 2025
52 'Masculinity and women's equality: study finds emerging gender divide in young people's attitudes', King's College London, 2024
53 'England's Tyrone Mings criticises Patel over racism response', BBC News, 2021
54 'Jacob Rees-Mogg empty desk note to civil servants insulting, says union', BBC News, 2022
55 'Hybrid working makes employees happier, healthier and more productive, study shows', *The Guardian*, 2024
56 Jonathan Aitken, *Margaret Thatcher: Power and Personality*, London, Bloomsbury, 2014
57 Moore, *Margaret Thatcher: The Authorised Biography, Volume One*
58 Peter Walker, 'Boris Johnson calls David Cameron "girly swot" in leaked note, *The Guardian*, 2019
59 Matthew Weaver, 'Supreme court chief's jibe at PM: let's hear it for the girly swots', *The Guardian*, 2019
60 Yvonne Roberts, 'Official: inequality is "natural"', *The Guardian*, 2003
61 Zoe Williams, 'What women want', *The Guardian*, 2003
62 Germaine Greer, 'Equality is dead: Long live feminism', *The Times*, 2003

63 Joan Smith, 'I'm a feminist, so I suppose I must be dead', *Independent on Sunday*, 2003
64 Slocock, *People Like Us*, p. 240
65 Ibid, p. 245
66 Ibid, p. 240
67 'Greater Expectations: Final report of the EOC's investigation into discrimination against new and expectant mothers in the workplace', Equal Opportunities Commission, 2005
68 'Small Business: Baby leave the mother of all issues', *The Sunday Times*, 2024
69 'UKIP's Godfrey Bloom under fire over "demeaning' joke"', BBC News, 2013
70 'The Equal Opportunities Commission Annual Report and Accounts 2005-06', HMSO, 2006
71 'Gender pay gap in the UK', Office for National Statistics, 2024

CHAPTER 7

1 Andrew Sparrow, 'David Cameron vows to tackle "secret corporate lobbying"', *The Guardian*, 2010
2 Katie Razzall, Sara Moralioglu, Nick Menzies, 'The 21st floor', BBC News, 2017
3 Theresa May, *The Abuse of Power: Confronting Injustice in Public Life*, Headline, 2023
4 'Grenfell Tower Inquiry Phase 2 Report: Government response', 2025
5 Andrew Woodcock, Dan Bentley, Ben Glaze 'David Cameron: I will kill off safety culture', *The Independent*, 2012
6 Laura Mark, 'Cameron claims victory in bonfire of the Building Regulations', *Architects Journal*, 2014
7 'Grenfell Tower Inquiry Phase 2 Report: Government response', 2025
8 'Grenfell survivors criticise ex-PM Cameron for claiming inquiry agreed fire regulations were excluded from "red tape challenge"', *Inside Housing*, 2024
9 See http://assets.publishing.service.gov.uk/media/69c3fd574a0660f085441cd/POA_Bill_-_Duty_of_Candour_Fact_Sheet.pdf
10 'Prime minister to scrap spy chiefs' Hillsborough Law veto', BBC News, 2026
11 'Delays to justice after disasters such as Grenfell are 'stain on society', says new victims advocate for England and Wales', *The Guardian*, 2025
12 Andrew Sparrow, 'David Cameron vows to tackle "secret corporate lobbying"', *The Guardian*, 2010
13 Keir Starmer's introduction to the King's Speech, 2024
14 Andrew Sparrow, 'David Cameron vows to tackle "secret corporate lobbying"', *The Guardian*, 2010
15 The Transparency of Lobbying, Non-Party Campaigning and Trade Union Administration Act 2014
16 'Lifting the lid on lobbying', Transparency International UK, 2015
17 'Greensill had extraordinarily privilegedcess to government, says inquiry', BBC News, 2021
18 Rupert Neate, 'What is the Greensill scandal overshadowing David Cameron's return to cabinet?' *The Guardian*, 2023
19 'Greensill: State bank risked £335m to back lender, say MPs', BBC News, 2023
20 'Treasury Committee reports on "Lessons from Greensill Capital"', Committees, UK Parliament, 2023
21 'We owe it to Epstein's victims and to British democracy to demand historic change', *The Guardian*, 2026
22 See https:// assets.publishing.service.gov.uk/media/69b172bf95b746516034 964d/ 11_March _2026_-_Letter_from_the_Prime_Minister_to_Doug_Chalmers_CB_DSO_OBE.pdf
23 Dan Alexander, 'Trump Jumps 118 Spots On The Forbes 400 List Thanks To Presidency, Forbes', Forbes, 2025
24 'Frank Hester: Tory donor accused of racist Diane Abbott remarks', BBC News, 2024
25 'Winner of huge public contracts becomes Tories' biggest ever donor', Good Law Project, 2024

26 'Health tech boss Frank Hester becomes biggest ever Tory donor with second £5m gift', *The Telegraph*, 2024
27 'Tories accepted £5m from Frank Hester days before election called', BBC News, 2024
28 'Keir Starmer received more clothes worth £16,000', BBC News, 2024
29 Sam Bright, 'Tories Ditched Net Zero Commitment While Receiving £250,000 from Oil Investors and Climate Deniers' DeSmog, 2025
30 Adam Barnett, Sam Bright, 'Revealed: Reform's £24 Million from Fossil Fuel Interests', DeSmog, 2026
31 'Nigel Farage faces standards probe into £5m gift', BBC News, 2026
32 Rowena Mason, 'Crypto investor gives £9m to Reform UK as donations exceed those to Tories', *The Guardian*, 2025
33 'Prime Minister: I will reshape the state to deliver security for working people', GOV.UK, press release, 2025
34 Rob Preston, 'Starmer reveals plans for 'fundamental reset' of relationship with civil society', Civil Society, 2024
35 'David Cameron's Big Society Speech' GOV.UK, 2010
36 'David Cameron's speech on the Big Society', GOV.UK, 2011
37 'Evaluation of the Early Legal Advice Project: Final Report', Home Office, 2013
38 'Labour's pledges on migration: the data' Migration Observatory, 2026
39 'Jo Wilding chronicles deepening immigration and asylum legal aid crisis, with failure to recruit staff an "existential threat" to the sector', Electronic Immigration Network, 2025
40 Margaret Thatcher, 'Interview for Woman's Own ("no such thing [as society]"), Margaret Thatcher Foundation, 1987
41 Frances Clarke, 'Tower block residents need justice. History shows they must lead the fight', *The Guardian*, 2017
42 'Building a Bigger We: insights from our network', A Better Way, 2022
43 'The Big Society Audit 2012', Civil Exchange, Democratic Audit and DHA, 2012, supported by the Joseph Rowntree Charitable Trust and the Calouste Gulbenkian Foundation; 'The Big Society Audit 2013', Civil Exchange and DHA, 2013 and 'The Final Big Society Audit', Civil Exchange and DHA, 2015, both supported by the Joseph Rowntree Charitable Trust and Barrow Cadbury
44 Peter Walker, 'Cameron's £1.5bn 'big society' youth scheme reaching few teenagers', *The Guardian*, 2018
45 See https://blogs.lse.ac.uk/politicsandpolicy/the-truth-about-tmos/
46 'PM speech at the Civil Society Summit', GOV.UK
47 See https://natcen.ac.uk/sites/default/files/2023-08/bsa30_key_findings_final.pdf
48 'Trust and confidence in Britain's system of government at record low', National Centre for Social Research, 2025
49 See https: //democraticaudituk.wordpress.com/wp-content/uploads/2013/06/ trends_in_political_participation_in_the_uk-1.pdf
50 'Party memberships fell in 2023 despite looming election', BBC News, 2023
51 'Grayling: charities put too much emphasis on campaigning', Civil Society News, 2014
52 'Third Party Election Campaigning – Getting the Balance Right', The Lord Hodgson of Astley Abbotts, CBE, HMSO, 2016
53 'A new hope: SMK Campaigner Survey Results', Sheila McKechnie Foundation, February 2025
54 Caroline Slocock, 'A Shared Society? The independence of the voluntary sector in 2017', Civil Exchange, 2017
55 'Defending our Democratic Space: a call to action', Civil Exchange and the Sheila McKechnie Foundation, 2023
56 'Campaigners claim victory as judges quash Braverman move against protests', *The Guardian*, 2025

57 'Richard Sharp: BBC chairman resigns over report into appointment', BBC News, 2023
58 'Ministers look at depoliticising top BBC jobs as Farage rides high in polls', *The Guardian*, 2025
59 'Local elections 2023: Voter ID backfired on Tories, says Rees-Mogg', BBC News, 2023
60 'Refugee charities install safe rooms and relocate amid rise in far-right threats', *The Guardian*, 2025
61 Paul Ovenden, 'Talaa Abd el-Fattah has shown supremacy of the Stakeholder State', *The Times*, 2026
62 Tim Shipman, 'We will use the power of democracy to blow you away: Reform plots a path to No. 10', *The Spectator*, US Edition, 2026
63 Danny Kruger, '12 Propositions for a New Social Covenant, section 2: Nation: "the state should safeguard the customs of the country"', The New Social Covenant Unit, 21 March 2021
64 'The change we want to see', A Better Way website
65 'Illegal Children's Homes', Children's Commissioner for England, 2024

CHAPTER 8

1 Tim Shipman, 'We will use the power of democracy to blow you away': Reform plots a path to No.10', *The Spectator*, US Edition, 8 January 2026
2 Rishi Sunak, 'My friends don't dare tell me if they vote Reform', *The Times*, 2025
3 David Smith, 'Britain's "deep state" thwarted my plans, Liz Truss tells US far-right summit', *The Guardian*, 2024
4 'Boris Johnson after No 10: files reveal troubling secrets of the ex-PM's pursuit of profit', *The Guardian*, 2025
5 'Interview with the Prime Minister', *Sunday with Laura Kuenssberg*, BBC One, 2026

CHAPTER 9

1 '"Move fast, fix things": Darren Jones sets out plan to rewire Whitehall and incentivise innovation in the civil service', Government press release, 2026
2 'Democracy on the Brink: Immediate Action to Safeguard UK Democracy', 99% Organisation and Unlock Democracy, 2025

INDEX